TEACH YOURSELF TO *Write*

Evelyn Stenbock

Writer's Digest Books

Cincinnati, Ohio

 Published by Writer's Digest Books, 9933 Alliance Road, Cincinnati, Ohio 45242. First edition.

Library of Congress Cataloging in Publication Data

Stenbock, Evelyn, 1929-
Teach yourself to write.

Includes index.
1. Authorship. I. Title.
PN147.S78 1982 808'.02 82-13703
ISBN 0-89879-093-X

Design by Maria Carella.

Dedication

To my crazy, creative family . . .
You've put up with me,
inspired me,
made me laugh,
And made writing about life EASY!

Acknowledgments

All along in my personal journey into the magical world of professional writing, people appeared who were willing to cheer me on. Some made outstanding contributions to my life.

For training in my novice years as a magazine editor, I'm indebted to the late R. J. Reinmiller, then president of Gospel Missionary Union, Kansas City. Ernest E. Pearson (of GMU) and Lew Hart (of The McWhirter Co., Kansas City) taught me the basic printing requirements, and Billie Courtney (of Dayco Mailing Service) shared with me her knowledge of clever copywriting and enthusiasm for creative advertising. Her confidence was contagious.

When I dropped out of full-time editing, M. A. (Bud) Lunn (manager, Nazarene Publishing House) expressed concern that my skills would be lost. He heaped home editing and writing jobs on me to keep that from happening.

Throughout the writing of this book, John R. Harrison, Ph.D. (of *Consensus*, Kansas City), looked over my shoulder. John was tough and unrelenting in his criticism, but incredibly supportive in pulling me through difficult spots. He, along with Carol Cartaino and Howard Wells of Writer's Digest Books, kept up my zeal for the project, making it possible.

The knowledge I pass along to readers has been absorbed through more than thirty years of reading and studying, coupled with on-the-job training, advice from consultants, seminars, and conferences. Many speakers and writers, some of them forgotten, have had important input into my life. I am grateful to all of them—all the way back to Emerson and Poe!

If you meet at dinner a man who has spent his life in educating himself—a rare type in our time, but still occasionally one to be met with—you rise from the table richer, and conscious that a high ideal has for a moment touched and sanctified your days.

—Oscar Wilde

Contents

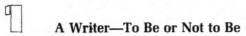

er." You'll be surprised when you see the easy methods for turning your articles into fiction and your personal experiences into the kind of objective, captivating articles editors are looking for. Does your writing habit pay its own way? While you climb the ladder to bigger success, sell to the mini-markets. Your options are so exciting that after reading this chapter, setting goals is going to be pretty hard!

7 **"To Market, To Market"—Which Market?** 118

Everybody says "study the markets," but nobody does it. It sounds dull and difficult and nobody knows where to begin. Start with a look at a publisher's slush pile. Do you know what slush is and how editors feel about it? Slush editors are treasure-hunters. They want writers who understand the stiff competition and set out to write better because of it. You'll learn what to look for in publications you want to write for, where to find them, and how to study them. You'll discover that studying the markets is fun and learn why it brings success.

8 **Those Awesome Editors** 139

When you bundle up your baby and ship it off, SASE dutifully enclosed, who receives it? Those awesome editors and their habitat are a fascinating study for aspiring writers. The editor is not a silent bookworm who sits in a stall devouring manuscripts, spitting out the bad ones. You're walking into a zoo full of talented adrenalized people. Peeking behind the scenes to understand the system and the people in charge of it is bound to increase your zeal for learning. You'll be inspired to become a major member of the team—a successful writer!

9 **Now the Sweat Begins** 163

Back to the drawing board. We not only think about writing, gather ideas, and learn where to sell our writing. We write! What about? You'll choose your subject, learn how to narrow it down, decide on the proper approach, outline it, and learn how to write it. Finding the right beginning (to hook the reader), organizing

content (to keep him reading), and deciding on an appropriate conclusion (to satisfy him) will help you break the deadlock so you can *write*, instead of staring out the window.

10 How to Spin a Yarn 199

Once upon a time there was a writer who wanted to sell stories. . . . Stories do sell, you know. The problem is that most stories sort of "happen." Ancient storytellers sat on the hillside thinking their stories through, and you will, too, once you learn how. You have an idea, but—what's a plot? a theme? a viewpoint? You'll learn how to describe the people and places, how to put rocks in the heroine's path to trip her up, and how to find a good balance between narrative and description. The basics of good fiction apply to a story of any length. The chapter concludes with what editors want—and don't want.

11 Poetry: Pleasure or Problem? 230

Are you walking around hugging an oft-rejected bundle of poems? Or would you like to write poetry, but haven't dared try? Tennyson was called a "hearthside rhymer," and many hymnwriters churned out verses that became immortal. You're in excellent company if you're comfortable here. The Psalms are poetry. So is some prose, when it's written in artistic, free-verse style. Free verse? Is it true poetry? How do you increase your chances of seeing it in print? Edgar Allan Poe tells you one way to write a poem—James Dickey adds his advice. And Ralph Waldo Emerson, who has the first word, also has the last.

12 The Art of Editing 256

What we're aiming for is accuracy (getting the facts straight), clarity (saying what we mean to say), and unity (tying the whole thing together). All too many writers weep over rejection because they've submitted their material before it was finished. You learn to correct details, edit (trim off the fat and check both content and flow of words), rewrite dull or foggy spots, and rearrange material. One of the writer's biggest enemies is his hatred

of retyping. This chapter shows you how to take a "finished" manuscript and whip it into better shape. Yes, Arabella. Retype it.

13 **Everything You Always Wanted to Know About Writing a Book** 280

To author a book! What a prestigious pinnacle for any writer to reach! How do you know if *you* ought to write one? Three questions are answered to help you decide: 1) Why should I include writing a book in my writing goals? 2) Is the material I envision of book magnitude? and 3) How does one get a book into print? You'll get a glimpse of "common losers" and learn why some books fail. The chapter gives excellent insight into today's opportunities and shows what kind of a hard-working, starry-eyed fool it takes to tackle writing a book.

14 **Wrapping It All Up** 312

What good is devouring a book about writing if you lay it down and go back to your knitting or TV? This chapter separates the doers from the dreamers with a challenge to shoot for the moon. You're given plateaus to aim for en route to success and tips on how to reach them. Best of all, this book becomes the basis for a writing course you can cover "all by yourself" in three years, two years, or eight short months.

Index 333

1 A Writer—To Be or Not to Be

Two checks in the mail in one day! I rip them open with excitement as I run down the driveway toward the house. One is for fifty-five dollars, payment for a play I wrote; the other—what is it? Forty dollars! For a simple inspirational article!

Two joys crown the life of the professional writer: seeing his or her very own words on a printed page; and receiving payment for writing—proof that someone else saw that it was good!

To be a writer, or not to be? I decided TO BE a writer.

Words spill out onto paper when I'm angry, when I'm elated, when I'm amused. When I'm bored, I write; when I'm sad, I write; when I'm happy, which is most of the time, I write.

When I'm not writing, I'm probably thinking of something that *could* be written, *should* be written, or *must someday* be written. Most of my writing, even on the job, has been done for my own pleasure, because most of the time, I'm writing to entertain myself, even when the work is done at the request of other people. Some major projects I have written for myself, only to have them picked up and published because others read and liked what I had written. Enough books, articles, stories, plays, and poems of mine have found their way into print to assure me a solid reputation as a professional writer, a person who writes for a living. I love it. Writing is profitable—and fun.

But I didn't emerge as a writer overnight. Becoming a professional writer has been an inch-by-inch process. I grew into it, studying and asking questions along the way, learning because I wanted to write well. I had no formal training in either English or journalism. I taught myself to write.

My father was a writer. We had a great deal in common, my dad and I, despite the fifty-year age difference. The years have dimmed my memory of him, but it doesn't take much to bring back flashes of nostalgia. One day, in a small Missouri town, I stopped at an antique store to browse. There in the midst of dust and clutter, buried under chipped saucers and coverless sugar bowls, was a table. Round. A sturdy pedestal, four stubborn castors. White paint slapped on, but all too obviously my father's old oak dining table. No—not his table. His desk. The circular shrine in his study to which he crept to pour out his heart onto sheaves of paper at the end of each day.

Some of us were born with a love for writing. Deep in our hearts a yearning to express ourselves lies dormant. Now and then it wakes up—at least long enough to pen words of love to someone we care for so much that just "saying it" isn't enough. Or it stirs us to write to "Dear Diary"—at least for a few weeks. This inner longing to write can blossom under the tender care of an understanding parent or teacher. (It can also be stifled in childhood by mishandling or neglect.)

But very often even exceptional writing talent gets buried in the gigantic task of growing up. Suddenly as an adult we feel the old yearning to scribble thoughts on paper. We ache to do it, and to do it well. We begin thinking, "I'd like to write," or even, "I'd like to be a writer!"

But can we? Are we talented enough to write professionally? Over our morning coffee we scan the newspaper, spending a little extra time analyzing the work of our favorite editorial writers, the sports commentators, regular feature writers. How did these people get where they are? How do you break in? Could I ever write something someone would think publishable?

We'd probably give up the whole idea, but suddenly we notice a short item about the local theatrical group, the gardening column, a book review, or an article about a subject of special interest to us. We set our coffee down so sharply a wad of napkins is needed to save us from disaster as we exclaim, "I could do that!" Something about the item makes us feel on eye-level with the writer—maybe even superior.

Just knowing we could do it doesn't make us writers. That's accomplished by *doing* it. And therein lies the problem. Our minds tend to wander back to school days. The school had a paper, but we didn't work on it. There was that writing club, but we didn't join. When a writing contest came along we were too timid to try. And tenth grade English? Wow! How long ago was that? College—if there *was* college—was no better. So many other interests crammed our young lives we never got around to learning how to write.

Now a new question slips in. Is writing something you *can* learn? Maybe people like Corey Ford and Erma Bombeck were just born writers. They have so much to write about, it just flows naturally; not many of us have lives *that* exciting. But the yearning won't go away. "I'm a born writer, too," we reason. "I've just had too much to do to pursue it."

People who love to write come to this point many times in their lives. "I really should get busy and write something," they say. Then the excuses begin: "I'll wait . . ."

Until I retire.

Until vacation.

Until the kids leave home.

Until I have more time.

Or we say:

"It's too late. I've blown it. Look how old I am!"

"With my job I can't go back to school!"

"I can't afford a correspondence course right now."

"I wouldn't know how to begin!"

To this vast audience of potential writers I want to shout, "Stop!" You can do it. And do it now. You can *teach yourself* to write!

How do you do it?

Perhaps that question is premature. Maybe you're asking, as did a musician-friend of mine, "*Should* I do it?"

"You mean," she asked incredulously when she learned the title of my book, "*anyone* can teach himself to write?"

I started to reply, but she butted in, answering her own question. "Maybe I could write if I tried, but I doubt it. I'm just not a writer."

I wanted to applaud. She's a singer, a busy piano teacher, an organist at a big church; she dabbles in songwriting, and she has other creative interests, as well. She could write. Of course she *could*. But should she? Thank heaven for all the people who decide not to. If everyone talented who had a hankering to write were to try his or her hand and succeed, those of us who have attained some small measure of success would suddenly be very tiny fish in a great big pond. Not everyone *should* write, and not everyone *can*, even though they may do very well at producing necessary compositions and papers to get through school. "True ease in writing comes from art," philosophized Alexander Pope in "An Essay on Criticism." Creative writing *is* an art, and one that demands a great deal of time, as well as skill.

Writing can be learned. But our talents vary and our time on earth is limited. Of all the things you'd *like* to learn in your allotted three-score years and ten, you'll have time for only a few that you'll learn well enough to be considered professional. Writing is a good choice. It's one of the nicer things to dabble in as you climb the hill to middle age and start the downward slope toward retirement. It's also a valuable tool on any job and could land you a good one if you improve your ability enough to be noticed by employers. And whether you are fifteen or fifty—or fifty plus fifteen—writing, for the born writer, is pure pleasure on the job and off.

To succeed in professional writing, certain factors have to be present:

YOU MUST HAVE A NATURAL BENT

Obviously you do have at least some natural writing ability because you are out to learn more about it. For you to achieve success as a beginner, your knack with words must be brought out into the open. It has to show. Others must see it and like it. Polishing skills comes with study and practice, but a certain amount of talent and desire is needed.

Throughout this book you will be given the kind of exposure that will lead you to examine yourself. In addition to musing about my thoughts, you will be given assignments that you can do at your leisure to test your ability and to start the daily writing habit. Although I don't necessarily recommend a daily journal, I do push hard for constantly putting words on paper, because the bottom line is this: To become a writer, you must write.

YOU MUST LOVE TO DO IT

This is perhaps the most universal trait of successful writers. Writing is hard work, and if you're writing on spec, as most of us are most of the time, you're virtually gambling away hour after hour, hoping you'll eventually get paid. Whether you work full time and write now and then, or write regularly and "work" now and then (like when you get hungry or the rent looms due), you have to like it a lot, or you'll never stick with it long enough to learn. Alex Haley worked days as a coast guard cook—exhausting work, as any chef will tell you—and wrote on board ship after hours, late into the night after the other men had gone to bed. He didn't begin with *Roots*, by the way. His eye for the unusual picked up stories many other people would have missed. He wrote for the love of writing, but he wrote well enough to sell, even back then.

Alan Alda is a professional writer, as well as an actor/producer. He loves writing, and he's exceptionally talented. Alda wasn't an overnight success. He wrote for years facing one rejection after another. His record of odd jobs to keep food on the table while waiting for a break probably beats all others. Appearing on the Mike Douglas show, Alda—oozing with exuberance as if he had just received his first small check—explained he had waited so long for opportunities such as those he's enjoying now he can't bear to turn any of them down!

YOU MUST SPEND A SIGNIFICANT AMOUNT OF TIME PRACTICING IT

There's a sense in which writing is a talent: Either you have it, or you don't. But not even talented musicians play beautifully without practicing. The pianist sits down to play regularly—even the one who plays by ear—and the more you play, the better you become. Some have a marvelous touch that seems to be a gift from God. Others stumble along rather choppily and never in a million years would play in public. But they can entertain themselves for hours when they are alone, and often, in a pinch, they are the ones willing to play at some nursery school or nursing home, if no one else can go.

There are various levels of talent in writing, as well—and various stages of learning—and divers ways to use them. To become a writer, you must practice, wherever and whenever you can—by yourself, for your own pleasure, and here and there, as chances to show off come your way.

Wherever you are, you'll have to get busy to get anyplace as a writer. To become a writer, you must write. The more talented that people are, the more they practice (writers, artists, athletes, musicians). They practice every day, some of them. You work at the task regularly; certain spare moments that you've planned into your schedule, an hour a day, or two or three hours a week. You write, even though you're not in the mood (though you generally will be), just as you practice anything you want to do well.

This does not automatically mean sales. It means scribble. Scribble—save. Scribble, scribble—scrap. Writers use 50-gallon drums for wastebaskets. Scribble—scrap. Scribble, scribble—scrap. Scribble, scribble, scribble—save!

Before you know it, you'll be saving more than you scrap. Then you'll be on the road to becoming a writer.

GO WHERE YOUR TALENT CAN BE USED

One doesn't *begin* writing with the sale of an article or poem. One begins by grabbing every opportunity in the world of literature one can get. And for every challenge you accept, another one or two or three will develop to help boost you up the ladder.

There's a certain amount of luck in the background of all successful writers. Somewhere along the line, they had an opportunity to write for someone who appreciated the effort. Someone encouraged each professional writer at just the right time, influencing him and unobtrusively guiding him to his full potential. A teacher, an editor, a parent, a contest sponsor, a friend—somebody believed in him, plugging him in to get him going.

For me it was R.J. Reinmiller, late president of the missionary organization I worked with many years. He always had one hand in the inkpot, directing the most minute details of preparation, production, and distribution of missionary publications. To him, good writing was the heart of all communication between the missionaries (who went away for life in the early days) and the people back home who supported their work.

For many years I had dabbled in writing. Within a few weeks after I joined the home office staff as a secretary, he asked me to author a form letter thanking donors for their contributions, and it wasn't long before he was encouraging me to submit various articles. Then I did some editing, and I began to see myself as he saw me—as a writer! When he was appointed president of the organization, he offered me his important sideline job as director of publications. This opened new opportunities for me, resulting in the publication of my first book and leading to the ones that followed. The job involved full responsibility of getting a monthly magazine together, overseeing all advertsing, and undertaking numerous other duties and experiences of inestimable value.

Looking back, I'm amazed a woman was ever allowed to invade the territory of those old-time letterpress men, hard-nosed printers and editors who demanded perfection of themselves and everyone who worked with them, gentlemen who opened doors for ladies and tipped hats to them. Those were great men, and Reinmiller chief of them all—men who locked horns over where a comma should be placed, *if* it should be placed, or if perchance a semicolon might be more suitable—subjects crucial enough to call in all executives and perhaps members of the board to decide the outcome. These were the men who shouted loudly, almost angrily, STOP THE PRESS! when they spotted some obscure flaw that had to be corrected, whatever the cost.

Not knowing any better, I walked in and took it on the chin with the best of them. And I dished it out, tearing apart the president's writing as he tore apart mine. Mr. Reinmiller's death was a personal blow for dozens of missionaries, for his rarest quality was making each person who entered his life feel like his best friend. I don't know what he bequeathed to the rest of them, but he left me his appreciation of historical archives, his love of good writing, his demand for quality work, and a few of his picky editing skills.

What about you? Whom do you know in the delightful world of publishing? I believe in hanging around newspaper offices and print shops, making a nuisance of myself until they put me to work. I work part time for a weekly newspaper doing routine deadline jobs: proofreading, making coffee, and flunkying around as needed.

The benefits of such contacts are numerous. For you, as a budding writer, one of the best is that you will meet people from whom you can learn grass roots journalism. Television stations and newspapers hire a variety of help, from janitors to copy typists to persons who stuff newspapers into plastic bags in rainy weather. Getting your foot in the door is important. The best journalists have the degree of POHW: Plain Old Hard Work; on-the-job experience, learned from the ground floor up.

Every chance you get, you should rub shoulders with the press. Carrying a press card won't get you anywhere (except on official assignments, where one may be required to get in free), but knowing the right people will. Philip E. Rawley, textbook editor at Moody Press, made his first article sale "cold turkey," but his love for writing led him to talk to writers whenever he could and to make friends in the publishing business. He built a circle of friends "who knew what they were doing," friends who could be counted on for sound advice, and friends who eventually knew his writing talent and editing ability well enough to recommend him for jobs. Peter E. Gillquist of Thomas Nelson, Inc., was encouraged by Robert K. DeVries of Zondervan. The book that resulted, *Love Is Now,* has sold nearly half a million copies. His next major step was ghostwriting *Man In Black* for Johnny Cash, and from there he was hired by Thomas Nelson.

Where do you meet "the right people"? You meet them by gravitating to "the right places." At the newspaper, I hobnobbed with the owners and managing editor, a freelance cartoonist, a freelance business writer, and a freelance typesetter who had coincidentally typed my books. And they hobnobbed with me!

At 4:30 one morning, Abe Goteiner, a freelance sportswriter, heard over his car radio that anybody listening to the station to which he was tuned was invited over for coffee and donuts at 5:00. He sped out there, a distance of several miles, and met a number of interesting personalities.

But, you say, "I don't live in the city," or, "I can't run off here and there to odd jobs or 5:00 A.M. kaffeeklatsches." Okay, for a start for you, here's another angle. Let's imagine all you want to do is write to entertain yourself. (Of course that's not true. All of us really want to write the greatest bestseller of the century.) You'll need nothing to begin except a tablet, some scratch paper or 3x5 cards, and pens or pencils. (You *could* get up and run to the typewriter every time a thought comes to mind, but it becomes cumbersome after a while.)

To entertain yourself with writing, all you need to do is turn your mind loose and write things down. Your past life is a story in itself. And what a story some lives are! One woman who wanted desperately to make her story known struggled over this very thing.

"I want my children to know what my life has been like," she explained. "They have no idea, and I want them to know."

I encouraged her to go ahead and jot things down as a beginning.

"But I don't want to . . ."

I waited. After a moment she looked at me helplessly.

"Oh, I don't know. I guess I'm just not sure I should share my story with the whole world. I just want my kids to know."

I understood. Some things are not meant for the whole world to know. Revealing one's secrets is one of the biggest struggles many writers go through. Shall I tell all? Or shouldn't I?

There's a place for confession. First of all, buried in the heart unknown even to those who care about us and love us best, are painful events of our past life that can sour and cause distress of mind needlessly. Intense feelings need to be expressed. One ought to take the cork off and pour it all out. Anger, grief, disappointments, guilt, and frustrations should never remain bottled up inside, unshared. What a relief to get it all off our chest!

But who can be told? In some cases, no one but God! Ben Franklin is credited with saying "Three may keep a secret, if two of them are dead." Once a thing is told, it's told. Whether you want to tell it or not is up to you, but you bear the consequences.

I have my own way of getting rid of ulcer-causing matters. I write a letter—and I've written some humdingers in my day—pouring out the whole story, sparing no details. It helps get the bad experience out of your system. Dump it all out on paper. Hold nothing back. Give vent to the angry feelings, the sorrow, the feelings of rejection, or whatever is eating away inside. As you write you'll begin to feel relief, for the process is like letting the steam out of a pressure cooker . . . slowly . . . until it's all gone.

I've lost friends ignoring the second part of the instructions. Don't mail it! Burn it up! Many times—innumerable times—I have stood over the kitchen sink with a flaming sheaf of papers and washed all my grief down the drain.

What does this have to do with writing?

Quite a lot. Our past experiences, for the most part, are valuable to us only after we're far enough away from them to look at them objectively. As long as bitterness remains, our writing will be plagued with I-ism and a totally subjective view—not very worthwhile reading for anyone, and certainly not exciting copy for an editor to receive. Manuscripts plagued with indulgence in self-pity are written by people who still feel destroyed by their failure, whatever that failure may have been. There comes a time when you know in your heart you're up out of the pit and ready to live again. Then, maybe, you can write, with hopes of producing sensitive, gripping copy worth submitting.

The year my father died, he wrote a chapter a week of his life story in a letter to my sister, Viv. He told some very personal family history that she buried in her heart for years. (Dig into any genealogy and you'll turn up a scandal!) Finally, though, Viv decided to share the letters, and what a treasure they are. Now we can pinpoint the tiny village in Sweden where he grew up. Sometimes I think I could walk right up to the tree by the lake where he buried a pair of skates for safekeeping and dig them up! My grandmother, who made bandannas for a living when he was a little boy, created hats when the style changed so she could stay in business. She stiffened them by soaking them in sugar water. (Wasn't that a sweet bit of information to pass on to posterity?)

But we don't live in the past, interesting as it may be. We live in the here and now—or at least I do, very much so. Writing to entertain yourself, as a launching pad for your career, means writing about things that are happening around you every day. You might be thinking, "My heart is bursting with happiness!" Or, "I saw the craziest thing yesterday—I'm still laughing about it!"

Well, for goodness sake, write it down. Write a poem, write a paragraph, write a letter, but write down your happy thoughts. Gratitude, answers to prayer, humorous events, funny sayings of children you know, all should be written down. The world never gets enough things to smile about, and the best time to write them is when they happen, or shortly thereafter. And what about expressing appreciation by writing a few love notes to your parents, your mate, your good friend? Or writing a thank-you to someone? You'll surely make that person's day.

So what if you're writing only for yourself, to entertain yourself? (Though you're not kidding me!) Writing whatever comes to mind is the way to start the creative juices flowing—to prime the pump, for you oldtimers.

Prime the pump! What memories the old pump stirs up in my mind! Hot and dusty after a long afternoon playing by the side of the potato patch where the adults were picking potato bugs . . .

Really. Picking beetles off the potato plants to save the crop. Gangly, long-legged, I would skip down the hill ahead of the rest of the family, singing every step of the way, and start to pump.

Even a little kid knew it took a can of water poured into the top of the pump to get it flowing.

Then, ah bliss, icy water gushed out, splashing over my dirty, bare feet.

Priming the pump is not just a cliché. You have to do it. You must write something, even if it's only a "little canful."

I suppose someone is snickering, thinking that if I knew how dull her life was, I'd never expect her to produce anything other people might like to read. I smiled when a receptionist who loves to write lamented that she was stuck in a doctor's office with no opportunity to get out and gather material for her stories. How often I have sat in just such an office noting clothing, smiles, eyes, hairstyles, actions and reactions of people who came and went. When I pointed it out to her, she laughed at her own lack of awareness of the world around her. Patients were such a routine part of her life she had completely overlooked them!

I've had an incredibly rich life. In a sense, of course, it's been uniquely my own, because many of the outstanding events I've experienced have been experienced alone, without companions to share the exciting moments, or the frightening moments, or those moments that were recorded indelibly as lonely moments, or moments of infinitely eternal value. They're my moments, and I can recount what happened in them any way I want to, with nobody to say, "That's not how it was!"

But no one's life is uniquely his own. When I was twenty-six, I crossed the Atlantic on a tiny freighter, the only woman on board. A hurricane at sea scooted the ship up and down huge swells while rocking it back and forth sideways, tipping it to terrifying angles. Mammoth walls of water crashed over the decks, loosening the cargo and threatening our lives. If I can write about the storm, or about the pudgy sea captain who calmly guided us through it, or about other events of the nine-day journey, then the cook, the crew, and the captain himself could turn out page after page of far more interesting material based on the same trip. And they might add a scene about the idiotic landlubber traipsing around on board wearing spike sling pumps, who stumbled when the ship lurched, falling headlong down the stairs into the arms of the startled steward.

Nobody's experiences are exclusively his own. Our lives are intertwined a thousand times over. Like the blind men who examined the elephant, each describing it in terms of the section of the body he was feeling, each of us has a viewpoint—a slant—all his own. From that viewpoint we write, telling it like it is from where we see it.

What does this all mean to you? It means that if you earn your keep selling socks at K Mart, you can write from the vantage point of one who sells socks at K Mart. I might write about the grocery carryout boy my dog nipped, but there is no way I could describe the event as the boy saw it. Whatever you do for a living, your life is probably full of colorful characters and recordable events you can turn into readable copy, characters and events as seen through your eyes, and maybe yours alone.

You are perched in the crow's nest looking out over a sea of humanity—human beings who are *really* characters, in the true sense of the word. Once you recognize this immense wealth, once you see its literary value, you'll see some improvement in your writing. People watchers are winners. Animal watchers, birdwatchers, fashion watchers, market watchers, science watchers, watchers of anything and everything under the sun are the writers who turn out readable copy. "Eyes open; ears alert," is the cardinal rule. You will see how much you really have to write about when we get to Chapter 3, where we will go into this in more detail.

Is your confidence still lagging behind your growing interest in writing? About the time I went freelance—a giant step of either faith or foolishness—*Writer's Digest* carried a cover article entitled "The Gutsy Road to Success."[1]

Oh, how I needed that! The title, I mean. Gutsy I am not!

You have to develop a little bit of gutsiness to make it as a writer. It takes a lot of nerve to offer something you have written with the utmost care, with the fear clutching at your heart that someone, somewhere may roar with laughter over your cherished piece.

That someone in the business might make fun of the efforts of a beginner is so unlikely it's ludicrous, but how does one know? Some of us refer to our creations as children, for they become like our kids—a part of us. We don't like to think of their being criticized, not even a little bit. You aren't alone in feeling this way. Practically every writer has hidden beautiful prose or poetry, sometimes to be discovered after his or her death and brought to acclaim. It's very hard to be objective about your own children. Unfortunately, it's difficult to know what's good and what's bad, and about the only way to really find out is to ask somebody else.

One last thought: When I talk about my wonderful dad, I often become very aware of people who have grown up with no such great moral support. It seems as though more parents than ever before are denying their children self-confidence; but even in the past, many busy people had no use for creative talents, and they scoffed at attempts their offspring made to write.

An episode of the TV program *Trapper John, M.D.*, featured a child of whom Trapper could only exclaim, "What precocity!" Thanks to the doctor, the child's father consented to putting the boy in a school for gifted children. When he learned of it, the child shouted gleefully, "Gifted! You mean I'm a genius? I thought I was just a smart aleck!"

"You are," growled Trapper.

Maybe you grew up a smart aleck because nobody recognized your special genius. Prisons are filled with people whose keen minds were overlooked in crowded schools, whose parents were too busy with their own problems to recognize the potential in their precocious kids, and whose environment and economic level excluded the unique training they needed to set them on the right track. If many such children grow up to spend their lives behind bars, how many more are locked up in jobs they hate, trudging the treadmill of meaningless tasks.

Let's face it: Childhood is hard. Kids' thoughts and feelings get overlooked, and few people are skilled enough at picking the complex brains of youngsters to help them develop their talent. If you have the impression that you missed opportunities because nobody saw your potential, you're definitely not alone.

Your early environment can be blamed for some wasted brainpower, but you are no longer a child. You are an adult, free to make your own choices and run your own life. At this point, untapped talent is no one's fault but your own. It's not too late to take hold of the situation, turn your mind loose, and begin to grow. You can break out of the mold.

Do you dare to do that? Being intelligent isn't popular; people often consider a genius downright disgusting. Since creative individuals can be touchy, and quickwitted people are all too often slapped down, a good many above-average folks opt for the easy way out. In a desperate attempt to be just like the rest of the world, they deny their true abilities, deny their genius, and try not to let their intelligence show. Longfellow mused that, "Men of genius are often dull and inert in society; as the blazing meteor when it descends to the earth is only a stone."

Of course they're dull. Nobody has ever been interested in what they had to say, nor have they been intrigued by the trivia and gossip of the crowd around them. After a while, they quit trying to play society's game, so good old society (that's you and me, in real life) dubs them "dull and inert."

An editor-friend with interests much like my own had an opportunity to attend a dinner at which a nationally known columnist spoke. I was envious! "How was he?" I asked her later.

"Dull." She grinned. "You didn't miss much."

I was shattered. She was talking about one of my favorite writers. I could hardly believe her. But it's so typical of writers. I have been accused of scaring people to death by my confident words on paper. In person the opposite is true. Though a part of me is garrulous, I've been bludgeoned into being quiet in a crowd. I'm apt to be a listener, rather than the loudmouth you'd expect me to be. Even in high school I failed speech because I was too timid to give my well-prepared talk. Although I've since spoken publicly numerous times to large audiences, I do it very rarely now, preferring, to borrow from Will Rogers, "to sit on the curb and applaud" as the parade goes by.

You wonder how many public individuals are in fact shy. Dickens begins "The Holly Tree" by saying:

> I have kept one secret in the course of my life. I am a bashful man. Nobody would suppose it, nobody ever does suppose it, nobody did suppose it, but I am naturally a bashful man. This is the secret which I have never breathed until now.

I suspect he was musing about himself when he jotted down those words. Then, clever man that he was, he built from them a fascinating tale in first person about a young man so insecure he left his bride-to-be just before the wedding because he thought she preferred his best friend.

Still waters run so deep they're dangerous. Even some of us average Jo's can get lost in thoughts of our own out of context with the gibberish hammering in our ears. We withdraw our souls, while leaving our bodies in the middle of a crowded room staring glassy-eyed into space. Our mouths hang stupidly agape. Our minds are only dully aware of the conversation of which we are supposed to be a part. We've not turned idiotic. It's just "Genius at Work."

If I've struck a tender spot with you, take heart. You can break out of the shell and be yourself, totally free, on paper. If you have to hide behind a pen name to do it, find one. Mine is going to be Sarah Alice Vasa, if I ever feel I need one. Watch for it.

Talent can be crushed temporarily, but suppressing a creative bent forever is like cutting down an unwanted tree. We have several in our yard that refuse to die. Each year we hack them down, but each year the old stumps just sprout again, bigger and better than before. A carpenter who stopped by to give an estimate on some work exclaimed, "What a secluded house!" He found me in the hammock where I lay exhausted, nursing muscles made sore by chopping, clipping, sawing, and hauling brush away so we could see the light of day. I just moaned.

Secluded! Yes, it's secluded, in spite of all our valiant attempts to keep a path cleared to the world beyond our doors. There's one compensation. Ralph Waldo Emerson put my thoughts into his "Good-bye, Proud World!":

I'm going to my own heart-stone,
Bosomed in yon green hills alone—
A secret nook in a pleasant land,
Whose groves the frolic fairies planned;
Where arches green, the livelong day,
Echo the blackbird's roundelay,
And vulgar feet have never trod
A spot that is sacred to thought and God.

Most of the time I'm "safe in my sylvan home," among the squirrels, coons, and a kaleidoscope of colorful birds; lost in thoughts of my own; buried in an avalanche of paper and books. I've yet to experience a writer's block so stubborn I can't break it by raking mountainous piles of leaves; and when I tire of that, I have only to crawl out through the brush with a cheery "Hello, Proud World!" to be ready and eager to write again.

Edgar Allan Poe is a prime example of literary genius that refused to die. Poe was raised Edgar Allan, known as the son of John and Frances Allan, who sheltered him from age two, when his mother died. Although Edgar had every advantage as the son of a wealthy merchant, John Allan was terribly disappointed when his foster son developed into a poet with literary goals. In fact, it seems quite likely the legend of Poe's strange, mysterious character stems from this discord between them, for young Edgar could only temporarily be chopped down. His literary talent demanded an audience. He *had* to write.

After a final quarrel, Edgar stormed out of the house and moved into a hotel; financial aid from his foster father virtually stopped. Edgar left Richmond, Virginia, where the Allans were living, and arrived penniless in Boston, where he wrote under his assumed name, Henri le Rennet. Boston was then the literary capital, but Poe couldn't get his toe in the door. Time and again the young writer was humiliated, and he was often flat broke.

But more than a century after he wrote "The Raven," we still get goosebumps reciting it.

Poe said of this and other poems which "went at random 'the rounds of the press' ":

> It is incumbent upon me to say that I think nothing in this volume of much value to the public, or very creditable to myself. Events not to be controlled have prevented me from making, at any time, any serious effort in what, under happier circumstances, would have been the field of my choice.

Ah, yes. John Allan did his best to smother the budding writer, but talent like Poe's burning in the heart is a passion that will die only with the man.

To succeed as a writer, you'll need that same kind of passion. The more intense your desire, the better will be your success. So come along with me. I'll do what I can to get you started, but after we've traveled together for a little while, you can teach yourself to write!

ASSIGNMENT 1

Here are some projects anyone can complete. The goal is to get words on paper. There are no rules or regulatons. No teacher is looking over your shoulder.

BEGIN A PERSONAL JOURNAL

If you're a rank beginner, the thoughts you write down daily may be as simple as "dog followed me home. Hungry. Dog hungry I mean. Me too." (Who cares about punctuation? It's *your* journal, nobody else's.)

A personal journal is a diary of events, thoughts, and transactions—a record of things that happened in your daily life and what you thought about them. You need not buy a diary (but you can). A notebook, file cards (probably 4x6), sheets of paper in a file folder, or even a scribble pad will do.

To begin with, getting words on paper is what counts. In time, your journal may grow into a sophisticated log in which your whole life story is recorded. Eventually you might want to look back at certain areas of your journal to draw material for writing projects or to get ideas. Trips you've taken, birthday parties, or holiday preparation—and certainly the big events of life—will become valuable material to you. Record the date (including the year). In addition, you might want to find a way to color code your journal: green paper for the Christmas season, yellow for Easter, blue for birthdays, pink for love affairs, orange for travel, and white for everyday routine reports. Colored bond paper (8½x11) is available at office supply stores. If your store is out of it, inquire about color mineograph paper. Hint loudly, as your birthday draws near, that you could use a three-hole punch.

Spiral notebooks also work well. As years go by, and the notebooks fill up, they can be indexed with tabs.

WRITE SOMETHING

Even a letter that's long overdue. If you don't want to write a journal (it's *your* life!), write a paragraph of a letter before you go to bed tonight, and another tomorrow night. It doesn't have to be good. Just write something down. Anything.

Here are seven suggestions to prime the pump for the first week. You can use these ideas either in writing colorful letters (keep a copy for your files) or for your personal journal. Use one a day, or if you prefer, try to answer all the questions briefly at the end of each day (or early the next morning).

1. Where are you right now? Who is with you? What are you/they doing?
2. What did you do today? Did something special happen? Did anything bad (or scary, or memorable, or sad) happen? What about good or exciting things?
3. How do you feel about events of this day—this morning—this evening?
4. What sounds do you hear? What colors/textures do you see? What odors do you smell/wish you did not smell? Describe your surroundings. How are they affecting you?
5. What are you worrying about? Hoping for? Planning? Praying for? Saving funds to get?
6. Who is dear to you at this moment? Whom do you love (or dislike)? Describe your feelings. If you could tell them what you're thinking, what would you say?
7. What have you read today (book, newspaper article, story) that impressed you? What happened on your favorite TV show? Write down your reactions and deepest thoughts about the subject.

READ THINGS YOU WROTE IN THE PAST, IF YOU DID

Write down what you think about them, even if your first sentence is: "I have never written anything good." If you're thinking "I have never written anything," write that down. Then think, "Why?" and write down your answer: "I've never had anything to say." Ask yourself why not. "I thought I didn't have enough education." Why do you think a person needs to be educated to write?

By asking yourself questions (any questions that come to mind—it's *your* assignment), work through a paragraph. (Who cares about spelling? Forget it, and write.)

SPEND SOME TIME THINKING

Contemplate your situation. Determine where you are as a writer. Identify your writing assets. What do you do well; whom do you have to encourage you? What does your schedule or locale have to offer? Think over your past writing accomplishments, dreams, and plans and jot down your thoughts about them in your daily journal.

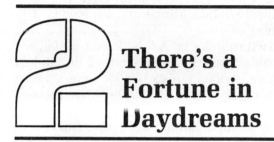

2 There's a Fortune in Daydreams

How long has it been since you sat on the patio with no portable radio at your side, no magazines to read, no one to talk to, no toenail clipper or nail file to entertain you, no one to watch, and no one, not even your own conscience, to tell you to get up and do something? How long since you sat in the recliner on your day off, with no TV, lost in your own thoughts? How long since you stretched out on the grass amid the violets to watch the clouds float by, only vaguely aware of the ladybug on your tee shirt, too wrapped up in daydreaming to tell her to "fly away home"?

The whole world revolves around daydreams. In just the past century, dreamers have picked up one ball after another and run with it. We've gone from the Wright brothers' "hang glider" all the way to the moon—and back again to the hang glider, just for fun. From Lindbergh's daring flight across the Atlantic we've progressed to NASA's successful spaceship adventures. Ford's first idea may have been wild fantasy, but he and other dreamers with "better ideas" put the whole world on wheels. Dreamers tore down cities and cemented acre after acre of rolling farmland to make room for the speeding traffic. Dreamers created amazing cloverleafs to join here to there. Increased transportation soon proved them to be so grossly inadequate that other dreamers were challenged to develop them into a network of highways so intricate that a high, winding stack of overpasses and underpasses tangled together in Duluth, Minnesota, was immediately dubbed "the can of worms."

When compared with my elegant Adler SE1000, my father's cherished little portable typewriter seems out of the Middle Ages. Dreamers who understood typists like me came up with the best idea yet: lift-off tape. And as I write, some dreamer somewhere has his feet on the desk and his head in the clouds, antiquating my investment by creating a word processor I can afford.

Inventors, artists, and writers all have the magical ability which Mayme Rice Smith, a *Childcraft* writer, calls "the magic power of your thoughts to make pictures." Webster breaks imagination down into *reproducing* and *creating*.

Mental creations may be consistent with reality. One dabbles with real situations, real places, and/or real people, or one creates situations, places, and people who seem to be real.

Fantasy is traditionally defined as "the unrestrained creation of the imagination," although this definition has been broadened to include creating mental images of people and places in the real world: "freely envisioned thought." You might fantasize becoming president of your corporation, for example. It's true fantasy if you're a young person starting out as a file clerk, but it is a possibility if you're already near the top, perhaps handling all the president's complex and confidential affairs. Romantic fantasies include the proverbial Prince or Princess Charming, the dream character who may never appear. Fantasies may be mental pictures of unreal situations bordering on whimsy, hallucinations, or grotesque scenes out of character with the dreamer in real life. But they might also involve real situations with people close enough to make the dream come true.

The expression, "What's your fantasy?" often brings a response that is quite feasible. Mine is to win the Sweepstakes, gaining enough riches to last a lifetime so I could buy the house I live in and hire my landlady as permanent caretaker, so nothing would ever have to change.

Fantasy, in the modern sense, is useful as hindsight. Long after all opportunity to respond is gone, one can think of witty replies to a remark, clever contributions to a brainstorming session, or superb solutions to important problems. If frustration results from thoughts having come too late, one can turn to foresight: The next time the occasion arises I will say thus and so. Of course, such thoughts are *pure* fantasy. Life is too complicated to fall into such a predictable pattern. If ever we do chance to meet again, my next conversation with the same person will be on an entirely new subject, and I may be lost trying to recall what I wished I had said the last time we met!

What kind of mind do you have? One that tends to boredom? One that leans toward loneliness? A very active mind, always darting here and there, always thinking, thinking, thinking? An extremely creative mind? A scientific mind? A mind full of ideas, or memories, or plans, or orderly thoughts?

LEARN TO USE YOUR MIND

Most minds are continually active, and people find a variety of ways to cope with the pressure of thoughts. You can drug your mind and not think; you can occupy your mind: turn it over to the media to fill it, entertain it, exercise it, or keep it too busy to have time to wander elsewhere; you can turn it over to merchants or companions who will tantalize it with trinkets to buy, places to go, and things to do; and you can close your mind, either by blocking out uncomfortable thoughts, or by going to sleep.

Or, you can *use* your mind.

For the past quarter of a century, twenty-five years (maybe that doesn't sound as bad), I have lived alone. Many of those years were spent as a missionary in Morocco. I lived most of eleven years at a mission-owned retreat on the rolling fields near the foothills of the Atlas Mountains. My neighbors were North African Berbers, seminomadic people whose biggest event in life was Tuesday market day and whose household moves came about by a need to begin life anew in a spot where fleas of seasons past had died.

Life began early in the morning, just before sunup. All day long the whole family worked at tedious, backbreaking chores on their primitive farm. At sundown, after a meal of pancakes and mint tea, they lay down together in their tent side by side on a handmade straw-and-wool mat, the entire family blanketed with one heavy, homemade rug. The fire in the corner of the tent burned out. Someone extinguished the tiny carbon lamp. The dogs sneaked in and huddled close to the family, as did kittens, chickens, sick lambs, and maybe a baby goat or two. By eight o'clock the whole community was asleep, and I, in my clean, comfortable, American-style abode, was left all alone with my thoughts.

During those long, dark nights by myself, away from family and friends, with neither a telephone nor electric lights, I experienced my share of loneliness, fear, and insecurity. To keep my sanity after everything available to read had been read, and all the letters to write had been written, I sat by the flickering kerosene lamp and jotted down page after page of whatever came to mind—like:

> The rays of the sun burst through the morning fog, dispelling it. God is! God is! God is! We may be devoid of human companionship and we may be desperately lonely, but we do not need to be disconsolate. God is! And we who experience many silent hours alone have the unique privilege of getting to know Him better. We can feel His presence in the stillness of the morning. And when the sun goes down, we know He is there.

I've told you that I went to bed every night as a child with the comfort of my father's study light still on, lulled to sleep by the sound of his typewriter clicking away. He was a scientist, a professor, a minister, and a poet. Any hat he might have chosen to put on would have required a certain amount of study and typing. But I know now that often he was not working on a required project. He was deliberately roping in his mind, controlling his thoughts, and putting them to constructive use.

Writing does just that. The most distressing days of my life surrounded my decsion to leave Morocco. I went to the home of missionary-friends—a sanctuary for all of us when we needed it. Clem Payne was a listener more than a counselor. His wife, Dot, was a good cook and a down-to-earth, faithful friend. Their door was always open, and there was always room for one more at their big oak table. You could talk or not talk, share or not share, work or not work.

In this remarkable home I found immense support and the answers I was looking for. Recalling those days I realize that my decision fell into place because I controlled my mind two ways. I sewed the most fantastic wardrobe any Barbie doll had ever owned—tiny, elaborate garments of velvet, satin, and bits of lace. And I wrote a story.

It was totally unplanned. One morning I was tired of crying, tired of struggling to decide. I began to put pen to paper. The words marched along in orderly fashion from page to page. A couple of years later, far from my Moroccan home, I expanded my story. What I had used as "therapy"—backing away from my problem so my subconscious could work out a solution—taught many Americans something about Moroccan life. Eventually *King of the Vagabonds*, a little paperback in print only one year, earned more than $1,000 in royalties.

That's what you call constructive thinking. Roping in your mind, whether to save your sanity or to deliberately choose to make better use of your time, is important to becoming a successful writer. Left untamed, the mind is like a wild kitten, wandering way out of bounds, but scurrying for a hiding place in fear when some intelligent human being appears. Left untrained, it becomes obnoxious, of no use to anyone, and disliked by all, like a half-grown mannerless pup.

Taming and training the mind requires self-discipline. I can waste a whole day daydreaming. Early in the morning I snuggle down in my warm robe with a hot cup of freshly brewed coffee. My morning chair faces the dining room window, which overlooks our large, wooded backyard. I lean back and put my feet on the windowsill. In summer there's a birdbath to entertain me; in winter it's suet on the clothesline, and a piggish flock of starlings all trying to eat at once. The sassy blue jays work together, one guarding the distant spot where they plan to hoard their pile of leftover dogfood, another flying back and forth, trip after trip, to move the whole supply to safety. The male cardinals spend the morning fighting, chasing one another away from the birdseed, all going hungry. The little downy woodpecker, fat as a plum, scoots up and down the tree trunk waiting his chance at the suet. Then he darts to the clothesline, where he hangs upside down by his feet, relishing the thought of another feasting day. At last he hops onto the net bag and pecks away, oblivious to all the feathered activity around him.

Oh yes, I can easily spend a day, a whole day, watching the birds, mind roaming here and there. The next day the thoughts are gone. Even if they were good thoughts, some of them, they are gone, never to be recalled.

Daydreaming can be turned to profit if you learn to control your mind: analyzing your thoughts, recording what's worth keeping, and dumping the rest. My niece, Jan Markell, has been a birdwatcher, too. Her first published poem is about a tiny sparrow. She decoupaged an original copy of it, and this treasure inspires me regularly from its top-priority spot on my dining room wall:

You out there . . .
Feathers ruffled with the wind and snow,
Perched on a branch
Nearly bent in two,
Clutching to it calmly,
Swaying, almost in time
To the beat of the winter wind.

Why do you, a tiny sparrow,
Peer into my window . . .
And almost into my mind?
What is it you would say,
   should we communicate?

And if I should make a warm nest for you,
Would you leave your perch

And forsake the winter chill?
I think not.
Yet you are speaking to me
With your tranquility,
steadfastness,
and courage.

The sun shines now to warm your icy wings.
The wind and snow have ceased their cruel sting.
You jubilantly echo a new song . . .

"This storm He has seen me through . . .
Would He do less
through the storms of life
for you?"[1]

Jan's writing was not only good from the start, it also happened to be timed right. She studied the markets and sent things to the right places; and she persevered. In a sense, it all began by her watching the birds and doing something constructive with the thoughts daydreaming produced.

Daydreams fall into three main categories: reminiscing about the past, reflecting on present situations, or dreaming about the future. Daydreams are light, misty, and changeable, as if the mind were flipping without interest through a magazine or photo album. They differ from imagination, which can unearth the past to study all its ramifications, examine the present, make plans and solve problems (or create problems that don't exist), and categorize the future into things to do, things to hope for, and things to worry about. Daydreams can disappear all too easily, but imagination keeps on working even when pushed to the back of the mind. Fantasy may begin as a daydream, but it is guided and directed by the imagination. Fantasy can relive the past, enliven the present, and envision a future too good (or too bad) to be true. Fantasy paints her pictures in splashes of brilliant color, like giant murals on a wall or multimedia presentations created by synchronized projectors flashing on and off in perfect time.

We may say the author of *Robinson Crusoe* had a good imagination, for he did have. He entertained Crusoe, stranded on his desert island, year after year, bringing in the companionship of a dog and some cats as an afterthought, since he had earlier neglected to say they were carried across the channel on Crusoe's makeshift raft from the sinking ship during the first few weeks. He entertained his readers for twenty-five years before bringing Friday into the picture. By that time he was winding down, preparing for Crusoe's eventual rescue.

The author of *Alice in Wonderland*, on the other hand, employed more than imagination. Lewis Carroll was a master of fantasy. Carroll is said to have written *Alice in Wonderland* (as *Alice Underground*) for three little sisters, one of whom was named Alice. He wrote the story by hand and illustrated it himself. Later he enlarged it for pubication, and it was an instant success. He tells us the story was inspired by a river trip.

Imagine, then, the three little girls in the rowboat with their friend, laughing and poking fun all along the way. "Tell us a story!" pleads Alice. "There will be nonsense in it!" cries her sister. And Carroll plunges in:

> Alice was beginning to get very tired of sitting by her sister on the bank, and of having nothing to do . . . Suddenly a white rabbit with pink ears ran close by her . . . the Rabbit actually *took a watch out of his waistcoat pocket*, and looked at it, and then hurried on.

With such a fanciful start, Carroll takes Alice through a fantasy world. As in a dream, the oddest things happen, combining with a bit of common sense, as also happens in dreams. He weaves a story endurable enough to be translated into one language after another; a story well loved enough to be reprinted many times during the last 120 years.

Jules Verne, the French author who is known for the tales of his imaginary voyages, used his keen imagination in an entirely different way. Writing in the late 1800s, he succeeded in turning out fascinating science fiction travel stories. His novels, among them *Journey to the Center of the Earth, Twenty Thousand Leagues Under the Sea*, and *Around the World in Eighty Days*, read like the diaries of a seasoned traveler whose eyes are wide open to the world around him.

Verne's eyes saw well beyond what most eyes of his day were seeing. He wrote amazing accounts of scientific advances that were only in the fantasy stage for scattered inventors of genius. In *Twenty Thousand Leagues Under the Sea*, for example, the protagonist is aboard a submarine, the *Nautilus*. Though the story is said to be for children, the modern-day reporting style intrigues adults. In the mid-1800s, clipper ships were at their peak. Submarines came into practical use decades after Verne's story of the *Nautilus*, which traveled as far, as fast, and as deep as his clever mind wanted it to.

Verne, probably building his book from whatever bits of information his creative mind could use as a foundation, looked beyond the known and wrote about what was to be as if it had already been done. The inventor of the submarine is all but forgotten, but Verne, the science fiction writer, lives on.

MEMORY IS A KEY FACTOR

We've spent some time analyzing the shades of difference between daydreams, imagination, and fantasy, and the ways they've been used by writers of the past. One other thing should be mentioned: memory—the ability to remember.

Obviously, writers who rely on imagination and fantasy are blessed with good memory: the ability to draw on information stored in their minds to create or vitalize their writing. The absent-minded professor is not a myth, however. Creative writers, those who draw up ideas from the deep wells of their minds, can be quite scatterbrained in everyday life. I certainly can be. If I do write notes to myself and manage not to lose them, I wonder later what in the world they mean, because their messages are grossly ambiguous. The best creative writers are more organized than I am, though I'm beginning to surprise myself with new tricks I've learned to stave off total chaos.

Oh, to be neat! My carelessness hinders my progress, because my files are in disarray and my memory can't fill in all the gaps. The market is crammed with humorous material, stories, drama, soap operas, science fiction, western thrillers, mysteries, and gossip columns (which are purely creative) because the public demands them. Advertisers capitalize on this demand, too, relying on creative writers to produce clever copy guaranteed to grab John Doe's wallet while he has his head back, laughing. Careful, organized writers, using their God-given memories, are more apt to get the job done than are slobs. The message is shape up or ship out. I intend to do better, as soon as I finish this book.

In addition, myriad opportunities in nonfiction await the writer: news articles, textbooks, research articles, instruction manuals, job descriptions, resumes, catalog copy, and technical articles. They require precise reporting skills, accurate notes, and a keen memory for details. Memory is a key factor for successful nonfiction writing.

There is a point at which daydreams disintegrate as either imagination or fantasy breaks in. The moment the skilled writer has been watching for has arrived. He feels it coming on. He shakes himself to vigilance as his mind prepares for action. He grabs a scribble sheet. As creativity takes over, the memory goes to work exploring the brain, playing out whatever facts are needed for the writing at hand.

Creativity, though highly valued and coveted by all writers, may be a hindrance when what is needed is a step-by-step account of facts. Sometimes I find it imperative to tell my creative self again and again to get out of the way, until at times I finally get cross with myself. Ghostwriting, for example, should be in character with the person for whom it is done. It requires stepping into the other person's mind, thinking as he thinks. I have successfully completed many ghostwriting assignments, but I recall one when I decided at the last minute not to allow the article to go to print under another byline. My creative self had gotten out of the cage, and I wanted credit for what it had done.

You might end up writing serious, factual material which, if it is top quality, is a commendable and satisfying achievement. At a funeral, an elderly friend asked me slyly, "What are you going to put in *my* obituary?" She had guessed my secret: I had written the eulogy! I can also get excited about selling nuts and bolts, and reporting news, both of which require a repeating of sometimes colorless facts.

If you choose the route of no-nonsense nonfiction, let me remind you that you have a creative self, too. Later you may prefer to leave it caged, but I want you to let it out and to get acquainted with it before making that decision. To excel (and no other goal is worthy of consideration), the writer must be in touch with his creative self, able to transmit life and feeling to paper when the occasion calls for it.

Now the obvious question comes: If there's a fortune in daydreams, how can you, as a budding writer, cash in on it?

EXAMINE YOUR MIND

Test your imagination abilities and think about your fantasy potential.

People afraid to be alone rush for either the *TV Guide* or the telephone when forced to spend an hour by themselves. Shoveling snow, mowing the lawn, and doing other routine jobs provide wonderful opportunities for thinking, but earmuff radios provide a way of escape for folks who prefer not to. Memories can be rotten. Starting the process of imagination can be a distasteful job because, "imagination is the power of the mind to re*produce* concepts or images *stored* in the memory, and recombining *former experiences* in the creation of new ones." If you refuse to get out the old memories and look at them, you cripple the process of imagination.

A few years ago, I was bitten by a brown recluse spider (in Missouri, not Africa). Since this spider's bite is lethal (second only to the black widow's in deadliness), the illness that followed was quite severe, and my recovery was hindered, as well, by side effects from various drugs. We have a healthy respect for the old shed where Madam Recluse and I met.

If you've been stung a time or two in your life, you may want to approach the dusty relics in your mind very carefully.

So how do you work up courage to begin?

When it comes time to clean the old shed, I put off thinking about it. No one would know I was aware an old shed existed. Suddenly, unplanned, early one cold spring morning while the spiders are still sleeping, I bundle up with boots and a hooded sweatshirt, spray can in one hand and broom in the other, and tromp down there. Out come lawn furniture, hoses, tools, gas can, trash, and lawnmower, and in go I and my broom.

Once you get started spring-cleaning your mind, you'll find the process invigorating and fun. Find the right time and the right place. Beauty is inspiring. A comfortable chair in a peaceful room, or a deck chair on an ocean liner if you can arrange that—a cabin in the Alps, maybe . . .

The Alps! You see? My mind, trained to sniff memories for their possible literary value, jumped on that one and I had all I could do to hold it back. My home in Switzerland was not in the Alps, but in the Jura Mountains: cowbells tinkling all around, wide expanses of lush green pastures with walking paths cutting right across them so I could stop and pat the cows—aged cheese, strong sausage, fresh milk, big pink peonies, the odor of wood smoke from the pot belly stove, nice people . . .

What are *you* finding? Do you have a recorder handy, or tools to write things down? Is your mind digging through the treasures in your past life? One way you can start the process is to think:

> *First grade:* We lived (where?). Our house was (recall what it was like). Our family consisted of (who?). My best friend was (an adult, a child, a pet). I liked (doing what? going where?). I feared (what?). I wanted (what?). I didn't want (what?).
>
> *Second grade:* What do you remember about school? (We had a rhythm band. My celluloid rattle was cracked, so I opened it and hooked it on the ear of the boy in front of me.)
>
> *Third grade:* Who was your teacher? (I remember recess: sliding down the school hill on hunks of tin or cardboard. This is also the year our house burned down, and we moved to the city, where instead of walking to Sunday school, we were hauled, standing up, in the back of an open cattle truck!)

If you're half as old as I am, you'll soon have enough seed thoughts to keep you daydreaming for ten years. After that it will come naturally. Let's imagine you are a teacher or parent, as well as having been a first grader yourself. All those recollections should also come out for contemplation: your children's first puppy; the children in your classroom, one by one, their faces, the clothing they wore, the homes they came from, the curtains on the windows of those homes; the zoos you've visited; the trips you've taken and memorable experiences on those trips; the games you've played or watched; the people you've met down through the years, their peculiarities and what they meant to you.

Allowing your mind to wander through the past also helps you to examine your feelings and evaluate your self-esteem. This is important, because to be a good writer you must be in touch with yourself. Are you comfortable in solitude? Do you enjoy your own presence? Do you like being you? If so, what influences in your past life built this self-confidence into you? If not, why not? Writers must be able to describe intangibles so vividly that others can share them. How might you record you attitudes toward others, your methods of coping with anxiety, fear, hatred, grief, or pain? What would you hate most to find out about yourself? If you discovered you were a phony, a coward, or cruel, how would you react? Have things happened in your life to make you feel dumb, ugly, or helpless? How can you describe that feeling?

Your present life is worth daydreaming about, too—your job, hobbies, neighbors, home, pleasures, future plans, dreams, possibilities, and hopes.

So much for material to prime your daydream pump. If you have any imagination at all, you can take it from there. How about fantasy? What direction does your mind take? Jules Verne's went to science fiction. Lewis Carroll created stories children love. I—shall I admit it?—tend toward the morbid. I die, or lie near death, surrounded by friends or all by myself. My neighbor's dog dies. Those I love, my dog, my relatives, and my special friends, never grace my morbid fantasy. For fun, I've tried to put them there. They won't stay. They burst the bubble and escape.

Where does your mind go when you turn it loose? Practice doing it, keeping it on a leash so you can pull it back for examination. Keep a diary of fantasies for a while. If you dare.

DECIDE WHAT IS CLASSIFIED INFORMATION

Some part of your thought life is classified, naturally. For one thing, other people are involved. If you write about your mean mother, flaunting her faults, you embarrass her and the rest of the family, which you may or may not want to do. Your mother might overlook your libelous comments and keep on loving you. Others may sue you for libel. Obviously, you can't tell all. (But you can *use* all. We'll get to that later.)

You can lose good friends exposing your feelings and beliefs! This brings up the awesome realization that you, if you pursue writing, will go public with your thoughts and opinions, bare your heart, and allow others to feel what you feel and know what you think. Even in the most detached forms of writing, you are putting *yourself* on paper. If you are right, someone may disagree with you; and if you are wrong, the world will know it.

Part of you must remain private. Everyone needs space of his own, a place to which he can escape mentally, if not physically, when the mad, mad world gets to spinning crazily about him. As you turn your mind loose to dream, to plan, and to envision, remember that you own all those memories, all those amazing original thoughts which have grown out of your own life. Since you own it all, you must control its use. You do stick your neck out in creative writing. How far out is for you to decide.

WHAT CAN YOU DO WITH WHAT YOU'VE GOT?

In an article entitled, "Doing Nothing Better," Thomas W. Klewin said:

> My son was sitting there, doing nothing, staring off into space, lost in thought, in daydreaming, or in the world of his imagination. I intruded into his world of silence with a question: "What are you doing?"
>
> "Nothing," he replied.

> My response was automatic, triggered by an old adage . . . "An idle mind is the devil's workshop." And my parents had added, "So are idle hands; they do nothing but get you into trouble."
>
> So I replied to my son, "Well, why don't you find something to do?"
>
> His answer made me pause and reevaluate the old adages . . . He simply asked me, "Why? What's wrong with doing nothing?"[1]

In the same article, Klewin refers to the comment of a friend who mused that King David's *Psalms* were written during quiet moments out on Judean hillsides. Said the friend, "The American has a strong feeling he must somehow justify even his leisure . . ."

Klewin used his memories as the jumping-off place for an article on constructive daydreaming. I used a memory of a friend on a patio recliner clipping her toenails. Big deal, you say. Well, it's something constructive to be busy with. The Morocco memories are obvious. We've already said that Jan's poem about the sparrow was a product of daydreaming. We've talked about the creativity of various authors and inventors who dared to dream.

The best way to use your memories is unobtrusively, weaving them in as illustrations to back up what you have said, or drawing colorful thoughts, vocabulary, or expressions from them. I recalled an old lady saying "fat as a plum," and it seemed to describe my woodpecker.

I've coauthored books in which I used numerous anecdotes out of my life. Writing to you, I feel comfortable saying "I this," and "I that." It's as if we're sitting together wherever you are, and I'm telling you what I know about writing. But in the books I wrote with others I couldn't do that. Instead, I created some Molly Boggleswoggle, had the things happen to her, and slipped them into place as if they belonged there. If I hadn't told *you*, nobody would know.

Memories can creep into fiction unobtrusively. For example, I recalled that in second grade I had used my broken rattle to pinch a boy's ear. You can bet that will show up in some children's story now that I've remembered it, as well as the sliding at recess in the third grade. I don't anticipate using our family house fire (I was away at school, so it isn't vivid), but that home was down the hill from the potato patch. I checked recently during a visit to the vacant field where our house and barn once stood. The pump is gone. The house, with its candlelighted Christmas tree, still stands in my mind, waiting to become the setting of a novel yet to come.

INSOMNIA

Insomnia, of course, is very frustrating. Daydreaming can be pleasant, but insomnia rarely is. Somehow, at night, the mind tunes in to morbid, unhappy channels. Some people are plagued with waking up in the middle of the night. "I couldn't sleep a wink last night," they moan. I know the feeling, but I express it a little differently. I say, "I woke up early this morning." If it's after midnight, it's morning. I get up, make coffee, and think. Even at 3:00 A.M. Even at 2:00 A.M.!

One of the best ways to use the hours of daydreaming and the nights of insomnia is to attack them with vigor, pen in hand. If you begin to jot your thoughts down, you will find that before long you'll have a rich source of ideas for future literary endeavors. The most important thing to keep in mind about daydreams is that they are only seed thoughts. From them ideas sprout, and from the ideas grow meaningful prose and poetry. You will find, as you begin to allow yourself the pleasure of doing nothing, that you'll jump up with increasing frequency to write down what has popped into your head.

We call that inspiration. But the truth is, it can be learned.

ASSIGNMENT 2

WARM-UP: If you have already been writing, get out your material and read it over. Praise yourself for whatever you think is exceptional, circle clever phrases, and mark really good paragraphs or sections you can use at some later date. You might think some things are poorly written, but don't throw anything away. Sort everything you have written into two boxes or drawers. Label the small one "GOOD" and the big one "GARBAGE." Hide the garbage but keep it, because we will use it from time to time. The writing may be unorganized or downright dumb, but on the other hand, the basic ideas could be very good.

NEXT: Organize the notes you have jotted down. As you go over them, open your mind to the writing possibilities they offer. If you come up with ideas, make a list:

SUBJECT	TYPE OF WRITING
Woolly brown dog	News article on stray dogs
Daydreaming	Short story about a dreamer
New baby	Article on child-rearing
Vacation trip	Travel article, or article about a dreamer

Before this day is done, write something. It doesn't have to be fancy. You have a garbage file now, you know. You can practice all you want, and hide it there.

IN ADDITION: Don't neglect your daily journal. For the present, that may be your most important writing.

FINALLY: Spend plenty of time "meditatin'!" And check your writing supplies. If an idea pops into you head, can you get to a pencil and paper fast enough to write it down?

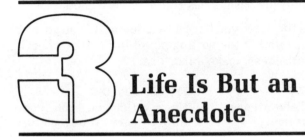

3 Life Is But an Anecdote

A prolific writer of romances said in a TV interview that she gets up every morning before dawn and writes furiously from 4:00 A.M. until 11:00 A.M.

I could do that if I were better disciplined, for I, too, am a morning person. Unfortunately, I'm addicted to the call of the wild, so when weather permits, I'm more apt to don suitable ragtag clothing and set out with two Old English Sheepdogs, Barney and Brandy, on a hike through the woods. Not far from my home there's a gravel pit that joins an undeveloped hillside overlooking a busy freeway, and beyond, the east bottoms of the Missouri River. One favorite vantage point allows the dogs and me to enjoy a breathtaking view of downtown Kansas City. Another hilltop affords a marvelous resting place from which to gaze at the ever-changing sunrise. We stop there so often that the dogs race ahead and lie down to wait. Huffing and puffing, I soon join them. After I pause a few minutes to let my soul catch up with my body, we follow an up-and-down motorcycle trail carved through thick woods—woods so wild that we've seen, on a lucky day, a quick red fox dart across our pathway.

One such morning I left the house wearing sandals. It was a mistake, because the temperature was in the low 30s and there was a light frost on the ground. I started up Sunrise Mountain, which is a dirt cliff worn smooth by the daring bikers, but about halfway up the steep incline I ran into trouble, because it was slippery. After a short struggle, I took off my sandals and threw them up over the crest of the hill. I still couldn't make it. It would have been possible, of course, to sit down and slide back to the bottom, but my shoes were at the top. The dogs looked down at me, panting huge grins. I clawed unsuccessfully into the sandy trail, but made no progress at all. At last I gave up trying that approach. On my bottom I scooted over to the nearby brush and timberline and struggled up through the briars and weeds to the top of the hill.

As I retrieved my sandals, a "moral to the story" came to mind. The whole article fell into place as I hiked on home, but the dogs needed water and I needed a cup of coffee and a few minutes in the easy chair with my feet on the windowsill. When the chores were done and I had recovered sufficiently to begin writing it all down, I glanced at the clock. Too late. Time to get ready for work. Writing was out of the question for that morning.

At dawn the next day, in the mood for writing, I tackled the article. It was gone. Though I have pondered, meditated, and even run that route again to try to recover it, I have never found the beautiful thoughts given me that frosty morning.

To preserve "inspired" thoughts, you must write them down while you have them. The creative process seems to run in cycles, like an evening's round of television programs. When the set goes off, the thoughts that have been projected are suddenly gone. The screen is gray and lifeless. When you do turn it on again, even if you're lucky enough to get a re-run of something you wish you could see again, it comes through the second time far less captivating than the first.

Life is full of moments worth recording for later use as anecdotes—mini-stories relating incidents, small glimpses into private lives, short narrations of interesting facts. Editorial guidelines can be obtained from prospective publishers. Requirements may vary in every other way: the field of subject matter, the scope it covers, the length required, the vocabulary level, the approach, the preferred writing style, and on and on; but one stipulation is almost always noted—"Give us anecdotes!"

Successful writers record everything worth keeping when it comes to them. Like a bunch of pack rats they hoard treasures they run across, storing them in a safe place. The collection might be orderly, or it might be in total disarray; but they can go to their heap of goodies and dig things out. The mind recalls only that there was such an incident. It must be down on paper in black and white to bring it back in full detail, as it happened, when it happened. This means pulling off the freeway at the nearest exit to stop and write down an important thought. Or stopping your grocery cart to pull a card out to jot something down before it leaves your mind. It might mean putting your boss on hold a couple of minutes so you can scribble out your idea before he boggles your mind with his own thoughts.

If you're at all serious about writing, you've already been doing this to some extent. Chances are you have some kind of a collection of your attempts at putting words on paper. Quite possibly, you've got a box or drawer into which you poke articles or book ideas, or you have a few poems framed.

A tenth-grader who called herself a beginner asked if she could bring me some of her poems. She came lugging a thick, three-ring binder. When I expressed surprise at how many poems she had written, she admitted to having three more notebooks just like it back home. As I glanced over the poems, it seemed clear to me that this was much more than poetry. It was the story of her life, expressed with deep feeling in free verse, a rare treasure, indeed.

By the tenth grade I, too, had several spiral notebooks filled with poems. Everything significant that had happened in my life and many things I had hoped would happen merited two or three rhymed verses. Only a few survived the journeys of my adventuresome life:

I sometimes wonder how it would be
If I were you, and you were me.

If I should look just like you do,
And you should look just like me, too,
'Twould be a mix-up, I should say—
I'd rather be me, any day!

My college-level education was missionary training, which began a new era in my literary zeal. I fell in love with the poetry of others: deep, moving religious poems that expressed my heart's awakening realizations of God's awesome power, His right as God to guide my life, and my willingness to let Him do so. Another notebook, a black, three-ring binder, was quickly filled with these treasures, many of them read so often I could quote them to you now. And well that I can! Somewhere along the line, my college notebooks were lost, too.

My third serious collection I mixed with an office illustration file. When I left that job, the collection had to stay behind, because it was not possible, at that point, to determine which clippings were mine, and which were theirs.

In the ensuing years, I've recovered from various sources many of the poems. I've built up a pretty extensive file of illustrations and ideas. My first leather Bible (which contained a wealth of irreplaceable notes) was stolen from my car in Morocco along with most of my personal belongings. I was packed for a two-week vacation, so you can imagine the loss! One poem I've yet to find was written in the Bible:

Let me hold lightly things of this earth;
Transient treasures—what are they worth?
Moths can corrupt them, rust can decay.
All their bright beauty fades in a day . . .

—*Author unknown*

Transient treasures! Someday we'll leave them all behind. But until we do, we have a heap of work, and some of the transient treasures are necessary tools. Flood, fire, moths, mold, mud, kids, thieves—nothing can stop a true writer from picking up and starting all over again, building up a new storehouse of illustrations and ideas, including anecdotes of his own, and borrowed ones. I call it the "i and i file," and I consider it very important.

My present collection, mostly tucked into manila folders in a four-drawer file, includes notes beginning with my stormy start in missionary life. I arrived at Newark Airport at 2:00 A.M. filled with all the horror stories of the Big Apple a midwestern youngster could collect, took a terrifying taxi ride to Hoboken (certain it was not really our destination), and discovered that my trunks were missing. Everything I owned in the world had missed the boat! In addition to all my own notes, I have all the letters I wrote my mother about that experience and the years that followed, a fairly extensive diary she kept for me. After my mother died, Helga, Jan's mother, took up that cause.

It took me a long time to re-enter American middle class life—to adjust to materialism (the clamor for more, more, more) and to find meaning in the Mad Dash Syndrome after living with the easygoing Berbers for so long (I still don't wear a watch!). To ease into suburbia, I worked weekends in the inner city; so I have in file security reports from my stint as housemother at a Job Corps lounge, a life too foreign for most Americans to comprehend. I wrote (and saved) the dedication for a book that never got written about those midnight escapades: fifty, sixty, seventy toughened teenage girls (black, white, Indian) against me and my armed guard, a huge black man from Mississippi they loved and hated in turn. Just glancing at it flooded my mind with at least fifty pages:

> This book is written in the hope that nice suburban ladies will stop rolling bandages for African lepers, and bake a few cookies for inner city kids. Because nowadays, bandages don't count. But cookies do.

From my suburban hilltop—safe enough to hike to at dusk—I often gaze at the twinkling lights of evening traffic on the bridge and the familiar tall buildings downtown silhouetted against the western sky. I know the peaceful view is deceptive. After one such outing I scribbled:

> Somewhere, as rats waddle past unnoticed, women curse, men cry, kids steal, dogs cringe. Somewhere a switchblade flashes, a fist is clenched, a gun whips out. Somewhere a

> youngster drops his first filthy needle into the vein. Somewhere a teenager struggles to free herself from hoodlums. Somewhere a child gives birth to a child.
>
> Somewhere in the darkness, sirens wail. Anger, hatred, fear, lust, poverty, and cruelty rule the night. Sickness. Sadness. Screaming. Grief.
>
> Somewhere. Tonight. Somewhere in your city. Not very far away.

So much for my i and i file. What should yours contain?

YOUR OWN THOUGHTS

I've given you a few samples of anecdotes I jotted down and filed, thoughts I had when certain things happened in my life. In the previous chapter we discussed daydreams, imagination, fantasies, and memories, all of which hold potential for your file.

Your i and i file, from which you'll draw anecdotes for years to come, can begin as a print-out of things your mind produces as you free yourself to think. Later we'll discuss your writing options, but keep in mind the varied forms of writing you see, remembering that the whole gamut of thoughts has value for one kind of writing or another.

The first step to setting up an illustration and idea file is to arrange quick, easy access to something to write *with*, and something to write *on*. Scratch pads or file cards and workable ballpoints or sharpened pencils belong in your car, boat, and pickup truck; by your TV chair; beside the telephone; in your purse or pocket; near the kitchen sink; close to the bathtub; certainly by the bedside table; and anyplace else you might need them. Nothing kills creativity so quickly as frustration. While you scrounge around hunting for proper tools, the tremendous idea you had is apt to float right back to where it came from. Or someone will come along to interrupt your flow of thoughts, inadvertently bumping the erase button.

The second step is to write down enough to make the illustration or idea worthwhile a few weeks or even years down the road. Many of my ideas were written out in full as they came to me—the thoughts on inner city, for example. When I finally use them, they might be taken out of context and changed so much you wouldn't recognize them; or I might pick them up just as they are, dropping them into some article in their proper setting. One's mind learns to cooperate beautifully, becoming, in time, versatile enough to fetch those forgotten treasures so they can be utilized in amazing ways. If you record them carefully when they happen, you practically guarantee a steady flow of anecdotal material for future use.

CLIPPINGS, PHOTO COPIES, AND NOTES

What others have written or said makes up a large portion of better i and i files. You are not the only rose on the bush. Others, too, have thoughts worth keeping. You are already aware of this, I'm sure, because almost all writers love to read. But do you keep choice items with a view to using them in the future?

Here's one for your file:

PERSEVERANCE

Don't Quit

When things go wrong, as they sometimes will,
When the road you're trudging seems all uphill,
When the funds are low and the debts are high,
And you want to smile, but you have to sigh,
When care is pressing you down a bit,
Rest if you must—but don't you quit.

—author unknown

From *The Best Loved Poems of the American People*
Selected by Hazel Felleman, Copyright 1936 by
Doubleday and Company, Inc.

Writers fall in love with the mailbox very quickly and, if they're smart, with the library, so you might appreciate this one:

> LIBRARY
>
> After returning an overdue book at the public library,
> a small boy stood at the desk with his past due notice
> in one hand and his fine in the other.
> After he had paid his fine he asked,
> "Please, can I have the letter back? It's the
> first one I ever got."
>
> *The New Catholic Treasury of Wit and Humor,* edited by Paul Bussard; from *My Third Reader's Notebook,* Compiled by Gerald Kennedy, Copyright 1974 by Abingdon Press.

And here, especially for writers, are a couple of gems which might help you become a better one:

> WRITERS (CONTENT)
>
> The reason why so few good books are written is that so few people who can write know anything.
>
> —Walter Bagehot
>
> Writers seldom write the things they think.
> They simply write the things they think other folks
> think they think.
>
> —Elbert Hubbard

Start right at the beginning to write down the source of your information. Where did you find it? What newspaper? What date? Who wrote it? The following should be included: title of the book or magazine, author, publisher, and copyright notice, if there is one. Record the name of a speaker, where he was speaking, and when, as well as the thought you consider worth keeping. If there is newspaper coverage or other printed matter that seems significant, clip it to the card.

To incorporate such material in future writing you'll need to write the copyright owner for permission to use it. Under the new copyright law, if a publication is not copyrighted, the author of the material is still protected if the author makes sure that his own copyright notice appears with the piece (good news for all of us!); so in order to quote from it you would need permission from the author. Generally it is best to write him or her in care of the publisher.

We writers must be most careful to extend this golden rule courtesy to one another, never reprinting someone else's material without acknowledging it, always asking permission to do so if the quotation is substantial. Less than fifty words out of a book or a couple of sentences out of a long article is considered fair use. Poetry and songs require written permission from the copyright holder. As to prose, even a fairly short quotation should have either an acknowledgment of the sources or a credit line. This can be typed at the bottom of the page of an article, but in a book manuscript a sheet of notes for each chapter should be typed separately. (This makes typesetting by the publisher much easier.)

It's the writer's responsibility to obtain permissions. On down the line you'll thank yourself for every bit of information you have kept on quotations and clippings in your initial i and i file; and keeping up the practice consistently is a habit you'll be glad you formed.

To be quoted by a fellow writer is the highest compliment one can receive. The question is not so much one of "Can I get by with using this?" as it is remembering that if it were your own writing, you would appreciate knowing your words were to be reprinted. No one likes to learn that his toothbrush has been borrowed. A written work is just as personal a property. Most writers find it disheartening to learn that their work has been used in a book or an article without permission having been asked. When a writer is handed some article that includes unacknowledged or stolen words he knows he has written himself, he's apt to contemplate either suicide or murder.

Copy quotations correctly, word for word, retaining the punctuation, using ellipses to indicate where words have been left out. On typewritten copy, ellipses are three periods only: . . ., with a space between each, and with a fourth dot for the period if you include the end of a sentence. Other punctuation depends on what you have omitted. If you file quotations correctly, you have the option later of loosely rewording them with something like: "Eisenhower had a hard time keeping in step with band music during his first few weeks at West Point." The actual quotation in your file would be:

> CONFORMITY (Or: GREAT PEOPLE)
>
> Military drill was a problem for me.
> I had had no training in marching,
> and to keep in step with the music of the band was difficult.
> For days I was assigned to the Awkward Squad.
>
> From *"AT EASE" Stories I Tell to Friends*
> Doubleday and Company, Copyright 1967 by
> Dwight D. Eisenhower.

At this point we need to stop and take note of a flashing red light. When you draw on others' writing for anecdotes, everything depends on:

1. *What* you borrow from others.
   You have to learn to be very selective, spending some time analyzing why some things look good, or why they do not.
2. *How* you use it.
   Anecdotes are not filler material. They are chosen with care and strategically placed.

By studying critically the articles and books you read, you can begin to recognize this skill as employed by others. We'll get into it more deeply later on, but for now you can begin opening your eyes to what is before you. People lay some reading material aside with a ho hum. Other things grip a person, holding his attention to the end. Many factors contribute to a captivating piece of writing; one of these is the author's wise choice and careful use of anecdotes.

You would do well to circle anecdotes as you recognize them, thinking through why they were or were not a good choice, and whether their application was proper or out of place.

The main warning I want to give you is this: Don't fall into the trap of collecting old, worn-out illustrations from someone else's dumping ground, and throwing them in to pad the piece. Editors and readers, the two groups of people you want most to please (besides yourself) have seen all the oldies. What they want is fresh, new approaches and new insights: striking ideas they haven't thought of before, or haven't thought of for a long, long time. Anecdotes that sell are brand-new. Even though you might have discovered them in a book five hundred years old, they are something you located yourself through the sweat of your brow, something you discovered, dug out, and put where you did because you thought that was the very best illustration you could use.

THINGS YOU HEAR, SEE, AND FEEL

As you are learning to analyze what you see and hear, getting in touch with how you and others really feel, and paying closer attention to what you and others are experiencing, your notes will grow more colorful. Practice expanding your first efforts to add interest to them. Listen to yourself and others as the events of the day are recounted. How exciting, how frightening, or how disgusting they sound! When the same events are put on paper, you have no sound effects to color them and your readers will not be able to see your facial expression or the objects you may be showing them. Your choice of words will have to be both show and tell, so to make the anecdote valuable to you in years to come, you must record the whole thing: what you saw, what you heard, what you felt, what you smelled, what you experienced; what others saw, heard, felt, smelled, experienced; and how you and they acted or reacted.

A beginning writer can fall into the trap of overwriting: using too many colorful descriptions, too many adjectives, too much color. Your first attempts may sound "cutesy"—death on an editor's desk—but take heart. We'll work on that problem before long, and we'll learn how to improve them by cutting out some words and replacing others. For now, you must get more on paper than you will ever possibly use, lest you leave out details you'll later wish you had.

We're talking about picking up illustrative material from everyday life, but even when I go out for the purpose of gathering material, even during detailed interviews, I rarely use a recorder, not that I write fast enough to get down all the details (although I think I can). Talking to someone who is less interested in me than in writing down what I'm saying is one of my pet peeves. I think, "Where was he when God gave out brains?" Practice remembering. A few key thoughts jotted down will suffice until you are free to finish up your notes. I've driven away from many an interview and pulled into a parking place a block away to fill in the details. Good writers are good listeners: *courteous* enough to look the other person in the eye and pay attention to what he or she is saying, and *smart* enough to keep the information on hold in their minds for at least a few minutes.

Since our minds respond to sounds, recordings can be useful tools. (And they do have a place in major interviews.) The cheer of the crowd on opening night at the ball game puts you back into the ball game mood. Music holds special magic. You can use it to break a writing block, putting on the kind of music that creates the atmosphere of which you're writing. My recordings from foreign trips put me back into the overseas atmosphere. One forgets the bleating of the sheep, the sound of camels' hooves, the raucous cries of the marketplace, the beat of the drums, the breakers at the seashore, the sounds at a wharf. An ancient, toothless Indian sang song after song into my recorder because he thought it was fun. The experience was delightful for me, but I thought it of little value until I got home, where I learned I could return mentally to his country simply by replaying his mournful chants. Slides and photos serve the same purpose.

But your most valuable source of information will probably be the words you write down close to the scene. Keen observation of details should be followed by careful recording procedures. When you look around you, what do you see? An old man? Or a man hunched over with age, silky white hair tumbling down over a rumpled collar, blue eyes sparkling, careful grin revealing shrunken gums and ill-fitting teeth?

A big dog? A big, woolly, brown dog? Or a feisty brown Saint Bernard puppy?

A middle-aged lady? Or an outspoken brunette, in high top boots, plaid wool skirt, and wrinkled velvet jacket—probably old enough to be your mother and acting as if she were. Her voice might have been soothing, or it might have been soft and melodic, or harsh and commanding, or sharp.

As the young woman stalked through the discount store, did she "yell at her kid"? Or did her angry reprimand crush the heart of her little son, leaving him wounded and alone even though she held his hand?

When something unpleasant happened, how did you react? Did you feel bad? Or did you feel as if somebody had poked you really hard right in the pit of your stomach? Jabbed you in the belly, maybe?

To create your i and i file, you will need to begin to view the world in a new light. If your life touches other people, you will need your pencil and paper to sketch exaggerated descriptions of the characters who surround you and their reactions to what goes on. Maybe you're chained to a loud, routine job, mesmerized by an assembly line, bouncing around in a bulldozer, or mopping endless hospital hallways. It matters not where you spend your working hours, whether locked in a boiler room, in a prison cell, or in a coal mine. Your mind is free, things are happening, and you should be ready to record them. If the work-a-day world fails to ignite your creativity, your i and i can fill up with relaxing experiences out of your evening and weekend life—whatever those joys away from time clock and supervisor may be.

Adding to your i and i file is like putting money in the bank. The more you have in file to draw from, the better you will become at pulling articles and stories together in record time. Notes; ideas; clippings; illustrations; quotations; book, movie, and lecture reviews; poetry—all of these serve to prime the pump. With them you can create colorful writing, make articles come alive with human interest anecdotes, and back up statements you make that need clarification or verification. A rich i and i file can become your most valuable resource.

If you really get going on your illustration and idea file, you won't limit it, neat as this sounds, to one simple card file, although this is probably the best way to begin, or, if you're organizing an old file, a good way to start sorting out the bits and scraps you have on hand. For one thing, 3X5's are convenient for carrying. For another, cards can be shuffled and filed easily under various categories, and incidentally can be found in a file much more easily than can a collection of napkin corners, paper plates, and torn bits of newspaper.

You ought to set up your file by subject as soon as you have a few cards:

Angels	Bears	Canned food
Antelope	Blessings	Christmas
Ants	Books	Cleveland
Artifacts	Boston	Clowns

There's a system sometimes found on file card dividers which you can purchase at any office supply counter. The idea is to file by vowels: Aa, Ae, Ai, Ao, Au, Ba, Be, Bi, Bo, Bu, etc. This is said to save time locating items in a huge filing system, which yours will be if you're faithful and consistent. If you like the sound of the system, most stores have someone who can help you figure it out. If you file the traditional way—angels, antelopes, ants, apples, artifacts—you'll have to wade through a heap of cards to find the one you want. Of course, you might come up with ten good ideas along the way, sorting through all those cards.

To give you an idea of what a file might eventually contain, here are a few notes I have on file under Bees/Honey:

> Hayfever remedy: local honey and natural lemon juice daily, year round.
>
> Differences in honey depends on flowers in area. Narbonne honey of France white, bees feed on rosemary; clover honey light-colored; Grecian honey from Thyme-covered hills near Corinth said to be spectacular.
>
> Ill effects from honey: botulism reported; allergies from too much honey (overdose of pollen intake, so to speak).
>
> Extracting honey Moroccan style (at midnight, squeezing honeycomb by hand while bees are hopefully asleep). American wasp spray directions back up the "sleeping" theory: "Spray at night while wasps are resting."
>
> Bees guided by peculiar sense, probably sight as much as smell. Insect senses illusive. (Scientists in California intending to combat the Med fly released "sterile flies" only to discover they were not sterile, after all. Shall we call it insufficient evidence?)
>
> June, 1981, *Kansas City Star:* Missouri woman killed by swarm of bees; controversy whether killer bees, or honey bees she angered.
>
> Child stung by 24 wasps recovered. Seventy-pound dog killed by honey bees.
>
> Remedies for beesting itch: soda paste, mud pack, onion slice, Cortaid.
>
> Honey as sugar substitute: preceded sugar cane as world's sweetener. Still used in Middle East and Orient for confections. Moroccan "Shebbakiya" is pretzel-like snack soaked in honey until soft and sticky. Ancient delicacy was honey; mentioned in Bible as sign of wealth and abundance.

So much for bees. Candles is another subject, and the note about candles should be in both categories: *Bees/Honey* and *Candles*. The allergy notes should also appear twice: *Allergies* and *Honey*. Insect senses studies, while pertaining to bees, should also be listed under *Insects*, or *Scientists*, or both.

Collecting anecdotes is a preliminary step toward developing a "nose for news." A good writer learns to keep his eyes open, his ears ever alert to what is being said, his mind ready to jump on anything that sounds good, ready to sort out and store what is worthwhile. People love to recount incidents in their lives and to talk about things they are going through. Barbara Walters is said to tell her friends on occasion, "Remember, I'm a reporter!" That's a goal worth aiming for—being so in tune with the writer in you that everything around you automatically enters the scrutiny chamber of your mind to test its literary worth.

To be in touch with humanity, to be jostled by the crowds, to be caught in everyday traffic, to wait in line restlessly as do others, is to gather usable material by osmosis. How often I have run out on some humdrum errand on a busy day, wishing I didn't have to go, only to pick up some delightful anecdote along the way that fit perfectly into what I was writing.

Many times people drop marvelous stories into your lap. The best one I ever got was at a remote Alaskan village accessible only in good weather by ferry, and on clear days by seaplane. The lonely missionary couple was delighted to have guests, a rare treat, and they chattered like children while we were there. During the day-long conversation, they mentioned a frightening incident. One evening, while the men and boys of the village were at a basketball game, the mother heard a noise at the back door. She peeked out the window and found herself face to face with a gigantic brown bear! She grabbed up the children, ran into the front bedroom, and slammed the door shut. Before the men finally came out of the gym and heard her screams, the hungry bear had clawed its way into the back porch and had started scratching at the kichen door!

You can be sure I didn't whip out a scratch pad and begin taking notes. I sat, mouth agape, listening to the horror story; I felt the fear, heard the screams, saw in my mind's eye the confusion, rescue, and relief. My eyes recorded the size of the bear, towering way above the top of the window where I was sitting, the strength of its claws as shown by the gouges still evident in the wooden door. I could almost feel its angry, hot breath on my own neck. I wrote it all down during the long ferry trip back to the city.

A couple of weeks later a snowstorm grounded me at the Denver airport. A stuffed polar bear stood guard over the motel lobby—ghastly teeth, dreadful claws, cruel beady eyes. I looked him over with the greatest respect, imagining him brown, hungry, and after me.

I heard several brown bear stories on that trip, but brown bear stories didn't fit into my schedule at the time. I put the notes away, wondering how and when I would use them. Ten, twelve years went by, the file got very full, and many experiences were lost in the deepest recesses of my mind. But the bear never got very far away. Its beady eyes were always there, peering at me, pleading for a chance to get into print.

An assignment for a forty-eight-page book introducing Canada to church children nine to eleven years of age brought to mind places like Nova Scotia, Montreal, Winnipeg, the western Canadian plains, the Canadian Rockies. Canada is a very big nation. For a few days I pondered the problem. How could I create an exciting story for kids that would teach them about Canada?

One Saturday I awoke at 4:00 A.M. with other plans, but as I was sipping my very first cup of coffee, I suddenly sat up erect, slammed my cup onto the windowsill, and grabbed my scratch pad and pen. A story was coming. Up in the Yukon, close to the Alaskan border, a little girl named Cathy was trapped with other women and children in a house with a rickety back porch, a table beside the kitchen window, and a familiar wooden back door. A hungry brown bear rattled around the yard and finally started clawing his way in.

Twelve hours later, at 4:30 P.M., the story was finished. Cathy had traveled with her family from the Yukon all across Canada, had gotten lost in the big city of Winnipeg, had looked for agates along the northern shore of Lake Superior, had learned a few words of French in Quebec, and had ended up at her grandfather's home on the east coast in New Brunswick!

I was still in my nightgown and robe when I laid down the thick sheaf of yellow papers. *Cathy of Canada* had been born!

If you faithfully store information in your mind and consistently place anecdotes in your file, that information will be there when you need it. The more you store, the better you will write!

ASSIGNMENT 3

WARM-UP: Using *Encyclopaedia Britannica*, or other such sources available at the library, study the life of Leo Tolstoi. Pay mind especially to the effect that his inner search and his daily journal had upon his writing.

NEXT: The practice of poking scraps of paper into box or drawer is fine for a start, but now is the time to begin to organize your illustration and idea file.

If you've borrowed this book, don't highlight, underline, or scribble notes in it. Buy a copy so you'll be free to mark it for future study. Go back over this chapter and jot collectible information on 3x5 cards. Ten thousand books on down the line you're not going to remember where you read these good things. Start a file, lazybones!

As a result of reading this chapter you might include the following sections:

dogs
clever anecdotes
writing
inner cities
honey/bees
quotations from famous writers

Then again, you might not. That's my problem, not yours.

FINALLY "The Diary of a Mad Housewife" has already been done, but I'll bet the author began just like you'll begin. Okay. Begin. Don't put off starting your personal journal any longer. Supplies needed: pen, paper, and *padlock*.

4 Library, Here I Come!

A few pages back you read: "The reason why so few good books are being written is that so few people who can write know anything."

I hope that insult raised your ire! If it did, there may be hope for your writing future, because you've begun to ask questions. Who is Walter Bagehot? What right does he have to insult my intelligence? And, perhaps most importantly, what does he mean by good books?

Walter Bagehot was a nineteenth century Englishman who chalked up to his credit four large, enduring nonfiction books on the subjects of politics, anthropology, banking, and the economic structure of the world of his day. He thought deeply, but he shared his knowledge by writing in an innovative, free-flowing style that appealed to his readers.

Not only could Bagehot write, but he also had something to write about. By the time he was thirty-four he had gained impressive credentials. He had an education from England's Bristol College and a gold medal in philosophy from London's University College; he had studied law; he had spent several years in banking; he had written and published notable essays; and he had inherited control of a weekly paper, *The Economist*, from his father-in-law. Bagehot made *The Economist* the most influential economic weekly in Europe; he devised the British treasury bill; he served as consultant to leaders in parliament; and he kept close tabs on all the major controversies of the day. Admittedly, he was a very intelligent man, an active businessman who mingled with the crowds on the street, a man who "knew something." He was in a position to say what he did.

I assume what he meant by "good books" is top-quality journalism which (whatever the projected audience, the length, or the style may be) is drawn from a spring-fed well of knowledge: unique thoughts

presented in a coherent manner
using selected vocabulary
suited to the subject at hand

The author of a good piece of writing is in touch with the world beyond his own patio, understands the thinking of a broad spectrum of people, and has a thorough knowledge of the subject about which he is writing.

Aspiring writers have not improved since Bagehot's time. As any editor who faces stacks of manuscripts knows, most people who write today have flunked the test because they took it far too soon. They are woefully unprepared to be professional writers. They view their subjects as an ant sees a jungle trail: from a world about one inch in circumference, a world made up of built-in activities related to the anthill, as seen by other ants.

Ants can climb trees, you know; and although no ant will ever become a monkey, she can break loose from the crowd after hours and start the long, lonely climb to the top of the tree to see what the monkeys see.

If you're serious about teaching yourself to write, you'd better make plans to get started. I'm not talking about a Jonathan Seagull experience of leaving the flock (exhilarating in itself at times). I'm suggesting that you keep doing what you're expected to do at the anthill, but add to your busy life an exciting, never-ending search for knowledge beyond your own world in whatever spare moments you can find. You've already reached out to learn what you can about writing. That search coupled with steady practice must go on, at least for a while. You've begun to examine your mind, sort out your memories, get acquainted with your surroundings, and organize your notes. I suspect your assets surprise you. You've found much to write about. But you're still at the anthill. You know less—probably much less—than the vast audience of readers you hope to reach.

The competition is stiff. First of all, any writing you hope to have published must get past a person skilled at sifting through the slush pile of unsolicited manuscripts and mountains of queries to sort out the rotten apples and to tell the next guy up the ladder *why* the rest are worth looking at, or why they are not.

Next (and not many manuscripts make it beyond the initial scanning), a person with a little more clout rejects about 95 percent of what was sent to him. Finally, the remaining 5 percent at that point are scrutinized by the tough guys. Few make it. Out of 36,000 stories sent in to *Redbook* annually, the magazine accepts about fifty. *Ladies' Home Journal* buys two or three articles a year from their daily bags of unsolicited mail. The syndicates get thousands of submissions while adding about one new feature a year.

The good news is that almost all magazines take the time to comb through the heap because they know there are excellent articles and stories buried there, and they don't want to miss them.

We can learn a few lessons from this, most of them to be covered in the following chapters. For now, as foundation training to start you off in your budding career (you're a writer, remember?), let's focus on the facts at hand. The ant has to leave that anthill and climb that tree. You *must* broaden your base of knowledge, first of all in your own fields, but also outside your fields of interest. The trick is to examine the minds of your potential readers, narrow the gap between their level of general knowledge and your own, and be able to look them in the eye as you tell your story, as one professional to another.

You can accomplish this in part through personal contact: through meeting people socially by putting yourself into circulation; through interviews and grabbing opportunities as mentioned in Chapter 1; through television; through weekend courses or night school, to name a few available channels of learning. But you will really sell yourself short if you neglect keeping up on the world around you through a study of literature reflecting current thoughts and trends. And your journalistic ability wll remain at disappointment level if you fail to delve into the literary minds of the past.

What did you miss by goofing off at college? Or did you bypass college, studying instead the realities of paycheck-to-paycheck living? What does a journalism major know that you don't know? And how can you catch up? Or can you?

I believe you can. And you can do it right from your own home by turning some of your spare time entertainment into a planned effort to educate yourself by reading.

Your best friend is the librarian. If you're like me, when somebody says "library," you hold your breath until you've shifted into whisper gear. Libraries are awesome palaces ruled over by all-knowing queens whose lips have grown into a permanent "*Shhh.*" Right?

Only partly right. Libraries are quiet places, all right, but librarians are very approachable, eager to help, and glad to see a newcomer walk in. They're quick to say "*Shhh*" when someone disturbs other readers, but rarely does that happen. Betty Fuhrman, editorial coordinator at Beacon Hill Books of Kansas City, worked as a student librarian in college. She tells me that when college sessions closed, she and other part-time student librarians couldn't resist putting life back into the awesome atmosphere by laughing aloud and shouting to one another a few minutes before closing the operation down for the summer! That jibes with what I sense in the sparkle of librarians' eyes when I timidly open the door and creep in, trying not to breathe too loudly.

When I get inside a library I still glance furtively about to see who's causing the uncanny silence before stealthily slipping up to the desk to plead for help—quietly, of course. Living near the heart of downtown Kansas City I have so many excellent libraries to creep into it would take ten lifetimes to do them all justice.

The medical schools of the Universities of Missouri and Kansas, for example, have extensive libraries open to people with proper credentials; the University of Missouri, Kansas City Branch (UMKC) has an excellent law library (and Jackson County Law Library is available, as well, in downtown Kansas City); also at UMKC is the Linda Hall Science Technical Library; not to mention the very helpful and adequate general library at UMKC. Liberal arts colleges and community colleges surround me, all with libraries; several seminaries in the city offer a full range of theological books, many of them old classics donated by various estates. The Mormon Genealogical Library in Independence, Missouri, is not far away. Within a five-mile radius I also have four good public libraries, including the gigantic Kansas City Public Library. And someone is sure to say I've missed a few.

Your resources, depending on where you live, may be less impressive, but any small library is adequate for a start; and no library, no matter how wonderful it may be, is valuable unless used. Services at the library are extensive. Even though your library may be very small, it probably is tied to a system that allows you to request books and information from a larger one. Your librarian will be happy to tell you all about the marvelous services available.

As you get into writing, you'll discover numerous helps at your library, ranging from pamphlets on any subject you might want to research to extensive general reference works that contain the whole world of information from A to Z. Almanacs and fact books hold a stupendous amount of information. For both ideas and research, the microfilm library of newspapers and periodicals is a fascinating source. The *Book Review Digest* can be used in a variety of ways, including picking up ideas for articles, checking to see what reviewers thought of various books, and examining trends of various decades, not to mention the knowledge that can be gained from reading many of the reviews.

In Chapter 7, we'll be studying the markets to prepare ourselves for trying to sell what we've written. To properly do this, you'll want to become familiar with various indexes, of which the *Readers' Guide to Periodical Literature* is the most well known. There are indexes for specialized subjects: the *Art Index*,

Business Periodicals Index, Education Index, and many more. Your librarian will introduce you to *Ulrich's International Periodicals Directory*, and Chicorel's Index to *Abstracting and Indexing Services in the Humanities and Social Sciences*, and between the two of them, you can learn about almost every periodical published. There's an *Index to Free Periodicals* which covers company publications, among others. Added to these helps, you'll find film indexes, consumer indexes, Catholic and Jewish indexes, black indexes, sports indexes, and how-to-do-it indexes. And, of course, you'll find the periodicals themselves available at the library, a wonderful source of information and practical method for reading both to absorb general knowledge and to study the markets.

But our concern in this chapter is not studying the markets. (You will be doing that unobtrusively along the way, so keep it in mind every time you go to the library.) Our concern is to move into the coveted position of "knowing something." You can go into a library to obtain a bit of knowledge, or have a mobile unit come to your door, or arrange for a distant library to mail things to you for study. A writer who is out to succeed must establish a base of general knowledge. That's the point of this chapter.

Where in the world does one begin? Not with the bestsellers. Keeping up with what's in is certainly important, but your priority at the moment is education, rather than entertainment. Extremely busy people with heavy reading schedules find ways to squeeze in the books and magazines "everybody" is talking about. Even people who are not speedreaders can learn to avoid the temptation to plod through unnecessary material. One learns to move on, reading only what is really important. When I'm involved in projects that engulf me with required reading, I gulp thoughts from popular reading whenever I chance to see them, as one might glug down a glass of cold water on a busy, hot day. Education requires discipline, which in itself can be relaxing and fun.

A person who is not familiar with the library can begin by sniffing out books in areas of special interest. Starting out by asking the librarian to direct you to fairly familiar subject matter puts you at ease in the library. But remember, your assignment is to move out beyond your own anthill, to learn what others know that you do not.

A liberal arts education—which so many of us now regret having missed—is a combination of studies in the field of learning that includes humanities and the sciences. Humanities has been defined as humane feelings and the conduct toward others such feelings dictate. Studies in the humanities mold the mind and sensitivity and develop the aesthetic side of the individual.

The quest for cultural development through learning has been around a long time. Learning was a status symbol in ancient times. Men sought to be great orators, eloquent of speech. Speech was the fundamental form of communication because the common man was illiterate and books were laboriously copied on scrolls. Since eloquence could be enhanced by knowledge, one studied philosophy and history, as well as the mechanics of proper word use, to have something to talk about.

Ancient speeches were full of magnificent words and flowery expressions, whereas modern culture demands the fat trimmed off; but effective expression is still viewed as a sign of culture. Generally it is thought to be obtained through intellectual training based on literature and the arts. The difference is that in the days of the ancient philosophers, the joys of culture were only for the favored few. Average people were excluded, except as onlookers in the marketplace. In medieval times, the clergy controlled a great deal of such education, and early England, which gave us so great a heritage of good reading, confined it to the minority able to attend the well-known universities of that era. This was true in colonial America, too.

How times have changed! All you have to do now, even if you dig ditches or run the dishwasher at some greasy spoon restaurant for a living, is to walk up to the information desk at any library and ask where the humanities section is. From there on, you've got the literary world by the tail. "The key to lifelong learning," wrote Carl B. Smith and Leo C. Fay in *Getting People to Read*,[1] is:

skill
plus motivation
plus access.

You've got it all.

It's fine for me to say to you, "Just walk up to the information desk and ask them to lead you to the humanities," but does that really work? I decided to try it out. It worked!

The first books listed led me to the philosophy and religion section. Do any of the following interest you?

Studies in Jewish Thought (Rawedowicz)
Studies in Medieval Jewish Philosophy (Efros)
Jewish Philosophy in Modern Times (Rotenstretch)
The Japanese Mind (Moore)
The Latin American Mind (translated by Abbot and Nunham)
Harvard Oriental Studies (edited by Daniel H. H. Ingalls)

Hundreds of volumes of religious books lined several aisles: various shades of Christian theology—Catholic and Protestant—and non-Christian thought. As to philosophy:

Plato (Dialogue on Love and Friendship)
Socrates and the Human Conscience (Sauvage)
Thomas Aquinas (14 volumes)
Roger Bacon and His Search for a Universal Science
The Philosophy of C. I. Lewis (Edited by Schlipp)
Several volumes by or about Bertrand Russell
Main Currents in Contemporary German, British, and American Philosophy (Stegmuller)

Of infinite value to the writer's mind, too, were the rows upon rows of books on geography (studies of nations we hear about on the daily news, and some we don't); social studies (for example, *The World of the Blue Collar Worker* by Howe); equal rights from many viewpoints; extensive current books on women's emerging image outside the home; race relations; aging; and volumes of studies on various classes and races of people across our nation and around the world.

I can't walk from one end of the library to the other without interruption. I have to browse along the way. En route to the general literature section, I spotted the current *Curriculum Guide for Common Learning—Library Reading Sheet for Grades 7 and 8.*

"*Humm,*" I thought, turning my back on all the other goodies. "I wonder what sophisticated young teens are reading these days."

If I hadn't suddenly realized where I was and clapped my hand over my mouth I'd have guffawed aloud. (A grand jury would have given me about ten years for that, I think.) Louisa May Alcott was among the first on the "current" list: *Little Women, Little Men,* and *Eight Cousins*! There stood Bess Streeter Aldrich, big as life, *A Lantern in Her Hand. My Friend Flicka* by O'Hara and even *Paul Bunyan and His Great Blue Ox* (Wadsworth) still graced the list, as they did forty years ago. So did Hemingway's *Old Man and the Sea,* John Gunther's *Meet Soviet Russia,* Lew Wallace's *Ben Hur,* and George Orwell's *1984* (how far into the future that seemed when he wrote it!). His *Animal Farm* was on the list, as well, and several more familiar books, plus, of course, many I didn't know.

I hope that the books are on the list to stay! Writers in our day are churning out mountains of material, but few rise to the stature of Alcott, Hemingway, or Gunther. We *could* rise to that level, if we set our hearts to excel.

Kansas City Public Library's general literature is on a huge, marble-floored balcony. Right at the top of the stairs are delightful books such as Salten's *Bambi* and *Bambi's Children.* Not far from them are the *Saturday Evening Post Stories,* a volume a year from 1937 to 1962, and the *Saturday Evening Post Treasury,* published by Simon and Schuster in 1954. What wonderful short stories those were—and we grew up on them! Maybe the *Saturday Evening Post* died because all the good writers did. It has revived. Can we whip our minds into shape to produce the quality of stories they need today?

One of my greatest discoveries was that to educate myself to become a knowledgeable writer, I didn't have to pass a battery of tests. I only had to study. As we said earlier, the amazing human mind can learn to fetch information when it is needed, not because we have sent it to fetch, but because it knows what we need! Reading is like putting money into a savings account. You might not have to draw out the knowledge for a long time, but there it is, growing more valuable all the time, especially if you add to it faithfully. I think I forget far too much, far too soon. But what my mind wants to keep, it stores away in its memory department without mentioning the matter to me.

What freedom! Just dig in and learn for the pleasure of learning!

His concern for inspiring adults to read good literature led Charles W. Eliot to prepare the wonderful *Harvard Classics*, published in 1914. In his introduction to the Lecture Series he writes that the lectures "ought to do much to open that collection of library materials to many ambitious young men and women whose education was cut short by the necessity of contributing to the family earnings, or of supporting themselves, and who must therefore reach the standing of a cultivated man or woman through the pleasurable devotion of a few minutes a day through many years to the reading of good literature." He believed reading the series would give people "a taste for serious reading of the highest quality outside of *The Harvard Classics* as well as within them."[2]

Forty years later, Robert W. Hutchins, chancellor of the University of Chicago, served as editor-in-chief of a fifty-four-volume set called *Great Books of the Western World*, classics reprinted by Britannica which Hutchins and his committee of scholars thought should be made available to folks who wanted a well-rounded education. The *Great Books* grew out of a concern that by the late 1940s and early 1950s, too much specialization had crept into college education and sports were being overemphasized. The committee members, with Hutchins at the helm, hoped to arouse new interest in the classics to bring about a balance they, from their excellent vantage point, saw was missing.

I think the *Great Books* would gather more supporters from readers and reporters like you and me than from the all-star quarterback type. The list of titles doesn't get even me jumping up and down with joy, but among the fifty-four huge volumes are some I like to browse through. In addition to the early philosophers already mentioned, the volumes cover men like Augustine, Dante, Chaucer, Shakespeare, Milton, Pascal, Goethe, Darwin, Tolstoy, and Dostoevsky. At our library, the last volume, Volume 54, is missing. A Freudian slip, I presume: Volume 54 is Freud.

The *Great Books* are heavy in more ways than one. I don't expect you to wade through all that material—not now, anyway, though I do believe you'll enjoy scanning any of the ancient classics you run across. In Kansas City, the *Great Books* and *Harvard Classics* are not available in some of the suburban libraries, but if you can't locate them in sets, you'll find some of the works in scattered volumes published by others either before or after Eliot and Hutchins compiled their remarkable sets.

For example, I found the works of some of the old masters in the philosophy section of the library, as I've told you. Goethe's entire works in German (as well as in English) are "on the balcony," which brings up another fascinating way to proceed once you've stepped in the library door. I find it intriguing to look at old literature nation by nation. For the writer, a selection of old books categorized by country introduces various authors both through diaries and biographies as well as through the things they have written. What a wealth of insight into good writing can be gleaned from those crisp old pages!

Russia: what were her people really like before Communism took over? What talent lies dormant behind the iron curtain? What thoughts have been crushed by fear? Our main library contains row upon row of old Russian books translated into English—stories of Russian life and humor; short stories; masterpieces of Russian theatre; *The Complete Works of Chekhov; The History of the Post War Years;* Russian songs, poems, and drama.

If you'd like to study Irish background, you might start with Stephens' *The Charwoman's Daughter,* and his *Crock of Gold.* Frank O'Connor, one of Ireland's foremost writers, put together a survey of 1,000 years in *A Short History of Irish Literature.* The writings of Yeats are important—and, incidentally, his statement that "words obey my call" is, too. Throughout his life he disciplined himself to writing, with that coveted result. James

Joyce wrote (from outside Ireland) some very important works, including *Ulysses* (a day in the life of three folks in Dublin) which was banned from some English-speaking countries, and his last and most controversial novel, *Finnegans Wake*.

Among the French books you will find Corneille's *Great Writings of France*, which will introduce you to French writing. Somerset Maugham concluded that the French are working writers, adopting the profession "without having any marked creative power."

French writer Alexander Dumas had plenty of creative power. He was a known plagiarist. In *The Life and Adventures of Alexander Dumas*,[3] Percy Fitzgerald recounts the stages Dumas went through, first borrowing from dead authors and adapting the work to his own purposes, then collaborating with two or three other writers to compose a piece, moving on to buying plots or scenes which he touched up and called his own, and finally stealing characters he liked, putting them into his own plays. He was sued, of course. When you're tempted to quote Dumas, remember he was considered a literary pirate, an ingenious crook who could piece together stolen work so beautifully you would swear it was original.

Among the most enjoyable of books are the English novels: One could spend a lifetime studying them. Obviously you don't have time to study all the marvelous classics at your fingertips; you can't even begin to read half of them. Your eyes would fall out. What you can do is set aside certain rainy days to slip over to the library; or if you vacation in a big city, schedule a trip to the library. Schedule your regular reading time now, while it's still fresh on your mind.

Greek and Roman rhetoric appeals to very few readers or listeners of the 1980s. Young preachers (and a few not so young) fall into the dreadful habit of displaying their budding knowledge of Greek by dropping it into their sermons one word at a time, until they've shown off their whole vocabulary. Vain attempts at pronouncing ancient languages maddens listeners and would drive a Greek national crazy were he to tune in. Your writing, likewise, can lose its appeal in a hurry if you use your growing wealth of knowledge in this immature manner. Acquiring knowledge is first of all for your own pleasure, to exercise your mind and keep it in shape. Enriching the material you produce out of a well-studied, well-balanced creative brain is a secondary benefit. True knowledge is unobtrusive background music enhancing what you write.

The classics do fall into everyday language, and your ears soon attune to them as if adding a new channel by attaching a better antenna. One of my bosses (I have had so many!) was recounting a hilarious incident from the *Barney Miller* show. "There was ole Barney," he said, "who came up through the ranks, trying to carry on a conversation with a guy who had a mind like Plato."

Screech to a sudden stop! A mind like Plato? What kind of mind did Plato have? I know he meant more than smart. How smart?

I'll let you run that one down.

Caution: If your reading leads you way out beyond your depth, unfamiliar words that might as well be Greek are bound to appear. Experts advocate stopping to look them up. I'm not an expert, of course: I'm a fellow learner with a long way to go. But I lean toward ignoring most new words if possible, at least in the preliminary stages of study, because one hinders the flow of thought by continuously jotting down notes or running to the dictionary to look up words one may very well never see again. Gain most of your vocabulary by saturation as does a little child. I maintain that your natural input will result in smooth, natural playout when you write.

When the classics lose their appeal (will they ever?), you still have the newspapers, the magazines, children's books, specialized nonfiction subjects, and choice books from the past five decades. To name a few of the latter:

1930s—*The Good Earth* (Buck)
Gone with the Wind (Mitchell)
The Grapes of Wrath (Steinbeck)
1940s—*Blood, Sweat and Tears* (Churchill)
Their Finest Hour (Churchill)
The Robe (Douglas)

1950s—*The Longest Day* (Ryan)
The City That Would Not Die (Collier)
Doctor Zhivago (Pasternak)
1960s—*My Life With Martin Luther King* (Coretta King)
Death of a President (Manchester)
I'm O.K., You're O.K. (Harris)
Happiness Is a Warm Puppy (Schultz)

Perhaps we're too close to the 1970s to make a judgment of any kind. *Eleanor and Franklin*, by Lash, had historical significance, and it would be very surprising if Haley's *Roots* didn't appear on "classics" lists of future years. As I write, *Passages*, by Sheehy, seems to be a household word and might be remembered on down the road.

You're probably familiar with authors I've omitted, possibly wondering why I've left them out: Updike, Spillane, Mailer, Vonnegut, Michener. It's not deliberate. We can't tell from our present vantage point which authors' works, if any, might last forever, but their names may live on, at least for a while.

Many books that do not last give readers hours of pleasure during the short time they sparkle. I personally liked *Airport*, *Kontiki*, *Kim*, *The Amazing Mrs. Polifax*, and *Bless the Beasts and Children;* and going way back, *A Tree Grows in Brooklyn*. A library expert told me they were not significant books, but they brightened my life when I read them. As a writer I take my hat off to anyone who writes a book good enough to be published, shelved, chosen, read, and remembered by anyone at all.

What will the 1980s contribute to the long list of good reading? My books, I hope. And yours.

Going to the library is a wonderful excursion, invigorating as a cool dip on a hot day, but I don't have time to do it often except in the line of duty. You might not have the opportunity to go regularly, either, much as you'd like to; but when one is in the midst of writing, packing it all up to go to the library is disconcerting. And let's face it—often I'd rather stay home.

The more literature you have at home, the more efficient you can be as a writer. A dear friend has given me *Reader's Digest* for Christmas every year since 1953, including the eleven I was overseas. You can pass the word around asking Santa for everything from subscriptions to *Saturday Review*, *New Republic*, *The New Yorker*, *The New York Times*, *Smithsonian*, or *Village Voice*, to lighter popular magazines you'd like to learn from and write for. When you're the birthday kid, let it be known you'd like certain reference books, or a contribution toward their purchase. Friends will gladly start a garage sale search for specific books. Places like thrift stores and charities that collect used goods may be willing to call you if a set of old books comes in, allowing you first chance to purchase them. Public libraries often have old books for sale at a token cost and sometimes sell choice reference sets. I'm drooling at the moment over a set of *Grove's Dictionary of Music and Musicians*, 1954 edition, which is gathering dust at one of our libraries. (To buy or not to buy: that is the question.)

If you have no other leads for old books, you can always check the Yellow Pages under "Books: New and Used."

I've told you there's a place for reading current bestsellers and a way to get it done. Obviously, if you put your mind to educating yourself as I've outlined in this chapter, as well as spending time writing, you're not going to have many hours left for reading nonessentials until you "graduate." But keeping abreast of what is being written today is important, too. Probably you already read the books condensed by *Reader's Digest*, especially those that appear each month in the magazine. (Old copies of *Reader's Digest Condensed Books* are readily available at thrift shops and garage sales.) The *Book Review Digest* is an annual volume listing books that have been published and what critics have said about some of them. This digest brings you up to date with a thumbnail sketch of books you missed before you began your pursuit of knowledge. Many popular magazines carry condensed versions of books you might like to read, and some magazines and newspapers are especially good sources for keeping one eye on the book market. One can browse through the microfilm library to locate various book condensations.

You'll find books of interest to you reviewed in publications you like—which is the beautiful part of it all. Someone else has gone through the stacks of books off the press in America in a given month, one hundred and more depending on the scope of interest of your reviewer, and has sifted a half dozen from which you can choose one or two if you have time for pleasure reading. I flip through magazines at the dentist's, the hairdresser's, the doctor's office, any place I find them, and read any book reviews I find. My best source of up-to-the-minute bestseller book reviews is the Sunday paper, but there are many others.

Just as I was finishing this chapter, I received in the mail Dean R. Koontz's book, *How to Write Best-Selling Fiction*. I opened it to the photo of a sharp young author clever enough to write books that have sold "25 million copies in fourteen languages." According to the biographical sketch on the dust jacket, one might read *The Vision* and *Whispers* to get acquainted with a writer of today who understands success and how to attain it.

Though I had to set the book aside for a few weeks, I glanced at a couple of pages. And what did I see? Delightful statement! Koontz says:

> The mystery has been in trouble because most of the current crop of writers have failed to engage and entertain their readers. . . . Even I have been disappointed by 98% of what I have read.[4]

To remedy the situation, he gives pointed advice to writers. It comes in three simple words: "Read. Read. Read." His book concludes with a list of writers he recommends, many of them mystery writers, most of them writing today. So you see, your next course of study, when you've completed all the suggestions in this chapter, is all set up for you!

Someday, when my eyes are rested and I have enough pennies for parking for a week, I'm going to move into the library and read, read, read. The complete works of Irving, James Russell Lowell, Herman Melville, Oliver Wendell Holmes, Longfellow, Poe, Emily Dickinson, Walt Whitman, and many, many more beloved writers await loving hands to take them off the shelves and let them come to life again.

What kind of reader are you? Readers seem to be quite varied. Some are skimmers, others are scanners, and still others are speed-readers; then there are the plodders, the slowpokes, and the browsers.

Not only does speed vary; so do comprehension, analytical ability, and retention. I read fast, comprehend rather well what I read, automatically analyze it, and promptly forget most of what I read. Ask me this afternoon what I read this morning. No matter what the subject, be it ever so dear to my heart, I can't remember. Let's not discuss mutual knowledge, because mine is unavailable for comment—my recall button is jammed. (That's why I have a filing system and insist on writing down significant facts and ideas I might want to use later.)

Our final word comes from veteran playwright/novelist Irwin Shaw, whose lifelong record of success is hard to beat:

> So many young writers I've met are uneducated. They don't read. They don't read what started things . . . produced the trends. They don't know the classics.[5]

No good writer will deny the value of establishing a top-quality reading program. Most of us don't reread our own books, we don't have a lot to say to one another when or if we chance to meet, each wanting to shine the brightest among our own little system of moons. But we do read the works of others, not to criticize, but to expand our minds.

Possibly you've spent years reading and rereading such bestsellers as *The Little Engine That Could,* or *The Pokey Little Puppy*. You must lay them aside now (unless, of course, you've *never* read them) and deny yourself other joys to catch up on reading you've either missed or forgotten during years of daily routine. It will be worth any trouble it takes. You can see you'd soon be really knowledgeable if you'd absorb the ideas of great writers consistently. Also, the vocabulary, sentence structure, style, grammar, and general knowledge picked up along the way are bound to improve your writing and increase your chances of success 100 percent. It's not a bad tool for building your anecdote file, either. I hope you keep that in mind.

You can't beat reading. All good writers read. Continuously. Nonstop. All the time. A broad variety of stuff.

It's hard to go back to the anthill after all that, isn't it!

ASSIGNMENT 4

Do I have to tell you what to do? Go to the library! Don't be afraid to ask for a tour. (Take along blank cards for your i and i file.)

I. Find the following and as you look them over, make notes on ways you can use them in the future.

Readers' Guide to Periodical Literature
Index to Free Periodicals
Ulrich's International Periodical Literature
Books in Print
Book Digest
Chicago *Manual of Style*

II. Find the current periodicals and browse through the following:

Saturday Review	*Smithsonian*
New Republic	*Village Voice*
Atlantic Monthly	*Wall Street Journal*
The New Yorker	*Time*
The New York Times	*Newsweek*

Make notes on items of interest to you which you can add to your i and i file. Remember to include title of publication, date of issue (including the year), and full name of the person who wrote the article.

III. Locate the small special interest magazines to discover the amazing range of subjects in print. Some of them will look especially interesting to you. List these on cards: title of publication, address of editorial offices, and editor's name, if it is given. You might want to subscribe or query them later.

IV. Find the card index, think of a subject or author that comes to your mind, and check to see what is available for the future research. (Have you looked up Tolstoi yet?)

FINALLY: As you leave, *shhh!* On the way home, buy a dictionary. (And before you go to sleep tonight, record in your personal journal a few thoughts about your library trip.)

5 Have I Got Style!

Have I got style! Or have I? What is it?

Last night one of those rare, crazy dreams entertained me. A friend directing a program needed a ride to his apartment to change into his tuxedo, and back to the theatre in time for the show. I offered him a ride in my jalopy and waited in the car while he changed.

The friend returned to the car dressed in a gorgeous dusty-blue tuxedo. "Look!" he shouted gleefully. I was panic-stricken when so close to showtime he pulled bunched up material out of his coatsleeve. But instead of our having to repair a disaster at that late hour, the material fell into a beautiful satin ruffle that matched the light-blue shirt I hadn't noticed until then. He outshined Liberace! Suddenly the ruffles were flying through the air as he flailed his arms directing a band which appeared from nowhere; and just as suddenly it was over, the ruffles gone.

A new style had been created—a tux with ruffles, sewed up inside the coatsleeve, that could be tucked back in if you wanted to wear it as a business suit!

Styles *are* ridiculous. In the 1960s I followed miniskirts around the globe. In Morocco one bought half a meter (19½ inches) for a skirt, allowing for the waistband and a good hem. I flew from Casablanca to Minneapolis, where before I recovered from jet lag my hem was let down, way down. On to Switzerland, where I felt dowdy indeed until the hem went back up. To Morocco—up again, a little more than before. You would be amazed at what is hidden by those kaftanlike cloaks and veils that Moroccan women wear!

Six months later I returned to Kansas City. The short skirt went into the closet, where it hung for two years unused. We're very conservative in Kansas City. Styles must be on the way out in Minneapolis, Houston, Chicago, and L.A., before we'll buy them. We consider anything new to be indecent, be it long or short.

Style in writing can be just about as varied as in fashion, but it changes from writer to writer, rather than place to place or from one generation to the next. Writers notoriously do not run with a herd. There are trendsetters and copycats among us, but writing style seems to develop out of one's personality much more than out of a desire to conform. In fact, very few good creative writers are copycats. They write what their own minds produce after it has digested whatever it has been fed, and if they turn out something brazenly different that the public happens to like, so much the better. A bestseller may be born.

THE TWO KINDS OF STYLE

So what is style?

We mean two entirely different things by "style."

1. The rules that are set down by the powers-that-be in journalistic circles and are a standard for writers, editors, typesetters, and proofreaders to keep them from fighting. If they disagree how about a word should be abbreviated, or where a comma

should be placed, some peacemaker runs for the stylebook, and whatever it says, goes.

2. The fashion in which a writer or speaker presents his material, regarding vocabulary, flow of words, sentence lengths, colorful phrases, and general tone.

Style as a standard refers to areas in which we conform if we want to sell our work. While every publishing house has its own little idiosyncrasies, most which buy freelance material basically follow the general rules set down by stylebooks such as the popular *A Manual of Style*, published by the University of Chicago. It's virtually the editors' bible. And you probably follow it, too, even though you may never have studied it, for you have learned by now to type your manuscripts on 8½x11 white paper; you punctuate more or less properly; and you follow standards of spelling, abbreviation, and proper use of words you see in all top national magazines and books. The better you do this, conforming to standard rules, the more professional your manuscript will appear.

Style as a standard (the rules of writing well) will be covered more thoroughly in a later chapter, so let's turn now to what the writing world generally means by style: *style as a fashion*—the manner in which the material is pesented. Donald Davidson, professor of English at Vanderbilt University, called composition "a subject Protean in all its manifestations, but, in its bedrock principles, firm and unchangeful."[1] The bedrock principles are the stylebook rules. The outward manifestations are "style," which is what this chapter is really about.

You can read and thoroughly digest every book mentioned in the previous chapter and still not write successfully until you practice writing enough to develop an acceptable style. To be acceptable, your style (whatever it surfaces to be) must flow smoothly enough to be readable; the content (whatever it is) must be presented in a manner understandable to the reader; and your form of presentation (whichever you choose) must conform to some extent to the style of the publisher you're trying to please.

It isn't easy to capture style and tame it enough to study it. It's like tearing down two old houses to see how they were built. You might do that and say, "Now I know the construction business."

No, you don't. At best you have an idea of how two people many years ago constructed their homes with whatever products were available to them. Currently the housing industry ranges from old-time bamboo, mud and thatch construction to nomads' tents and Eskimos' igloos, and beyond them a great many more ingenious, sophisticated, complicated, durable forms worldwide, designed and erected by brilliant people as different as the world is big.

Writing style varies in much the same way. People write in a manner with which they are comfortable and which is suitable for their intended market. They write with whatever vocabulary and knowledge they have, but outside factors determine the acceptability of their efforts. Some writing is elegant—intended for elegant audiences. Some writing is homey, comfortable, middle-class stuff. Some seems shoddy, but there are people who like it just the same.

Where does one begin a study of style? Perhaps a consideration of the two basic structures is the best method: creative writing and journalism. We touched on them briefly in Chapter 2, where we saw that creative writing relies on a feisty imagination, whereas most specialized journalism depends on memory and organizational skills to report the facts.

JOURNALISM

Journalism is writing generally characterized by objectivity, a recounting of happenings past, present, or on the planning board. It is an explanation or discussion of subjects, sometimes using editorial liberties to present one's own viewpoint, and often sprinkled with anecdotes.

In French (which is a Latin language), *jour* means day, so a journal is an objective account of daily events. In popular usage, however, "journal" has developed into meaning a publication that reports objectively, whatever the time period it covers. *Wall Street Journal* and *Journal of Commerce* are daily; numerous other periodicals such as medical, technical, and academic journals are monthly or biweekly; whereas news journals such as *Time, Newsweek*, and *U.S. News and World Report* are weekly. All these journals keep abreast of current events of interest to their audiences.

Among the most influential journals in the world are the national and local telecasts (to which most of us are addicted) and daily local papers. The names of the latter present an intriguing study:

—The *Times* (keep up with what's going on),
—*Sentinels* (stand guard; stay alert; keep a close watch on events),
—*Monitors* (maintain discipline; have the clout to enforce rules; keep their ears and eyes open),
—*Chronicles* (record the hard, dry facts),
—*Tribunes* (champion the people's rights),
—*Heralds* (tell the whole world),
—*Posts* (deliver the message).

I suppose *Stars* outshine them all, being good at all of this. And so must you be—good at all of it—if you want to become a top-rated journalist. The best journalists can write in whatever style appeals to their readers. They captivate our minds by telling us what we need to know in a style that keeps us coming back for more.

Some of this century's greatest American journalists surfaced as war correspondents in World War II, among them Ernie Pyle and Hal Boyle. Both men traveled the war fronts, writing columns that sounded like letters home, with a human interest style that developed in the foxholes, or, as Ernie Pyle once wrote, on the bridge watching London burn.

Pyle was a master of description, able to draw word pictures showing what places looked like and how it really felt to be there. He wrote to his good friend and editor Lee Miller about "my crazy style," which he counted on Miller to edit only for errors, and to leave otherwise untouched. Hal Boyle was a master of down-to-earth speech which folks back home understood and loved. Both men were reporting to farmers and blue-collar workers whose interest in those distant lands grew out of sons, grandsons, and neighbor kids being over there.

On the other hand, Stewart Alsop, famous *Newsweek* columnist, employed the conversational tone of New York businessmen he worked and lived among, combining it with familiar but bookish terms he and they were comfortable with. His style of writing did much to lift the literary level of all America, for instead of coming down to the conversation level of people scattered in mountain villages, along riverfronts, and in isolated farmhouses on the vast prairies, he and his journalist colleagues expected folks to climb to reading and therefore speaking proper English. Such writers introduced common people to a vocabulary a rung or two up the ladder from their own.

We are richer by far because men like Pyle and Boyle dared to write at gut level, but we would be poor indeed if there were no Alsops to balance it off—and we have many men and women like him today, still working at the task of keeping American English intelligible.

Good journalists rise above the colloquialisms of their own neighborhoods. They become leaders, setting the pace in style. Rudolf Flesch advocated "writing like you talk," and he did have some influence in cutting through gobbledygook. But newscasters overruled him, making us "talk as we write," instead. More than any great writers or orators of the past, today's journalists are molding language, as well as influencing thought.

How can you get on board, become a mind-molder? Since so many beginning writers first taste success in nonfiction, it is extremely important that we examine journalistic style to discover keys that might open doors to you. What is the common denominator among top journalists? And what makes them differ from one another?

Success stories begin with a good idea, but they don't end there. Many people have excellent ideas, but when it comes to presenting them on paper, they flounder. Rejection slips by the thousands are mailed out simply because people have submitted commonplace clutter.

Five keys to quality journalism immediately become apparent in almost any fine article:

1. Organization. You say, "Here is my idea," but you go on from there: "This is what I'm going to do with it." Of all there may be to report on a given event or say about a given subject, you decide what *you* want to say about it. Careful planning is the rock-bottom foundation. One can't eliminate it and succeed.
2. Knowledge. The broader your background, the stronger your writing will be. Successful writers exude confidence.
3. Vocabulary. This does not mean careless tacking on of words picked from Roget's *Thesaurus*, useful though that book may be. Vocabulary increases with knowledge and flows comfortably throughout fine writing.
4. Writing skills. As a builder must know what to do with all the material he gathers to erect his dwelling, so a journalist must be equipped with an eye for word beauty. Talent is strengthened by comprehensive study and diligent practice. It solidifies through experience and success.
5. Human interest. The most important key is understanding what grabs audience attention and holds people spellbound. Without it, all other effort is in vain.

Interestingly enough, these are master keys opening a wide variety of doors. Your journalistic style will depend upon how you use them and where. In this sense, style can be developed.

But style is also wrapped up in the personality of the writer. Everything about the writer helps to mold his journalistic style. You are equipped with a unique, all-encompassing birth-to-present-day background which colors your presentation in a singular way. Your writing style is you—you, on paper; you, presenting your thoughts in your own way.

Losing sight of the personal aspect of style accounts for a high percentage of rejection slips. Most nonfiction writing today follows a predictable pattern. Rather than saying what *they think*, writers say *what other people think*. To an editor, a pile of freelance articles begins to look like the "ticky-tacky houses all in a row" we sang about in the 1960s. All the writers think alike, and few dare to break out of the mold. The successful journalist breaks away from the commonplace crowd. He is alert, curious, daring, innovative, and his style stays fresh and appealing because he is alive and in touch with a broad spectrum of people and events.

Exposé and persuasion are two very important journalistic styles that give birth to whole new families. We think of exposé as startling exposure of secrets some celebrity has tried to keep hidden—or secrets that never existed but which some tabloid has blown up as big news, or some gossip columnist has dreamed up. It is all that; and judging by sales, the public never gets enough of it.

Exposé refers to things discreditable. If you put your mind to work on that, you'll recognize many wrongs that need exposure—Ralph Nader made a name for himself doing that. You could do the same by expertly investigating local situations and bringing them to light with a carefully documented but sharp-tongued (or poisoned pen) exposé, or with a sweet or funny approach that gets the point across even more effectively in some cases. You don't always have to put your head on the chopping block to let people know how you feel.

The same goes for persuasion. It can be a calm, deep river flowing through the hills year after year, taking a little of the landscape with it each day to the delta down below. Or it can be a bulldozer, wrecking and making enemies as it roars through to its goal. Readers need both kinds of persuasion, which are examples of very different styles.

While news reporting uses the most efficient method of getting current events to people who want to learn about them, journalism taken as a whole expands those reports, coloring them with human interest sidelines. It peeks behind the scene to see what's there, expresses opinions, editorializes, and drops in lighthearted punch lines and homey comments. These are all so closely related to creative writing that the two overlap and are synonymous in many areas. True journalism, though, begins with facts, and studies in journalism cover the how-to of transmitting those facts through the media, as well as how to write them down.

CREATIVE WRITING

Creative writing, while referring especially to poetry and fiction, encompasses a great deal of nonfiction as well. Any writing that taps one's creative resources falls into this category. An imaginative writer whose flair for words becomes apparent soon after he picks up his pencil can develop an attention-getting style using the same keys to success we talked about earlier. Add to them tough discipline, for creativity tends to get out of hand, splashing color wildly as captivating thoughts tumble out of the mind.

The creative writer plucks an idea, any idea, out of the air and builds on it. As an artist paints a prize-winning picture showing a bug on a weed, so the creative writer uses words to do the same thing—painting a picture a blind person could read in Braille or hear on tape, see clearly, and enjoy.

The creative writer excels in narrative and description. Both prose and poetry may leave blank spaces to be filled in by the reader's imagination, but narrative and description are not just filler. The creative writer learns to use them to advantage much the same as a speaker learns when to spell out an explanation, and when to allow the twinkle in his eye to do the job. Description, perhaps as much as word choice, determines one's style and reveals one's skill or lack of it.

For the writer to succeed in description, his mind must first create the image transmitted to it through the five senses. Perhaps even more importantly, the emotions get involved: the heart, the gut-level feeling, the feelings in the pit of the stomach exposed when excitement is high or when fear, tragedy, or trauma tear away the outer, civilized shell of an individual. Some writers have a unique connection between the funny bone and the brain, the rare ability to produce the laughs that keep a hurting world sane. Comedy is much more than a Band-Aid; it's a miracle medicine extracted from a rare type of creative mind. Other writers have a tender spot connected to the heart that transforms the ordinary into special, never-to-be-forgotten moments. There are the minds like Poe's, exuding an aura of mystery, widening the eyes in anticipation half akin to fear as they jot down a few simple words that require a gasp and a whisper to read them: "Suddenly there came a tapping, as of someone gently rapping. . . ."

Although the style of the era comes through in the following three examples of good narrative, the excellence in writing will never change, and the authors' styles are apparent, too. From Robert Louis Stevenson's *Kidnapped*:

> . . . we lay awhile, and panted, and putting aside the leaves, looked back . . . They had not spied us . . . and now and again, when a grouse rose out of the heather with a clap of wings, we lay as still as the dead and were afraid to breathe . . .

From Victor Hugo's *The Hunchback of Notre-Dame*:

> I do not think that there is anything in the world more delightful than the ideas aroused in a mother's heart by the sight of her child's little shoe, especially if it be a best shoe, a Sunday shoe, a christening shoe, a shoe embroidered down to the very sole, a shoe in which the child has never yet taken a step.

And finally from Charles Dickens' *A Tale of Two Cities*:

> The night deepened. The trees environing the old chateau, keeping its solitary state apart, moved in a rising wind, as though they threatened the pile of building massive and dark in the gloom. Up the two terrace flights of step the rain ran wildly, and beat at the great door, like a swift messenger rousing those within . . .

One good way to sense the variety in style is to read excerpts from these three books aloud. They require three different approaches, and they set three very different moods.

What determines style? Several factors have a bearing on it: the writer's personality and background, his environment, his own vocabulary and interests. But even more than the writer's natural contribution to his style, publishable style is determined by outside forces: the subject, the publisher's choice of style, and what the audience demands. The buck stops in the readers' hands, more often than not.

GETTING WALLED IN BY A SUBJECT

The question is, can the facts be colored or not, or is the matter at hand the type of material that must be stated dryly, without opinion or pun? If the subject allows touching it up, how much is appropriate? A discussion of new findings in cancer research, for example, could feasibly wrap up dry facts between a human interest anecdote and a conclusion of hope. Martin Luther employed humor in expounding deep theological matters. My favorite is his statement: "Here a bungling jackass of a sophist looks only at the outward appearance of the work, as a cow looks at a new gate."[2] (That was translatable, by the way, and has endured several centuries.)

THE PUBLISHER'S CHOICE OF STYLE

Every publisher has a range of style that is acceptable, borders beyond which he very seldom goes. Work is scholarly or it's homey, it's light and funny or it's heavy and somewhat dull, it's geared to people over forty or under seventeen, it's for college age or senior citizens, it's nonfiction or it's heavy on fiction or all fiction.

New magazines I've seen in the past few years in my fields of interest seem to fall into two categories: those filled with satire, out to change things by poking fun at somebody—a scoffing at the sophists, as Emerson and Luther did openly, and those aimed at lifting the quality of American literature to a higher plane, both in content and style. Both types of magazines appeal to me, and I could write comfortably for either one. (Whether or not they'd accept my work is another subject. Let's not talk about that.) We'll study the markets later, and you'll see more clearly that a style suited to one publisher might not please the next.

WHAT THE AUDIENCE DEMANDS

The publisher decides this to a large extent, so the writer has lessened responsibility. Market testing is tremendously important to any publisher, and results are carefully scrutinized. If you can zero in on specific audiences with some accuracy, and then write for them, all that remains is to find a suitable publisher. Knowing your audience is the message here. You've got to know Kansans to write for *Kansas*! and if you write for *Palm Beach Life* you'd better not view the world as a hobo from Minnesota living on a shoestring. You must do more than study the markets. You must write for people you *know*.

YOUR KNOWLEDGE AND ATTITUDE

There are times when you will disregard your own feelings about a subject, allowing the wishes of the publisher, preferences of the readers and slant of the subject to dictate the way you write. If you're a nut like me—and many creative people do march out of step with the crowd, not listening to any drummer at all—you'll learn to suppress some of your thoughts and refrain from expressing some of your ideas.

But by and large your style will grow best in its natural climate. You, the real you, the you you feel most comfortable with, will determine your own style, be it through heredity or environment or both. Only insofar as an education was part of your developing-years environment will it play a significant role in shaping your style. Education beyond your youth serves to sharpen, expand, and polish what has already been put into a basic form. The die is cast.

Sir Edmund Gosse, writing in *Encyclopaedia Britannica*, defines style as "an artistic arrangement of words." This puts it in the category of planning a flower garden, landscaping a yard, or decorating a house, where tastes vary immensely. He considers the personal aspect of style indispensable because: "Language is so used as to awaken impressions, and these are aroused in a way peculiar to the genius of the individual who brings them forth." Gosse points out the variance between "feeble rhythm by an inferior novelist . . . bad rhythm by a bad novelist and . . . no rhythm at all by a police reporter."[3] He is referring to mediocre writing, lousy writing, and writing that lacks color. The latter occurs because the assignment is to get the facts down accurately without speculation or slanting. It might be very good writing, if properly done.

If there are two basic structures in which to display style—creative writing and journalism—there are three ways in which to present the materials that mold the style to some degree: detached, sympathetic, and empathic.

DETACHED APPROACH

The police report is detached writing, not because the reporter doesn't care, but because the assignment allows no room for personal opinion or speculation that might prejudge the case in someone's mind, making a fair trial unlikely.

Detached writing is done by people who don't get all tangled up in their own heartstrings telling a story. They may certainly care deeply about what has happened. Few reporters can flip off the TV screen of their mind and go to bed totally free of haunting thoughts about traumatic events they've covered. It would be easy enough for me to fill the rest of the book with tales of people I've felt like crying over, only to walk away and leave them as bad off as when I met them, with nothing more than the memory of a smile, if they looked up from their troubles long enough to see that.

Although they care, detached writers tear themselves free

emotionally. They write with almost total objectivity, disclosing neither political leanings nor personal opinions. TV news anchormen excel in objective reporting. Subjective, you say? Yes, maybe, in the sense that the telecast might be slanted by station management or the network. But objective, since you cannot tell from the tone of their voice or the words they say how they personally feel even about touchy matters that make most of us want to throw a shoe through the screen. Newspaper reporting is done with the same skilled detachment.

SYMPATHETIC APPROACH

Sympathetic writing is like the governor touring the site of somebody's pet project. He's interested because he wants their vote, but the minute he turns his back his mind is switched to another channel. He doesn't toss and turn all night wondering how it's all going to be worked out, but he probably will see to it that some funds come through—enough to get the votes, at least.

A huge amount of writing is done by sympathetic writers. They feel the cause is worthy of a moment of applause, so they jot off an article, write a story, run out for an interview, scribble a poem, and reap enormous amounts of pleasure seeing their words, if not their names, in print. Working writers survive by being willing to tackle this kind of assignment regularly. Newsrooms would die of starvation without it. The headline stories, no matter how important, won't fill the whole paper, so the little daily (weekly, monthly) reports of this and that fill the news holes between one feature and the next.

Sympathetic also means to feel sorry for someone. The sympathetic you will be able to write stirring accounts of things you run across—deteriorating communities in your town, crime in the suburbs, the murder of a child, flood victims, tornadoes, fires, earthquakes, accidents—as long as they're across town, and not in your own backyard.

Writing from a sympathetic viewpoint has feeling because even though the events happened to strangers, your emotions are in some distant way tied to them. The events could happen to you. They could, you well know, strike anywhere. You respond and write in some sort of gratitude that you were not involved, and with that bold relief we all rely on that you and those you love are somehow immune—all the while knowing that's not true.

Much of what we call human interest material falls into this category. We humans still follow the fire truck, enjoying the thrill of the moment without feeling the pain. Think how many wild car chases there are on TV, ending in over-the-cliff plunges or fiery crashes. The public loves violence, although everyone turns coward in a hurry if the camera veers his way.

Sympathetic writing covers happy experiences as well. Stories by the score have been published that tell about the hectic/sad events of everyday life: weddings, love affairs, homecomings, a "grandbaby" (as they say in Missouri) to fill the arms of a lonely widow, a kitten that finds a home, a crippled bird rescued, a big happy family and how they all turn out, endless tales of the family mutt, and the college kid out of money.

All it takes to be a good writer with a sympathetic style is to be alive and in touch with everday affairs. The world is full of things almost everyone can enjoy, laugh about, cry about, remember, hope for, avoid, or worry about.

EMPATHIC APPROACH

Empathy differs from sympathy not so much in depth of understanding, as in depth of feeling. To write with empathy one must have been there. Stewart Alsop wrote a book, *Stay of Execution*, because:

> If a writer has had an unusual experience likely to interest a good many people, he has an instinct, and perhaps even a duty, to write about it.[4]

A good many readers did have an interest in his experience. He could write about dying of leukemia because he was facing death. He knew what it felt like. War correspondents write realistically because they feel the fear and hear the bullets whiz past their ears. They see the boys fall in battle and help carry the wounded to safety.

It might strike you as strange, but most articles and books

written by patients about their illness, by parents about the suffering and death of a child, or by widows about the loss of their mate, are rejected because the person is too close to the subject, writing out of grief, rather than with empathy for others. Impressive empathic writing requires a certain amount of objectivity, possible only in rare instances by the victim. Alsop could do it, thanks to a lifetime of trained writing that enabled him to know just how large a dose of someone else's grief a reader could bear. Dale Evans, writing about her mongoloid child in *Angel Unaware*, succeeded.

Empathy is both learned (through experiencing pain) and a natural gift (being born with a tenderness that feels others' pain). If you hanker to write another *Lassie, Come Home*, you will either need to have experienced the loss of a dog you loved, or know dogs so well you know how one would feel and what it might go through on a journey such as Lassie took. Horse stories, stories of children, stories of old people, and stories of painful divorce or of loneliness all require a certain amount of understanding of the feelings of the horse, the children, the old people, the lonely people, and the feelings of those who surround them.

One of the best books I've read to illustrate empathy is *Benjamin and Jon*,[5] a novel about an old man who escaped from a nursing home (bravo) and in the woods where he hoped to hide came upon the camp of an abused child who had also run away. Authorities didn't find the pair for months, and I loved every moment of their adventure. Without jumping up on a soapbox to shout her message to the world, the author, Mary Ellen Heath, effectively made it clear: a weak body does not indicate a weak mind; old people get lonesome and bored and need to get away from it all now and then; good kids are being brutally beaten for little or no reason and would turn out to be jewels if given half the chance.

Empathy is feeling what others feel. Take hunger, for example. People who have been lost in the woods or held hostage without food; people whose loved ones have come home skin and bones, or whose last pictures revealed skeletal forms; people who have suffered from real hunger or have dished out bits of rice to starving groups of skinny human beings—these people could write empathic accounts of starvation. Friends of mine visiting Timbuktu told about a starving desert nomad who trudged into the city for food while they were there, but died outside the mission compound because he was just too late. When trays were set before my friends on the plane homeward bound, they couldn't eat. *That* is empathy.

Writing is show and tell. You could talk and talk about the plight of both abused children and lonely old men in nursing homes, and people do spin out thousands of words on those sensitive, significant subjects. Painting a word picture of two lovables like Benjamin and Jon is another way of doing the same thing in a fresh, readable style. I give Heath an A+ for a job well done.

I'm reminded of a student who once asked me what style was. I went through a long spiel dumping on her everything I could think of, taking up half the class time to answer her question. When I finally stopped for breath she said, "I still don't understand what style is."

Style is not something you struggle with. It surfaces as you learn to write. The total saturation program you've begun will affect your style, increasing your versatility. A full brain soon overflows. You will find yourself with much to write about; thought building upon thought, idea upon idea, dream upon dream, as if you were putting the right ingredients into a mixing bowl. Once everything that's called for is in, you can mix it all up, place it in a pan, and pop the pan in the oven. When you pull it out, it's done—but it's not quite finished. You put on the frosting and decorate it according to your own skills and taste.

That's not hard, is it? Style is a piece of cake!

In another trip to the library (you'll soon have to start paying rent, you'll be going so much), you might take down all the magazines—I found about thirty at our suburban library one time—and spread them on a big table, shuffling into various heaps those whose styles match. It's a very educatonal game—one you can do at home, with whatever you have.

And while you're browsing, don't forget your anecdote file. Add to it.

Ready for a breather? Or shall we go on?

ASSIGNMENT 5

WARM-UP: You can do this assignment—at least part of it—while you read the morning paper. Study the style of various writers. When you are free to write, follow the suggestions below and write fifty to one hundred words in various styles, checking the categories off as you do them.

_____fast-paced reporting	_____in popular feature style
_____humorously	_____fiction (East Coast)
_____in editorial style	_____fiction (Midwest)
_____poetry	_____fiction (Western flavor)
_____as to a child	

The list is only a suggestion. You do not need to check every category. You might prefer not to try humor, for example; or possibly fiction for children is totally out of your line.

The idea is to try writing a variety of styles. Today you could tackle one or two; tomorrow you might be in the mood for something entirely different.

Here's where you get your material:

1. Lean back in your chair and recall some place you go regularly: a ball park, a supermarket, the barbershop, your home, office, farm, route, or plant. Picture surroundings. Examine details such as overloaded trash barrels, sky patterns, ground cover, size of rooms, cracks in the wall, arrangement of meat in coolers, food on the tray of the person in front of you, wall textures, fabrics, colors, condition of machinery or equipment. When you have it fixed in your mind, pick up your pencil and describe it.
2. Study the face of someone you know well. Watch the person's mood changes, note the eyes, the set of the chin, hairstyle, age lines, and facial expression. Describe the person on paper.
3. Think back over the most exciting or frightening

experience you can remember (it could be a dream). Write it down in third person, as if it happened to someone else.

FINALLY: This is *your* assignment, but if I were you, I'd leave the writing in the rough and not make a big production of it. Practice—and have fun! You'll have time later to finish the pieces that seem especially good. For now, keep the words flowing. I want you to become addicted to the joy of writing things down.

6 Examining Your Writing Options

Early one morning, as I was sipping coffee while gazing at the star-sprinkled heavens, a huge flash of gold streaked across the sky. I was jolted from my reverie, shocked; because although it was the color of a shooting star, it was so large: the size of a small plane; so close: right over the river beyond our hill; and so fiery: flames enveloped the object, which was on a definite downward course. The spectacle was so dazzling I sat for a moment frozen to the edge of the chair and barely breathing before thinking any rational thoughts. What should I do? Call the police? Call the newspaper? Jump in the car and speed to the scene?

Barney, lying on the ground outside my morning window, sat up and began to howl. I opened the window a crack. Sirens. Heading east. I gulped as I leaned back, deep in thought. I had a ringside seat. A plane had crashed, and I was one of few who saw it happen.

If I were working as a reporter, I'd have sped to the scene, because River Front Park is only spitting distance away and I felt sure that's where the plane had gone down. Allowing for time to pull on jeans and a sweatshirt, to stumble into sandals, to grab my camera and briefcase, and to locate my car keys I'd have been among the first to arrive. From the highway three blocks from home I would see the flames. If not, certainly from the bridge they'd be visible, as would the flashing red lights of the police vehicles I had heard. I might be able to follow the ambulance and fire trucks certain to be along any minute.

I'm not a reporter, except at heart. I flipped on the radio. The best news station offered only the raucous sounds of rock and roll drumming on and on. Five o'clock news came on. Six o'clock. Seven. No plane had gone down.

Or had it crashed into the swollen river and been carried away, with no one else seeing it? Perhaps it was not a plane. Maybe . . . maybe it was a UFO.

The dark night. Impenetrable blackness. The pitch black predawn sky. Magically, without a sound, the somber night sky is transformed into a jeweler's velvet draped across a carefree, slumbering town—black velvet cushioning the beauty of clear, glittering stars scattered like dozens of tiny diamonds as far as the eye can see. If one wanted to reach out to glom a jewel, it could be easily done. No one would ever know. The stillness of the night. The whole city enjoying the deep, quiet renewal of a good night's sleep.

Just as silently, unknown to earth dwellers lost in pleasant dreams, the sleek oval form glides downward from outer space, soft iridescent lights shimmering like colored pearls as they blink off and on. From 50,000 feet. Then 40,000 . . . 30,000 . . . 20,000 . . . Now it stops, hovering over the strange sights of our world. Inside the spaceship six creatures, excited but busy, pore over intricate maps photographed in detail by computers on the advance teams' ships. Fascinated by the sights below, they step now and then to the porthole, now to the charts on the wall, now to the table to check the maps, brainstorm their next move and bolster their courage. Thoughts dart back and forth between the keen minds. The decision is unanimous. Though the prospect is challenging—meeting humans face to face on their own turf—their mission must go on.

Zyxlen, leader of the team, moves to the controls, releases the brake, and touches "descent." But what has gone wrong? Instead of floating silently to earth, the spaceship jerks and jolts, rocking with such force the voyagers stumble about, grappling for safety bars, struggling to sit down and fasten safety belts to prepare for what now seems inevitable. Hawa, the only female on board, is with Zyxlen at the console, both of them punching emergency buttons. The ship veers to the east, away from the city. Lights on the console flash wildly. An eerie warning signal sounds and a forceful command from outer space pierces their thoughts: "Eject! Eject!" The six alien minds comprehend and try to obey.

From my peaceful dining room window I view the awesome scene only as a fiery meteor slitting the beautiful black velvet before disappearing by splashing into the river beyond the hill. But in reality a spaceship has burst into flame. Within moments it will crash to the earth to be buried nose down in the soft soil near River Front Park. Of the four creatures who successfully eject, only two will survive.

Kansas City is wide awake in moments. Imagine the frantic rescue efforts, the jumbled messages over police radios, the confusion throughout the city as word speeds from one precinct to the next! Who dares to lift the broken bodies of such awesome creatures—giant, dark beings clothed in metallic suits bright as stardust, but covered now with mud? Silent moments of horror precede the pandemonium that follows the discovery that Hawa and Zyxlen are still alive. The air is filled with shouts. The mayor is awakened rudely from his sound sleep. Every disaster alert in the city is sounded. Here and there lone night watchmen, isolated patrolmen, and bored dispatchers sick and tired of listening to meaningless crackles on their radios suddenly think their fantasies have unhinged their minds. A spaceship crashed? In River Front Park? Aw, come on!

Before dawn the national guard is called in to help restore order, see if there are other survivors, and guard the buried spaceship until digging can begin. By noon the city is overrun with telecasters stampeding to get the story.

But suppose I refuse to give it to them? I give it to you, instead, to take it from there. Instead of a children's story, you might create a short story for adults, written from whatever angle you see it. But remember, I'm giving you only the idea. Don't let me recognize my story. Your people had better not look like Hawa and Zyxlen, and their names will have to be changed. Your spaceship had better fall to the earth in some farmer's field; or on some sandy beach; or on a forested mountainside where Artesians dwell. Maybe it could land quietly in the backyard of a nursing home to be seen by a lonely old man who happens to be the only person awake. What a getaway you could create for him!

Suppose the national guard never finds the spaceship, or no one even knows it has gone down until two little boys out fishing run across the shiny silver UFO, embedded in the ground near the riverbank. Neat experience for a couple of kids way downriver on their bikes!

Maybe—yes I think that would be good—they find the one and only survivor of the crash, as well. Hawa communicates with them in a soft, soothing voice in choppy English she has learned from the computer. They have very little time to wait before the boys' fathers arrive to fish for a while before taking them home in the truck. Help for Hawa is already on the way! Won't the men be surprised at what the boys have to show for their day? The kids become Hawa's best friends and after she is claimed by the mother ship, following her hospital stay, they get to visit her planet!

Well, the incident—large golden object streaking across the black sky—did occur, but I didn't think of the UFO stories when it happened. Being a writer of inspirational articles, I thought along those lines and wrote a short inspirational article:

> War! How devastating to live in constant peril where falling planes and bursting bombs light up the night skies often enough to become commonplace! How dreadful the prospect of morning for those who survive, digging through the smoking rubble to locate bodies of neighbors and friends.
>
> Isaiah 25 seemed to remind me that, in spite of all our struggles and sorrows, God is in charge. I was calmed by the realization that in Him is our hope, no matter what happens. The verses of praise became the song of my heart:

> "O Lord, you are my God; I will exalt you and praise your name . . . You have been a refuge for the poor, a refuge for the needy in his distress, a shelter from the storm and a shade from the heat. . . . The Sovereign Lord will wipe away the tears from all faces . . ."
>
> (Isaiah 25:1, 4, 8, NIV)[1]

What would you do with a quiet night, black sky, huge flash of light, sirens, thick forested riverbank, and a city fast asleep? If you're a poet, you most certainly could weave a few lines together about a velvety star-filled sky. Your viewpoint, your personality, your mood, your general writing style, and the specific writing form you choose to approach the subject will determine the outcome. Undoubtedly you will find an angle for it entirely different from my own.

Poetry, newswriting, articles, stories: one incident can be the core of them all. A good, versatile writer can take the same event and draw reams of material from it to use in a variety of ways. The more I think about it, the more I believe I'll go fishing with the boys. We'll find that spaceship and the survivor, and while they keep Hawa company, I'll rush back to town for help.

Amateurs limit themselves by not experimenting with various kinds of writing. They tend to confine themselves to what felt good the first time they put words on paper. "I'm a poet," they say, or "I write children's stories," or "I'm our club reporter." From then on, they view everything from that vantage point, avoiding the risk of trying something new, but losing opportunities for expansion and growth.

Rarely is a crackerjack writer a one-talent person. Most are multi-talented, with interests as varied as their own small world has allowed them to develop, and generally much broader, as their creative spirit climbed up and reached out, finding one tree limb after another from which to spy on the world beyond their own. Since quite likely you have lived a few years as an adult before taking writing seriously, I have a hunch you have carved a few notches on your spear for past accomplishments in other fields. To settle down into a single rut in writing would be out of character, would it not?

Onward, then to consider the options!

One evening a three-year-old came toting a worn-out book. She climbed up into my lap as if she owned it and, ignoring my participation in adult conversation, jabbed the book in my face. We spent a long time reading such things as "The Three Little Kittens" and "Little Miss Muffet." Suddenly, as we turned the page, I saw Longfellow's name.

"Longfellow!" I mused (although I couldn't stop reading long enough to even snatch a breath lest a frenetic little voice plead: "Wead! Wead!"). "What's Longfellow doing in *this* book?"

I envision Henry Wadsworth Longfellow as a studious sort of youth who longed to be a writer. He begged his father (who had other plans): "I greatly desire a place of eminence in literature!" And he reached his goal, writing essays and books; deep, questioning theological works; ballads such as the well-known "Evangeline," "Hiawatha," and "The Courtship of Miles Standish"; and moving poems suitable to be set to music as hymns. As a professor he excelled in languages; translation was one of his major accomplishments, and he is remembered especially as head of Harvard's modern language department, a rather dignified position.

Small wonder then that I read with a grin the masterpiece before me (probably the most widely read of his works!):

There was a little girl who had a little curl,
Right in the middle of her forehead,
And when she was good, she was very, very good,
But when she was bad, she was horrid.

Longfellow wrote deep, significant material, but he also scribbled verse. Most good writers exercise all their options for both pleasure and profit.

So much recorded history of literary masters pictures them jumping from earnest university student to elderly, staid university professor, that we tend to overlook the years between. They were as human as you and I, involved in everyday affairs. You may remember that Kipling, whose ballads sometimes seem to have a humdrum sameness to them, wrote from lands afar such well-known words as, "You're a better man than I am, Gunga din!" and "If you can keep your head while all about you are losing theirs, and blaming it on you . . ." But he contemplated, too, his choice between Maggie and his cherished cigars!

> *A million surplus Maggies are willing to bear the yoke;*
> *And a woman is only a woman, but a good cigar is a Smoke.*

In "The Enlightenments of Pagett, M.P." the same man wrote in a serious vein (with nobody threatening his cigar supply) the following nonfiction defense of oriental life:

> You, perhaps, find it hard to conceive of people absolutely devoid of curiosity, to whom the book, the daily paper, and the printed speech are unknown, and you would describe their life as blank. That's a profound mistake . . . [The average Oriental's life] is bovine and slow in some respects, but it is never empty. . . . It is the man that is elemental, not the book.

Kipling's works, as much as anyone's, reveal that his flair for writing followed his moods and traced his travels. The talent was always there. What came out through his pen depended upon where he was and how he felt about it. Learning how to get mileage out of everyday events of life requires examining all the options. That's called "proficiency in the art of versatility!" You obtain it by knocking down any fences you have built around yourself, launching out to try new things.

DO YOU CHURN OUT RHYMES?

Stevenson's stories are well enough known, but his *A Child's Garden of Verses* has always been considered his masterpiece, head and shoulders above the rest. Interestingly enough, the verses are no more than ditties, and could have been written for (and maybe by) a twentieth century child anywhere in the world:

How would you like to go up in a swing
Up in the air so blue?
Oh, I do think it the pleasantest thing
Ever a child could do!

Most of us will fail utterly in writing enduring verse. "Da, de da da rhymes," which most of us can grind out in heaps and piles when in the proper mood, are not the world's hottest sales items, partly because:

1. The writer is thinking of meter and rhyme but is unable to produce quality content.
2. The writer is wrapped up in content but has no comprehension of the rhythmic value and little knowledge of rhyme.

We'll get to the basics of poetry in Chapter 11, but for now, let's use it as a jumping off place for examining our options, because there are many people walking around hugging oft-rejected bundles of poems who might succeed with other literary forms.

The writer able to fill page upon page with rhymes has one good thing going: a mind that loves words. The problem is, the words are much like the children who lived with the old woman in the shoe. Many of them are small, thoughtless, undisciplined, and unruly. They tumble into the midst of serious thought, bungling the whole creation by insisting on marching hand in hand, always on the lookout for others just like them who can get in step and march along in the very same, tiresome line. The mind may be full of little untrained words, but they can't be allowed, naughty as they are, to join in any new, bigger adventure.

Like the old woman who lived in a shoe, to get control of words that insist on rhyming you need to "spank them all soundly and put them to bed." The mind that loves words can begin to write as prolifically as a cat has kittens, one batch of winners after another; but to do so takes discipline, a deliberate separating of the naughty twins who insist on sticking together for the sake of rhyme.

A writer called me to read me a chapter from her book (oh

please, please spare me!). Her earlier calls had been pleasurable interruptions. Choice words flowed smoothly, recounting her story in a unique, creative way. But this call set my nerves on edge, so I finally interrupted and begged her to stop.

The chapter was prose, all right. But her style had stripped a gear. Ordinary sentences suddenly had the exact same beat, with an ending word that rhymed perfectly with the one before. The result was dreadful.

"I can't help it," she whined. "That's how it came out!"

The rhyming was not intentional, because she had never written rhymes. What she had said was good, so to remedy the situation I suggested that she first deliberately choose a replacement for at least one final word in each of the couplets: a synonym, a phrase that said the same thing, or some brand-new conclusion to the sentence. Thus:

I was thinking strongly of going to bed,
But sat in the recliner instead, and read . . .

became: "I sat in the recliner instead and browsed through a magazine . . ."

After she had wiped out all rhyming words one way or another, she was to go to work on the sentences, lengthening some and shortening others. The effect was to disrupt the timing so two good friends didn't inadvertently meet at the corner to join hands again. The final result was a tale well told.

You could do that with Stevenson's verses (though who would want to, except as an exercise!):

In winter I get up at night (before dawn)
And dress *by yellow candlelight* (by the light of a small lamp)
In summer, *quite the other way* (quite another problem plagues me)
I have to go to bed *by day*. (before the sun goes down.)

Thus, we read: "In winter I get up before dawn and dress by the light of a small lamp. In summer quite another problem plagues me. I have to go to bed before the sun goes down."

If you have reams of rhymes, you'll enjoy seeing how many ways you can turn them around to say virtually the same thing in prose that *might* have sales potential, if you polish them long enough. Free verse, blank verse, or any other form of poetry you write can be put into prose much the same way.

The mind that loves words is sure to cooperate. Our minds catch on to new games so quickly they soon take over and play alone, long after we've consciously turned to other matters. And they don't give up easily. Like a three-year-old, they hang on to a new idea with amazing tenacity. You'll awaken to find your mind chewing over words you've read or heard; and as time goes on, if you should be aware of what is happening, you'll see rich vocabulary crop out as your mind experiments with choice replacements for words that used to rhyme.

RIGHT CONTENT: WRONG PLATFORM

Writers of rhyme plagued with the other problem, poor ability to put the right beat to the line, have even more going for them, since excellent content is the whole idea of writing. We write because we have something to say.

Forcing good thoughts into rhymes and calling it poetry is like putting on a costly garment that is way too small for you. How often does a scanning editor have to note: "The thoughts in these verses are meaningful . . . show insight . . . touch on the realities of life . . . but meter is nonexistent, and the rhyming contrived. *Reject it!*"

Great thoughts need room to grow. With few exceptions, the day of long ballads is past, which limits your poetry to a few lines, not nearly enough to expand the magnificent thoughts flooding your mind. Although you may think rhyming verse clever—or you've never tried writing anything else—you'll soon discover, if you launch out into other forms of writing, a selection of platforms grand enough for your choice thoughts to really perform.

The method of accomplishing the switchover is the same as

for the other problem, where good rhymes without depth are churned out. The trick is to convince your mind you really mean to change. You are seriously going to turn those nice, worthwhile thoughts into readable prose others will enjoy. If you work at the project consistently, you'll soon begin writing good prose from scratch, but the unmarketable poems you have cried over because no one else loved them might hold a wealth of article or story starters. By carefully following the directions above, you can salvage some, but even more importantly, use others to create something new and exciting from the thoughts you have freed. Exchange rhyming words with new phrases or synonyms that do not rhyme, and vary the sentence lengths.

In some instances, you'll expand the whole idea, using the short original verse as a starter from which other thoughts will grow. Other material may be well suited for what editors call "filler," that is, nice little paragraphs dropped in here and there for browsing interest and to fill in space between longer articles. The best-known examples of filler are found in *Reader's Digest*, but all magazines and newspapers use short pithy pieces to fill in partial columns.

FACT OR FICTION?

You can become versatile in the use of other material you have written, too. The plane crash we began with was not fact, but there might be ways to drop it into nonfiction as an anecdote, because the experience was real. I *thought* I saw a plane go down. It not only *might* have happened, it all too often does. When it does, it can be reported as news or used in various ways in nonfiction. For example, it could be used in an essay on the delights of flying, in which you admit occasional crashes, but point out how infrequently they happen; or as an anecdote in an article about air traffic control. But notes from such a tragedy can also be seed thoughts to grow into a short story, children's story, novel, poem, TV or movie script, or play.

As rhymes can be transformed into prose, so fiction and

nonfiction ideas are interchangeable. The important skill to learn is to view the material from various angles. You can backtrack now, taking a new look at things you have written. Possibly you have articles worn thin from traveling from one publisher to another, so outdated by numerous rejections that not a whisper of a chance remains they would ever be accepted as is. What a shame to bury them forever! You need to think how you might recycle them.

If you had gathered material at the scene of a plane crash, you probably would have had far more than your little suburban newspaper could use. Perhaps you tried unsuccessfully to sell the story and photos elsewhere. You can see now that there's still hope for using it—not as nonfiction (though it holds possibility as an anecdote), but in a story. You can count on failure if all you do is rename the characters, trimming the feature article with a few lines of fiction. But if you look at the plane crash from several angles (as we did), a whole new story may surface. Since it's a story, fictitious and imaginary, you won't necessarily use all the facts and all the people, or the time, place, and chronological sequence of events. You might throw all the bits of paper into the air and pick them up in any order, and even if some key factors of the original account blow away to be lost forever, the plane crash would highlight the story. The nugget you need is the blazing streak across the night sky. Picking a few facts out of the wreckage, you give the fiction the element of possibility, making it believable enough for readers to tune into your channel and follow your fantasy.

Nonfiction is more salable than fiction. Ranging from small club and church news through well-researched articles written on assignment for top magazines, from no pay to the highest pay, nonfiction opportunities are as abundant as wild berries in the northern woods. (My father, out on a weekend research hike, came home on one occasion with *two washtubs* full of blueberries.)

There's a catch, naturally. To fill the tubs with berries, you must arm yourself to face the world's meanest mosquitos and friendliest bears, and set your mind to keep plugging away at the job even if it rains. When you get tired, you keep on working, filling the pail again and again. When you're discouraged, you keep on working. When you want to slow down, you push ahead. When you want to quit, you laugh and go on, thinking about the fresh homemade pie at the end of the line. The parallel in writing is obvious. To succeed in article writing, moving ever closer to the "pie," you arm yourself with courage, work hard, push ahead and as Winston Churchill said, "Never, never, never quit!"

Much excellent talent has gone down the drain because a person who loves to write and could have been good at it once wrote a story. The needle got stuck in that groove, and other stories followed. Alas! The stories were not good enough, so discouraged by rejection, the writer quit.

One must be extremely creative, but also well read and well trained to consistently write and sell fiction. The discipline of trying to succeed in other forms of writing enhances your fiction skills. The question might be, how well do you know your subject? Mary Ellen Heath knew nursing homes, old people, and abused children. If she had not, she could never have written *Benjamin and Jon*. To sit down and write a story about a foster child or a pilot because your neighbor has one or is one is to miss the whole point of professional writing. Fiction writers don't only *view* life, they live it. One day at a time, like the rest of us.

Some of our ideas are lousy. Dumping the whole thing in the trash to start over again is one of the writer's options. Learning *when* to do that comes with experience and is another skill to be learned. While it rarely is smart to send and resend rejected material hoping someone will finally see it as you do (as ingenious), it's always smart to hang on to unsuccessful material until you know without a doubt that not a phrase on the page has value. It may take years to drain out all the potential it holds, even if (as you see looking back from some pinnacle of success) it really was poorly done.

"FIRST PERSON" MEANS YOU!

I've already alluded to the fact that autobiographical material is terribly hard to sell. If you'll promise to keep that warning in mind, I'll give you another insider's tip: First Person articles are not only the easiest to write; dozens of publications open to free-lancers are looking for them.

First Person articles range from "I Caught the Flu and Here's How I Cured It" to "I Raise Sheepdogs," "I Build Boats," and "The Biggest Weekend of My Life." Successful First Person articles may be simply entertaining (with all that word encompasses, from gruesome to funny), or they may be tied to motivation: "I Made a Million Dollars—Here's How You Can Do It, Too."

The personal experience article begins in the personal journal. Your *illustration and idea file* contains notes on everything that goes on around you, as well as usable material from other people's lives and files. Your *personal journal* should be made up of notes about experiences that confront you personally: how you struggle through them, how they turn out, and what you learn from what happened. If you are building a boat in your backyard, you should keep a journal. A notebook on your work-bench ought to become well worn as you jot down the struggles you encounter: purchasing material, difficulties with storage of materials, coping with the problems of temperature variation, sudden downpours, or neighbor children who get in the way. You'll need to record all your costs, as well as getting photographs along the way; to write a top-notch article, you will also have to recall your frustrations and delights as the project progresses. Recording those feelings for future use might spell the difference between acceptance and rejection.

You can draw dollars out of your diary by learning to use it right. For example, let us say you have been passed by on the job, with a longed-for promotion going to a person who is younger than you, with much less experience, and a woman, at that. If you were to hold that whole ball of wax up to the light and turn it this way and that, you might discover several good possibilities for First Person articles:

> A labor-related article incorporating business trends that favor youth and women, perhaps focusing on how your union worked out a solution for you.
>
> An inspirational article showing how you coped with the anger, jealousy, and/or disappointment.

A humorous article telling your story of woe to a general audience for laughs.

An article which focuses on finances, tying in to the economic squeeze you feel as a result of losing the promotion.

Something on the psychology involved as you assess your emotional damage, showing how the experience affected your feelings of insecurity and weakened your self-esteem (or bolstered it, as you surmounted the obstacles).

A self-assertion article, explaining steps you took to change your unhappy situation.

Successful personal experience articles are often intense. They include confessions, testimonials, trauma accounts, how-to's, and reports on special events in a person's life. While the experience often makes up the entire article, it should always be considered for its potential as an anecdote or illustration, because it might be more valuable as an attention-grabber or as proof to glue an argument together.

To find ideas for First Person articles, answer the following questions and others that may come to mind. After you have settled on an answer for each, focus on some experience to illustrate your answer. To prime the pump and learn the skill of writing personal experiences, you can recount anything that comes to mind. As you progress, however, you will want to look for startling experiences, unusual approaches to common experiences, or unique conclusions to normal events.

How do I cope with feelings such as anger, grief, trauma, disappointment?

How do I succeed in overcoming obstacles (handicaps, poor relationships, financial squeezes, weight gains, drug dependencies, hard-to-solve problems, poor self-image, job discrimination, racial prejudice)?

What is my hobby? How do I spend my free time, weekends, vacations? On whom do I spend my mad money?

What is there about my job, my home, my family, my relationships, my car, my pets, my reading habits, my religious experiences, my illness, my life, that others would like to read?

Possibilities for personal experience articles are almost endless, especially when you turn to the lives of other people whose stories could be ghostwritten or fictionalized. In addition, you can approach the experiences from an entirely different angle and develop them into solid articles based on principles you have learned through living.

Most of us find that writing about ourselves is quite simple, but producing a smooth presentation of general interest material is much more difficult. A good exercise for learning top writing skills is to transform your personal experience into straight journalistic style. Take out all the "I's" and apply the principles of your experience in a general, objective manner.

Personal experience:

> When the phone rang, I had my hands in the dishwater. I grabbed the towel and dried them as I ran to answer it, but when I touched the phone, I stopped. How could I possibly pick it up and say hello? My heart was pounding. Was this the phone call I had dreaded so long?
>
> It was. "I'm sorry, Mrs. Jones," said a kindly voice on the other end of the line. "Your husband took a turn for the worse a few minutes ago, and has passed away."

Journalistic style:

> How does one respond to the dreaded phone call? With mixed feelings, as a rule. A person might dash to the jangling phone, but be unable to pick it up. As if refusing to answer might change the situation, the hand may rest on the receiver through two or three rings before responding to the mind's command.
>
> The human heart holds on to hope long after all hope is gone, and hearing the words "Your husband has passed away" is a dreaded blow one avoids as long as possible.

PROFILES ARE FOR BEGINNERS

One of the easiest forms of nonfiction is the biographical sketch, the profile. It is easy because the subject provides you with the material (although you might have to sniff the story out through multiple interviews and complicated research, of course). I say easy, but I suppose some of us (like me) have minds equipped with sorters, and others don't. It's fair to say most subjects dump details of their life stories into your lap like tangled masses of yarn, and it's up to you to find the beginning of each one, and the end of it, rolling the remainder into a neat ball.

To do profiles, at least three skills must be learned:

1. Spotting the people whose stories are marketable (or whose lives contain some incidents that are worth applauding);
2. Gathering the right material, using only the best and storing what's left over for future use;
3. Sorting and writing it up well enough to catch an editor's eye.

RESUMES—BIOGRAPHICAL OUTLINES

An absolutely delightful method of getting started in serious interviews is to advertise one's ability to do resumes. The resume is, after all, the outline of an individual's life story. To write resumes successfully, one must ferret out the significant characteristics of the subject, his or her key interests, pursuits that have led to the subject's current capabilities, and come up with concrete evidence that this person is one of the best choices for the position.

Writing resumes is an all-around learning experience. The sharp writer gains much more than his fee. One simple resume can set a writer's head spinning with ideas: an article drawn from (or inspired by) the subject's hobby, a news report on the subject's activities, a story spun off some incident in the individual's life. I don't think I need to tell you again: Biographical material, when thoroughly recycled by the skillful writer, is a marvelous resource for fiction, since you'll be handed supporting characters (relatives, friends, children, spouses, employers, pets) and real-life situations and events to draw upon in future projects.

Most people requesting a writer to prepare a resume bring a sheaf of papers including birth certificate, awards won in childhood, and their first grade teacher's name. Some of course, come empty-handed, expecting the writer to pick their brains for the information that should be included. A few bring an orderly arrangement of facts which needs very little more done to it. A resume is just that: an orderly arrangement of facts. The trick is to spot *significant* facts and arrange them in a manner suited to the purpose for which the resume is being done.

WRITING DRAMA

Plays we write ought to be the quality of old-time closet plays. They ought to be better, as zip is added to make them delightful productions on stage. Our dialogue must be as tightly written as any copy we send out. Words need to be weighed just as carefully for drama as for an assigned newspaper story—more carefully, perhaps, because one can't replay the script during a performance as one can return to a badly written sentence and reread it to ponder the meaning. Write your plays so well that you can shout as Hamlet to the players (Act III, Scene ii): "Speak the speech, I pray you, as I pronounced it to you, trippingly on the tongue. . . . And let those that play your clown speak no more than is set down for them!"

The plot needs to be woven together with professional skill. Forbid that it ever "grow like Topsy"! Thoughts, worked and reworked, have to be placed in proper sequence giving the drama a good beginning, middle, and end. Word tempo must match the action, setting the pace for the one who is to play the part. Interplay between characters has to be fast moving, gripping, and believable; with language suited to the characters, whose very words indicate the varieties of their appearances and personalities. On stage the setting, costumes, body movements, actions, and facial expressions can color in whatever the script might lack, but you, as playwright, are required to weave in your own imagination and feeling to give the players the cue.

The best of drama, like the best of novels, walks a tight rope between reality and fantasy. While the audience wants something realistic enough with which to identify, they're bored by anything that sounds too much like home. You and I are not likely to reach Broadway with dull suburban living room scenes where various people straggle in, wrangle with the mother, and shuffle back out to live their pointless, uninteresting lives. Winning plays will be those with tightly knit plots, striking conversations that introduce new ideas or lift the audience out of their ruts, and characters that ooze charisma, arouse distrust, and make the audience think, grimace, cry, laugh, applaud, or groan.

WRITING FOR KIDS

Can you create exciting stories, scripts, games, activities, and informative articles for children? To do it well, you must know children. To assume a cranky teacher role, with a "you sit down and listen" tone of voice, is to lose the ball game.

As one studies conversation, three levels surface: adult to adult, adult to child, and child to child. You can acquaint yourself with this phenomenon by listening to conversations (even on TV) between parents and children, teachers and children, older neighbors or siblings and children, or kids' conversations with kids. It's a good idea to make mental and actual notes or recordings to compare later.

Adults visiting together use an adult tone of voice with adult vocabulary. Enter a child, the tone and vocabulary change to adult to child, while children chatter to each other as child to child. Puppets chatter happily as kids, but the puppeteer enters sounding like the adult he is. A ventriloquist is often an adult dealing with his dummy, a sassy kid. An adult talking to a pet assumes a parent role; a child sees the pet as a playmate and speaks accordingly.

To write successfully for children you must learn to distinguish these differences, which have more to do with the approach (the tone of voice, in speaking) than the vocabulary. Very few people write children's material of exciting quality, and the main reason they fail is that they are writing from a distant vantage point, instead of sitting in the sandbox, learning from their intended audience.

Children are not always noisy and boisterous. They sit by an anthill for an hour, watching the tiny creatures come and go. Holding a fishpole in absolute silence they glare at any adult who "scares the fish." Long before they shout "Mom!" they have struggled to button their own buttons, or tie their own shoes. They whisper, they tiptoe, they slip quietly onto a comfy lap and lean back to snuggle, rest, or listen to a story.

Today's writer is dealing with kids whose keen minds have been entertained and educated by top TV scriptwriters, so only the cleverest of children's journalism will win their attention. TV, America's babysitter, is our stiffest competition, and its effects reach down to affect the tiniest tots.

Preschool children relate to animated cartoon animals as well as fictional playmates around whom stories can be created. Finger exercises as well as action games interest the little ones, who also love picture books, puppets, and stories that require startling sounds as they are read or told: a puppy that barks, a kitten that mews, a firecracker that pops, a vehicle that roars, a siren that sounds.

Lower elementary grade children love to read and spell, so stories and other pieces done for them should contain a vocabulary at least a second-grader can handle. You learn it from their schoolbooks, which ought to be on your required reading list if you plan to write for kids. And what child doesn't love to entertain a visitor by reading aloud? I always ask youngsters if they'd like to show me how well they can read—and hardly ever get turned down. All such exposure to the world of children is excellent, needful training.

Youngsters of the lower elementary grades love jokes. If you can write stories or jokes to make this crowd giggle, you're in. They like action—in fact, to siphon off some of their boundless energy, they can act quite strenuously. They never run down. They fight naps and fight bedtime, falling asleep the minute their heads hit the pillow at night to enter a world of busy dreams.

Older elementary children love suspense, action stories, heroism—things like a mother trapped in her bedroom with a brown bear after her. They want the heroine rescued just in the nick of time. The more often a hero gets trapped, the better. They identify with courage.

Because their minds are developing complicated thought systems, pupils in grades four through seven enjoy science, science fiction, allegories, mysteries, and sports. They have an unquenchable thirst for knowledge: math, computer sciences, history, geography. Puzzles and thought-provoking quizzes of any kind are winners.

Adolescents and teenagers relate to experiences of others their age or slightly older. Best friends and secrets mean everything to them and they like situations which have a bearing on their growing up: the complexities of puberty, dating, parent-teen conflicts, friendships, and glimpses into the lives of older teens. The early adolescent, unsure of who he is, may be difficult to get along with. Confidence-building techniques filtered into writing for young teens wins readers. Rejectable material aimed at this group generally overlooks the fact that young teens are not children—although they may be kids.

The success level for children's writers indicates that the younger the child, the harder it is to write for him or her. Of course, you will write for the age group you are best acquainted with, but if I were to suggest an audience for beginning children's writers, I would recommend the older elementary grades and young teens as the most viable option.

With every rejection letter I write to neophyte children's writers, I suggest two helpful Writer's Digest books: *Writing for Children and Teenagers* by Lee Wyndham and *The Children's Picture Book: How to Write It and How to Sell It* by Ellen E. M. Roberts. I recommend them to you for further study in the art of writing for kids . . . and I urge that you further study—kids!

MISCELLANEOUS MATERIAL FOR THE MINI-MARKET

Program material is used year-around, not only for Christmas, but also for Mother's Day, Father's Day, Thanksgiving, Valentine's Day, and the patriotic holidays. A sensible idea is to spend time thinking and writing during every holiday season, because most publications work so far in advance that if you write a seasonal item while you're in the mood, get it polished and typed, and send it in, it should arrive just about when the editors are "thinking Christmas," or whatever the season may be. By the time you get your seed catalogs, it's too late to be thinking of an article on planting your garden. Think and write of spring a year in advance!

Poetry, readings, ideas for installation services, women's programs, dramas, skits, and ideas for costuming, decorations, banquet menus, and recipes are all possible mini-markets sales items. A clever writer keeps pen and paper close at hand during all seasonal celebrations—even Halloween, which holds endless possibilities for articles, stories, poetry, and fillers.

The mini-market is open to suggestions for game-time, puzzles that can be used as filler, quizzes, crossword puzzles, shower ideas, funny quips to enliven speeches, picnic ideas, sewing, gardening, and hobby tips. Anything goes. On one occasion I took a furry green frog, Oscar, home to mend him. He sat beside me on the front seat of the car bug-eyed, so real I had to talk to him. Later Barney spotted him in the rocker. Oscar screamed for help, but I was not quick enough. By the time I got there the dog had sunk his teeth into Oscar's stomach. It was nip and tuck to save his life.

The result was Oscar's firsthand account of the nightmarish experience, pinned to him when he returned to his ventriloquist. That script, which took only a few minutes to write, netted me fifteen dollars. Some places solicit such simple scripts for twenty-five dollars. Three or four of those would pay the service contract on my typewriter. You can't knock that.

The options for a good writer are so challenging one can hardly begin to set goals. They surface gradually in some cases, because of special interests: science, medicine, sports, politics, business, education, hobbies, and travel, for example. For an amateur to confine himself to one field early in the game is a mistake. No matter how specialized your interest, you have (as do all your readers) a twenty-four-hour-day life to live. Even the most technical writing will go faster and be of better quality if your writing experience is as well rounded as the average life.

The mini-market is the beginner's delight. You get to see your own creation in print, you're sometimes given a byline (your very own name in print), and you receive a check: payment for something you wrote! The benefits beyond that inspiration are numerous. Cutting your word count down to fifty or two hundred when you'd like to ramble on and on is terrific training in editing. Mini-articles provide the challenge of thinking, coming up with new ideas that will sell. They get you acquainted with the business side of writing and with research. The little checks coming just in the nick of time are a good incentive to try again, getting you into the habit of writing for pay. Nothing in the world breaks writer's block like a check in the mail!

It's hardly possible to conjure up all the options open to writers. A good many of us began by writing without pay, for the simple pleasure of creating publishable material and seeing our thoughts in print. For beginners, money is a by-product, not the purpose for writing. I can hear the opposition. Lawrence Block, in "Getting By on a Writer's Income," said, "I write for money, and if I struck oil in my backyard I can't be certain I'd ever write another line."[2]

If I struck oil, I'd write like crazy the rest of my life. That's the kind of freedom I've been dreaming of. Even on my spaghetti and rice income, living in my tiny basement hovel with a monstrous dog on his ninety-fifth sack of Purina dry, I give away excellent writing, sometimes putting more effort into volunteer projects than into the other things I might be chosen to do. Writing purely for satisfaction, for pleasure, is one of your options. I like to do it and will always be surprised that anyone would pay me for having so much fun.

Being paid to write proves one's skill. The ultimate test is, does someone else like it well enough to buy it? Will it sell?

Small markets are the best place to find out. Some people stay there forever, or keep dribbling small items out to keep the cash flow steady while working on more sophisticated writing projects. One of my favorite writers, already past seventy and churning gobs of odds and ends out of her schoolteacher mind, once told me she had sold more than 1,250 small items—some netting a dollar, some two dollars, three, six, ten dollars. Not a bad hobby. You wouldn't turn down what she earned, would you?

One word of warning. The smaller it is, the harder the piece may be to write. Study the market listings and the markets that buy mini-pieces. You'll see that the same tough standards apply for two lines, as for two thousand words.

Everybody says "study the markets," but few beginners do it. In the next chapter I want to discuss *why* it is so important, and *how* to do it.

ASSIGNMENT 6

The previous assignment, in which you practiced writing a variety of styles, was a good jumping off place for this one. You can play a matching game:

OPTION:	YOUR IDEAS:
short story	______________
children's story	______________
routine news item	______________
feature article	______________
poem	______________
drama	______________
political speech	______________
sports report	______________
advertising copy	______________
human interest article	______________
technical report	______________

Studying results of your previous assignment, come up with various ideas for using them. Match your ideas with this list and write them down. You can use the same material more than once. At your first opportunity, tackle writing one of the items on your list. It's probably premature to submit it to a magazine, but it's not too soon to *think* about who might use it. Look over your library notes.

Not everything will fit here. Some of the last assignment paragraphs may be best suited to your GARBAGE file. While you're in it, dig around for salvageable ideas for this assignment.

FINALLY: It's okay to dream big dreams, but include some realistic thinking, too. Make some concrete writing plans. Then:

get ready . . .
get set . . .
WRITE!

7 "To Market, To Market"—Which Market?

I wish it were possible to take you to an editor's desk to show you what a "slush pile" really looks like. Take your own manuscripts, all of them, old and new, and run them through the U.S. Post Office until the boxes are bent and broken and the pages dog-eared, the brown envelopes torn. Multiply the mess by about two hundred and you will have an idea of what lands on the desk of a major publisher's scanning editor each week. Keep in mind that the crew has yet to process mail from the past two months, and you begin to conjure up a mental picture that's fairly accurate.

Slush, according to Webster, isn't only the gray, melting snow we plod through each spring, or dodge as the speeding traffic showers the crowd on the curb, but slush is also "refuse fat, grease, or other waste material from a ship's galley." A "slush fund," incidentally, is a fund derived from selling this refuse, a fund used to buy luxuries for the ship's crew.

This is a book about learning how to write well enough to

sell, not how to sell what you've already written; but in either case, studying the markets separates the winners from the losers.

Every day, editors face a mountain of unsolicited mail; that is, material they didn't ask to receive and for the most part don't want. The slush pile denotes this heap of manuscripts someone has to plod through, read, and return; manuscripts which, though possibly worthy, are of no use to the publisher and are therefore considered slush. When they grumble about being buried in an avalanche of slush, you understand now that they aren't speaking of being "snowed under." They feel, rather, like the man riding the back of a trash truck when the driver stops and accidentally pulls the wrong lever. Editorial slush, by dictionary definition, is garbage.

When you think about the good things that might be buried in it, you don't feel quite so offended. I lost a valuable bloodstone ring and a friend lost her diamond during meal preparation. Plumbers could multiply such stories, as precious jewelry often goes down the drain. Other valuables are added to the dump both accidentally and deliberately, as any scavenger knows.

One evening the dogs and I topped a hill, surprising our neighbors who were digging through a pile of trash dumped illegally. Too embarrassed to face me, the wife turned toward the car as if ready to leave, but her husband held up a wire hanging basket. "Still in good shape," he called out sheepishly.

If they hadn't beaten me to it, I would have taken it home myself. We reminisced a while about the good old pre-garage-sale, pre-landfill days when friends often met at the dump at evening to hunt "treasure" or exchange trash.

Some days slush editors would love to call in a bulldozer to shove the whole mess over the cliff and bury it, because finding something good seems hopeless. But for the most part they sift through and sort as patiently as if they were panning for gold, always aware the next shovelful might turn up their reward. Since they are so busy doing this, it simply is not possible to write and tell you *why* your manuscript is unsuitable. You can read between the lines on most rejection slips and be fairly sure the main reason it is coming back home is that you didn't study the markets.

Here's what happens. Not knowing what has already been published has led to your assuming your own work is unique. This leads to careless writing, since you have no idea the competition is so stiff. Only the truly clever manuscripts get a second look, and then only if the writing skill has been sharply honed and the product has been presented to the proper publisher. What the reject slips don't tell you is:

> It's poorly written. (Needs a lot more work.)
> It's been done before. (Same old thing, seen every day.)
> It's sent to the wrong place. (Unsuited to the publisher.)

While all of us have been guilty of careless writing caused by lazy streaks, it would be unfair to lump all amateur writers' work into the first category. By the time they send it in, most beginners have worked hard to whip their writing into shape. Later in the book we'll show you ways to brighten and improve it.

More likely, rejected writing is either too ordinary to be noticed, or it's sent to the wrong publisher. Studying the markets is done primarily to avoid these two problems.

Slush piles are interesting. During the years I was Program Materials Editor at Lillenas Publishing Company, I was amazed at how often creative minds working on opposite coasts duplicated each other. From Seattle and Miami I could receive two almost identical dramas on the same day—or more than two alike—from authors unaware of each other's existence. Accompanying cover letters assured me nothing could be found on the market to equal the enclosed, which was totally original, dreamed up out of desperation because of the dearth of workable dramas. I heard that so often that the letters might have been bought in preprinted tablets.

If one play were purchased, the author of the other would surely scream "plagiarism!" But I knew it was individual creativity at work in minds accustomed to similar surrroundings even though living thousands of miles apart. In our own catalog of published dramas I could have pointed out several similar, not to mention what was available from our competitors. As King Solomon said, "There is no new thing under the sun."

During the months I've prepared to write this book and since actually tackling the job, I've avoided attending writing seminars and reading other writing books because I didn't want to assimilate the ideas of other teachers and turn right around to put them into my book as my own. If twenty-five years of writing, studying, reading, editing, and occasional teaching hasn't stuffed my mind with enough material to fill the required pages, last-minute crash courses aren't likely to fill the gap. I determined to confine my book to original thoughts.

Original? Hah! Every time I do peek into a book or article on writing, I find the author mimicking the words I've just written, words not even at the typesetters' yet! I assure you that if all the authors advising you on how to prepare, submit, and sell what you write sound alike, it's not because we're copying from one another. It's because all of us have learned the hard way, through trial, rejection, and trying again, that certain rules are inflexible. Only rarely will one who breaks the cardinal rules of professional writing succeed.

WHAT IS MEANT BY STUDYING THE MARKETS?

The rule most universally broken, even by writers who devour all available advice and follow it to the minutest detail, is the stickler, *study the markets*. Stacks of similar plays returned as "not suitable" are good examples of the breaking of this rule. Amateur playwrights have not studied the markets. They do not know what *is* available, what *has* been published. Being too uninformed to know where to look, or being too lazy to do so, they have written their own dull dialogue and have dubbed it "the greatest show on earth."

I picked up *Writing and Selling Science Fiction*[1] and read C.L. Grant's introduction, "Getting Your Feet Wet," in which Grant says, "I'm going to give voice here to my ego and show you me . . . " and proceeds to recount personal experiences of a beginning writer, including receiving "those blasted little printed letters which thanked me kindly for my submission but noted that it did not meet the current needs of the magazine."

Grant was set on the right track by editor Frederik Pohl, who took time to scribble a reprimand on the rejection slip, "telling me in no uncertain terms that perhaps I should read his magazine—*Galaxy*—before I tried to sell to him again."

The message was clear. Grant hadn't studied the market. To study the market is to familiarize yourself with the publication you want to write for by reading it, not just once, but several times, even regularly.

All alone here, staring glassy-eyed out across the backyard, I sat several moments after writing those words, mind having escaped to North Africa again. Forgive it. It lived there so long. Studying the markets! What a study! North African markets have changed very little over the centuries. Expressive, colorful people spread their wares on grass mats on the ground, and haggle with primitive customers from dawn 'til sunset.

There is the donut man, bubbly gray dough in a huge, flat tub on the ground inside his tent, kneading it with his knuckles as he kneels like a camel about to rise, while his opium-drowsed partner drops big globs of dough circles into boiling grease. My mouth waters. I want one so bad.

The markets are filled with colorful characters: orators shouting above the din to a circle of listeners; storytellers smothered by a crowd trying to hear; the water carrier, knobby knees sticking out from beneath his red, sequin-covered garment, offering cool, refreshing water for only a penny a cupful poured from the furry black goatskin he has tucked under his arm; the meat market with beef and lamb quarters freshly butchered hanging from huge hooks, a jovial, turbaned man swinging a palm branch back and forth to keep off the flies; and the egg market, with a few live chickens, legs tied together, nestled against the farm lady sitting on the ground before her wares. There are heaps of colorful spices, mountains of juicy oranges, and cloth merchants hawking their wares. And—ah!—the sellers of brass, of silver, have polished it so bright it blinds you in the morning sun.

GETTING TO KNOW YOUR READERS

An examination of potential readers, people you would love to entertain or educate someday, can be conducted just about anyplace you run across people: on the subway, at the barbershop, at the grocery store, at the bus depot, at a truck stop or shopping mall, at the amusement park or zoo (I said people). For example, you might be an avid reader of *Sports Afield*. At a crowded restaurant, look over the customers, viewing them as *Sports Afield* readers, as they may well be.

There sits a doctor or lawyer (several years in college and broad experience with people and events); a table full of business executives (a wide range of college degrees, years of experience in a variety of fields, and wide travel, both for business and pleasure); a crane operator (a war veteran with many years in the school of hard knocks); a cop and a fireman (veterans, too, with ten or fifteen years beyond that experience, responding to panic situations, dealing with human emotions in crisis).

You might be the best fisherman in your little town (or the biggest braggart at the office?), or, you might have taken a vacation at great fishing waters; but to surface in the slush pile of a slick sporting magazine, the whole tone of your fish story has to say, "This writer is a pro." The article will have to pass muster several ways:

1. The manuscript looks professional.
2. The lead paragraph grabs the first editor who reads it.
3. The writing flows smoothly.
4. The outline has congruity.
5. The photographs (if any) are full of action and are sharp, clear, and cleverly cropped.

In addition, the content will have to capture and hold the interest of the doctor, the lawyer, the crane operator, the cop, the fireman, and thousands of other men and women, hundreds of whom have fished longer than you, with consistently greater success, not only where your story takes place, but in much more interesting places in the world.

"Wow!" you say. "I might as well quit right now."

Well, if you can quit, then yes, you might as well; but if writing is burning in your soul, you're hooked, so you might as well come along.

Incidentally, I'm a fisherman. But though I love to fish, I rarely see a copy of *Sports Afield*, nor do I have some lead from an insider there as to what those editors are looking for. I have no more than you, a market listing, and I didn't look that up. What I do know is my profession. You can pick any publication worth its salt, almost any magazine you've got your eye on, and you'll find the basic requirements pretty much the same.

GETTING ACQUAINTED WITH TODAY'S LITERATURE

You might abhor some literature and find other types particularly boring, but there are two approaches to studying the markets:

1. Taking a general tour. (Checking the whole range of published work coming off the press right now.)

By this I mean going to two or three large bookstores to get the feeling of which books are currently being made available to the public and spending time at newsstands to acquaint yourself with magazines and other periodicals. If you're lucky, you might find the manager of the department to chat with, or even better, the supplier's delivery driver changing stock for the week. You can ply such people with questions about what seems to be popular; which publications move more slowly than others; what newsstands carry other magazines not available where you are; and, if the person you're talking to is well versed in his work, what the trends may be.

For several months I worked as an independent checker for one of the tabloids, covering seventy supermarkets a week to keep track of our own displays. I listened to delivery-boy and manager blues with interest: "This sells, and that doesn't, and *this* is so hot we can't keep it in stock . . ." More often than not I got a little free advice in the form of "I think what the public wants is . . ." Generally I spent an extra minute straightening up the competition's magazines, not because I'm nice, but because I wanted to see what they deemed important enough to print. (Thoroughly loyal, I hid their tabloid behind others before leaving the store.)

When one takes the general market tour, one also goes to the library. Instead of meandering through old literature, though, or specialized subjects, or research material, one heads for the current material: bestsellers and magazines. The general tour leads one through friends' magazine racks and even impels one to snatch schoolbooks from the hands of little children. A person involved in the general tour spots every printed page within eagle's-eye range, grabs it, and (if the reader will let go) looks it over carefully.

2. The personal tour. (Carefully examining publications of interest to you.)

A serious writer stays on the general tour for life. Glancing at book reviews, browsing at bookstores and grabbing magazines from fellow commuters becomes a way of life. But however it is done, studying the markets must become a matter of individual taste to become truly valuable. You read what you hope to write for, and you write for what you like to read.

WHEN SHOULD MARKET STUDY BEGIN?

Focusing on definite markets, as well as background study on the form of writing you have in mind, ought to precede any attempt to sell. Part of this is the obvious need to offer your wares to the proper publisher, part of it to assure that your writing is up to that publisher's standards and follows his style, and finally, referring to what Bagehot said, part of it is to "know something" before you try to write.

Taking drama as our example, let's analyze what studying the market might entail.

Not many amateur playwrights of today have studied drama to any extent. Most plays I have read appear to be thrown together with as much forethought as a child might have, but with far less imaginative skill. A ho-hum sameness marks them all: a wandering through a chosen subject with a colorless or invisible plot, uninteresting conversations between dull people often haranguing one another. No consideration seems to be given to the audience, probably because the writer is wrapped up envisioning himself as the star of the show, tossing all those clever words into the wind.

WHAT TO LOOK FOR WHILE STUDYING PLAYS

One of the most intriguing drama forms out of the past is "closet plays"—plays written not for performance, but for enjoyment in reading. Some were never performed, because the playwright believed no actor could do his baby justice!

To apply "studying the markets" to writing drama, you must create your own collection of "closet plays" by hunting through libraries and bookstores for good plays to read. If you have contact with people in the theatre, they can guide you to what they consider the better plays. Using your *Writer's Market*, write to play publishers for their catalogs, or ask bookstores for assistance in finding collections of plays you can purchase.

As your play collection grows, you'll need to closet yourself for the purpose of study. Since you've bought many of the plays, you can mark them up. Just because a play is in print doesn't mean it's good. You can circle and scratch the weak areas, highlight the good, and make notations throughout the play. When you come to the end and look back over the play, you'll have a pretty good idea of what makes it powerful or weak.

Studying what has been successful is a key to writing strong drama. You don't steal the playwright's characters, style, or design, but you learn from his work and absorb some of his skill to put you on your way.

If would-be playwrights have neglected studying drama, so have they neglected the theatre. Studying the market also means buying tickets to every play in town. If you're serious about writing drama, you have to be interested in attending plays.

SOME SPECIFICS TO LOOK FOR

Correctly written, drama involves compelling impersonation, strong dialogue, and action to match what is being said; so as you read (and watch) you'll need to keep your eyes open for these three things. Note the characters. How many are on stage at one time? What are they doing? How long are the sentences? How many lines does one speak before the other takes over—or does he or she interrupt? If several are on stage at once, how many are talking? Which conversations are significant and which are filler? Who, by what he or she says, surfaces as lead character? Is there a villain? A hero? What do they say? How do their words set the stage for their actions?

The purpose of the play might be the next thing to consider. Is it strictly entertainment, a change of pace from the workaday world? Is it satire, with a powerful message hidden beneath the surface? Is it the recounting of history? Is it realistic, or idealistic? Ask the same questons of your own play as you plan it (or as you critique those you have tucked away in some drawer). The purpose of the play determines a great deal about how it will be written; by studying the process you can learn how successful playwrights accomplished what they set out to do.

What is the plot? How has the writer drawn the audience into his mind to let them know where he is going and why? Has he humdrummed along as they might expect, or has he peeked out from behind a few trees to say "boo!" surprising them, making them think he was going in some other direction, only to come back in the end to the original plot? Are there obstacles in the paths of the characters? If so, how did he get them there? And having done it, how did he remove the obstacles?

APPLYING WHAT YOU HAVE LEARNED

So much for studying drama. A similar process should be followed as you decide to pursue any specific form of writing. Studying the market means analyzing every angle of the writing form you've set your heart to do (which helps you to write well), and analyzing the material being produced by various publishers in the field so you can decide which one best matches what you plan to write.

1. Study the background, the history of that writing form. Understanding where it came from and how it developed sinks roots to balance your skills.

2. Study early literature of that particular form: old novels or short stories, if that is what you plan to write: poetry; early forms of nonfiction. Study the classics.

3. Study current literature, analyzing it as we did the plays. Do picky things like counting the conversations (or in nonfiction, the anecdotes), circling adjectives or lively dialogue; highlighting strong points you recognize as good; mark in red the weak areas and jot in what you think would be a better way to say it. Rewrite boring narrative to see how you could improve it. Analyze the editorial trend, the age of the audience, the vocabulary level, and the style. Compare all this with your own.

4. If a related performance comes to town, rush for a front-row seat. I'll never forget, while I was involved in puppet plays, trotting down to a Saturday morning matinee of "Pinocchio." What makes stories like "Pinocchio," musicals like *Oklahoma!*, operas like *The Flying Dutchman*, and historical plays like *Shepherd of the Hills* live on and on? Is it the dedicated efforts of folks who love them?

I doubt it. Dedicated efforts even backed with tons of moral support won't breathe life into a manuscript doomed to die. No, there are ethereal qualities to them, qualities we should long to understand, and the only way to do that is to see them again and again.

While fiction writers and history buffs obviously benefit from attending such performances, all of us will find our lives enriched and therefore our writing bettered by taking them in, too. Nonfiction writers should keep their eyes open for great lecturers speaking on general interest subjects, as well as speakers expounding their special interests. Writers in any field of science ought to get used to seeing science fiction writers show up for every lecture touching on scientific advances. Whatever subject you're working on, you should watch the community calendar, to be sure you catch the experts when they go through town. Television is a marvelous tool for keeping abreast, too, as well as a good form of relaxation—a recess for the brain. Learn to differentiate between the two and keep your recesses short.

Once your general study has seriously begun (and you'll thank yourself later for any reading and entertainment diary you keep), you can begin to narrow your focus to specific markets.

MARKET LISTINGS ARE ONLY A GUIDE

Until you have read material the publisher has printed in the past, you have no business mailing in a manuscript. I know what you do, because I do it myself when an orphan I've produced needs a good home! You open up *Writer's Market*, put on a blindfold, and spin the wheel!

Great! Flipping through *Writer's Market* is one of the first steps toward studying the market. (After you've done everything else we've talked about, that is.) Your finger falls on some publisher you've never heard of before, who sounds pretty promising. She pays well for articles, plays, stories—whatever it is you're hoping to sell. Let's see. Wants articles 800-1,000 words. Mine is 1,500. Of course, I probably didn't count right. Reports in four weeks. That's better than some.

And you bundle up your baby—diapers, Pablum, and all—expecting the stranger to be so excited upon its arrival she'll pay you double for letting her keep it.

There are more sophisticated ways of getting results.

GOOD, BETTER, BEST

Good: Send for the writer's guidelines offered, and sample copies, which you may have to buy. (Enclose a big enough stamped envelope to receive them.)

Better: Send for the writer's guidelines, but not until you've checked the newsstand to see what kind of magazine this stranger is. Maybe she doesn't *like* babies. Or maybe you don't like her. If you do like the magazine, buy a copy and begin to study it.

Best: Subscribe, if you like it, to read the publication regularly. This tunes you in to the editor's pattern of purchase, eventually allowing you to write an intelligent query letter.

Does this sound like more work than you can handle? That's because all the advice is crammed onto a few pages, and you're swallowing it as one huge bite. I expect you to munch on it, to digest it slowly, and to come back later to munch on it again. If you're serious about becoming a professional writer, you must realize that it takes time. If you reach the top of the ladder in four years you're a genius. I would expect you to spend four years as an excited student (teaching yourself, of course!), increasing your skill and experiencing the satisfaction of small successes, followed by another three or four years of internship—bigger challenges, bigger wins—before striking it rich.

So you started late in life. Too bad. Starting is starting. You get no handicap in this race just because you're getting old. When our bodies start to feel a little decrepit, the mind is just coming of age. Once you get that into your head, you can forge on toward your goal with confidence.

CHOOSING YOUR PUBLISHER

Now you're ready to find a publisher. If you've done your homework, you are already acquainted with who publishes plays, because you've received the guidelines and catalogs, bought sample copies, and studied others at the library and store. You know how much detail they want in stage directions, and how this information should appear on the manuscript. You know the age group each publisher has in mind, the number of actors he prefers, the number of acts and scenes he likes, how much scenery change he will allow, the type of content he's looking for, and the length of most of the plays he accepts.

Here's one more tip (and some play publishers, as well as other editors, send you explicit directions on it). Following the proper typing style is a plus for acceptance. For example, while many drama companies use capital letters for characters' names, followed by a colon, others prefer cap/small cap, which is to be typed cap/lower case, followed by a hyphen. (No one wants quotation marks around dialogue but many playwrights madden editors by putting them in.)

Cap/colon:	MARY: I don't know how to write. JACK: You can teach yourself.
Cap/lower case/hyphen:	Mary—I don't know how to write. Jack—You can teach yourself.

You should underline only when the publisher's guidelines tell you to, unless you mean for it to be italicized. To a typesetter, underlining means "put it in italics," and as you probably know, underlining isn't removed all that easily.

Twenty pages typed in the wrong style may appear too formidable for the editor to read, because the immediate message is, "We'd have to retype the whole play." Time and money. Down the chute it goes, and out the door.

Studying picky details does help. No matter what you are writing, the style should match that of the publisher you hope to please. In some cases, you might as well count on retyping your submission for the next guy if it gets thrown out by the first.

BACK TO "GO"

You can bluff your way into the big leagues before you're ready, but all most beginners collect from national magazines is reject slips. Since you're going to start with mini-markets, you can do two things at once. Begin to study markets you'd like to write for "someday" by following the preceding advice. Meanwhile, gather mini-market material from various sources, study it, and start submitting give-away pieces to publications such as newsletters and suburban shoppers to test your marketable skills; enter contests; and, as suggested in the previous chapter, try to sell to low-pay markets or those that purchase suitable, appealing material either as filler or for compiled works.

To study the small markets, comb the neighborhood for old magazines (local, regional, or specialized, as opposed to national magazines), newsletters, church school papers, and suburban newspapers. The same analyzing techniques can be applied. What is the style? The approach? The content? What's strong writing in this publication? How can I do better? Circle flaws, highlight good features. Notice the editorial slant. Which side does the editor seem to take on various issues? If you're looking at a health-related magazine or newsletter, ask whether it is published for M.D.'s, D.O.'s, chiropractors, dentists, or health faddists. If it's religious, what doctrinal stance does it take? What has been published in the last five or six issues? (If you pick up one issue at the Laundromat or barbershop, you can run to the library to check out the previous ones.)

Studying the markets takes time at first, but once the habit is formed, you'll save hours of time, lots of frustration, plenty of postage and some of the disappointment of rejection, as well.

I KNOW MY RIGHTS

Studying the markets also means understanding before you submit your material what rights a publisher buys. The market listing might not be accurate (they're sometimes outdated and sometimes wrong) but if the writer's guidelines don't specify otherwise, you should follow what information you have. If it says they purchase "All Rights," you're wasting your time jumping into their slush pile by submitting material that specifies "First Rights Only." You can dicker and protest all you want; just be sure to enclose your self-addressed stamped envelope so you can get the reject back.

Personally I deplore the current fad of specifying rights on the upper righthand corner of the first page. I never do. Nor will I. When you get to the big leagues your agent will probably handle that detail. In the minors, that little note marks you as an amateur. Beginners don't have that kind of clout. I love to reject manuscripts like that, just to prove the point.

When I worked for an "All Rights" company, I sorted the slush getting rid of all manuscripts shouting "First Rights Only." They got a quick reply. One woman scratched out the offending words and sent her manuscript back with a sweet letter pleading with me to reconsider it. She had never sold *anything*, but she had come in the door with her fists up ready to fight for her rights.

I can categorically assure you that no editor with an evil grin is going to pull your piddley piece out of the slush pile, steal it, and pocket future returns. Large, sophisticated companies drop the accepts into the proper slot for proper processing and proper payment shoots out the other end. A few years down the road, if you've sold all rights, you can buy them back if you want them. I doubt that you will. You'll be amazed anybody even bought those early attempts! The matter of rights is one thing you can learn by properly studying the publication. If you don't want to sell all rights, don't.

Why would a company want all rights? If the mini-market is tied to a major one, the publisher probably doesn't want to fool with operating two processes. One playwright I dealt with wrote me several long letters trying to change this. It was a lost cause. She argued that the process was so simple. My reply each time was simple, too: "Do you want us to publish your play, or don't you?" Whether right or wrong, deciding what rights he wants to buy is the publisher's business. Paper work represents a lot of money, and publishing company employees, always close to a deadline, are among the most harassed workers on the face of the globe. Successful mini-market people are usually amateurs glad for a place to begin. One price they're willing to pay is—if necessary—selling all rights.

By the way, there is a market for reprints. But pity the poor writer who loves his one and only sales success so much he can never create a new one!

Incidentally, if a publisher says no reprints are accepted, or specifies only original, previously unpublished material, what are you going to do? Send it to him anyway? What are you, a glutton for punishment? Read the rules! And follow them!

HOW DO I KNOW THE RIGHT PUBLISHER?

I advise beginning with publications you subscribe to, beginning close to home. You buy them because you and they have common interests. It's a good foundation to build on.

Here are some guidelines to follow as you study the markets:

1. The philosophy of the magazine.

Do they think like you do? Do you agree with their opinions? Some magazines like controversy and allow writers to present opposing views for the sake of reader interest. But as a rule, if you disagree with a publication's basic philosophy, you might just as well keep looking because that one isn't for you.

2. Its social level.

Does it live pretty much the same as you do? Or are you (though in a different situation now) really familiar with its kind of life? An Idaho rancher's daughter living in some cement jungle could write about Idaho ranches in a believable manner, but some city person probably couldn't, except as a reporter during or following a visit.

Mark Twain is a good example of this. He saw the world and enjoyed great success before his mind went back to really reminiscing about Hannibal, the riverboats, and the rafts: the childhood we now know so well. John Updike wrote his "Rabbit" stories from New England, using his childhood Pennyslvania home as the setting, which he could do successfully drawing on memories, as did Twain.

3. The educational level.

What's the vocabulary and style of writing? Are you comfortable with it? Can you do it? In many kinds of writing (academic, technical, medical, theological, sports) there is specific terminology to learn. Some legal vocabulary is not commonly used in everyday life. Writing for teenagers is different from writing for children. Many publishers turn down heavy, scholarly works that the average man on the street wouldn't be interested in wading through. Other publications *are* scholarly, and they wouldn't want me.

4. The level of experience of writers.

Who writes for the magazine you're looking at? Housewives? Professional writers? Doctors? Professors? Ordinary run-of-the-mill freelancers whose work just happened to be picked out of the pot? If you've got no experience, and they're all way ahead of you, you're aiming a little too high.

5. The audience.

Do you feel at home talking to those people? Condominium dwellers yawn when I excitedly talk about my brush-cutting experiences. They don't understand my lawnmowing woes—except as a horrible memory. The editor of a magazine that caters to Georgia and wants southern writers won't jump for joy when a Maine housewife sends an article about tulips coming up in May. Few grandparents write well for teens—with some exceptions, but not many. A magazine that delves into building techniques won't buy the tulip article, either, even though the first thing the home buyer will do is plant tulips.The key to success is partly dependent on feeding the magazine into the computer and requesting a perfect match with *you*. If everything about the publication makes you nod yes, you're in the ball game. If everything has you shaking your head no, run like crazy.

PRETTY PLEASE, DON'T WRITE A PLAY!

I hate myself for always bowing to the wishes of flashing caution lights, but I think there's one more thing I must say.

Don't rush to the typewriter and pound out a play! If my editorial colleagues in that business get ahold of me, my head will be mashed potatoes, buried in the slush pile, maybe.

Beginners have a way of jumping on the wrong bandwagon. "Hey!" they shout. "There must be a *big* market for plays. And *big* pay!" The deluge—most of it garbage—can be devastating.

There's not a big market for plays, and sometimes the pay is hilariously small. There's a steady market for good plays, as there is for any good writing. I used drama as an example only because it's a field I know well and a good example of one that produces numerous reject slips because plays, not a common household item, are seldom studied before being written or submitted. If you don't attend the theatre, if you never rush to get tickets for the high school play, if you haven't thought of writing a play until I mentioned it, don't write plays! Forget I ever said the word!

But don't forget the message the example was trying to get across. Know what you're doing before you try to peddle your wares.

ASSIGNMENT 7

WARM-UP: Review Assignment 4, which took you to the library. (You did go, didn't you? If not, hightail it over there *right now*!) Your notes from the library should include a list of periodicals you found interesting.

1. CLOSE TO HOME

Whatever it takes to obtain them, scrounge up copies of small publications, special interest magazines, church school papers, suburban newspapers, and company newsletters.

1. Beg back copies of magazines your relatives, neighbors, or coworkers subscribe to.
2. Check the barbershop, hairdresser, and Laundromat. What do they do with their back copies?
3. Call church and synagogue offices to request copies of their periodicals. (Drive by to pick them up, don't ask them to mail the papers.)
4. If suburban newspapers do not show up otherwise in your search, drive to each newspaper office to

request sample copies. (You can make "friends in the business" while you are there.)

5. Check the Yellow Pages under "Periodicals" and "Publishers." Local magazines are often excellent markets for promising new writers.

As you sort your collection of papers and magazines, you will immediately see that some are outside your range of interest. After you have clipped from them tidbits for your i and i file, give them to the Boy Scouts paper drive. Arrange the remaining publications in order of importance, based on your first-glance evaluation. For example:

SUBURBAN SHOPPER: Uses new items about clubs and churches. Uses profiles of local people. Uses articles about local tourist attractions.

LOCALLY BASED NURSING MAGAZINE: Uses profiles of doctors and nurses; sometimes assigns articles to local freelancers.

CHURCH SCHOOL PAPERS: Use articles about significant people or programs; use stories for various age groups; use inspirational articles.

COMPANY NEWSLETTER: Uses profiles of employees being honored; uses articles about technical advance or equipment change. Needs reporter.

Take ample time studying each publication to determine what type of material is chosen and who has written it. The nursing magazine and church school papers might be listed in *Writer's Market*. See what the listing indicates. Then call the editor (if local) or write to inquire about current needs. Call the suburban newspaper editor to get acquainted and to make your services known. If the company newsletter is published in the same building where you work, talk to the compiler/editor personally about your desire to contribute something as a writer.

The newsletter and shopper will probably be gratis jobs—no pay, at least to start with. The magazine and church school papers probably pay by the word.

Following this pattern, study every publication you can locate, including the following:

II. THE MAGAZINE STAND

Spend time here each week for *at least two months*. Perhaps you can locate someone who subscribes to interesting magazines you locate here. Free back issues obtained regularly are a bonanza. Buy only what your budget allows but do buy or subscribe to magazines you plan to submit material to.

III. THE LIBRARY

Depending upon your newsstand, you will need to rely on the library for copies of some magazines. Remember that small publications (with limited circulation) and special interest periodicals are excellent targets for beginners. They are best obtained from subscribers (your friends and relatives) and from the library.

IV. THE PUBLISHER

Usually sample copies can be obtained by writing. If there is a charge, this will be indicated in the publication or in the *Writer's Market* listing.

FINALLY: As a beginning writer your best markets are local or special interest magazines and papers. As you progress, study whatever market you're aiming at. This assignment *never* ends.

8 Those Awesome Editors

In that seventeenth century classic *Pilgrim's Progress*, some women and children following the pilgrim's path entered "the valley of the shadow." All sorts of frightening things happened: They heard dead men groaning; the earth shook under their feet; serpents seemed to hiss at them; the form of a monster rose up to terrify them; and finally, just before they were forced to enter a dark, foggy pit, a lion roared.

As you contemplate entering the world of professional writing, your knees may be quaking, too. Let me play the part of "Mr. Great-heart" now, to reassure you, to encourage you. The journey to success is not as fearsome as it may seem. Rather than being roaring lions which keep the potential writer from being published, editors are intermediaries whose job is to get writers' material to readers. Their work is complementary: That is, it takes both parts to complete the whole. Editors and writers are reliant one upon the other. Editors love writers, and even in the most extreme cases, when hopelessly ridiculous writing projects are laid upon their desks, most of them show abundant patience and even compassion.

WHO ARE EDITORS, AND WHAT DO THEY DO?

The term "editor" denotes a variety of jobs within the publishing world. Editing is defined as (1) "preparing or revising literary work," (2) "supervising or directing the publication of a newspaper, magazine, or other printed matter," and (3) "adapting film for showing by rearranging, cutting, and splicing."

The publishing industry began with scribes copying written matter by hand onto papyrus or parchment. Such scrolls were circulated among literate people long before the birth of Christ (no doubt the Magi had access to them). In time, industries (sometimes with slave labor) were started by businessmen dedicated to selecting, reproducing, and circulating worthy scrolls. These men, the world's first editors, chose manuscripts, took the risk of paying authors in advance, determined the length, price, and format, and found markets for this rare, handwritten literature.

Codices replaced scrolls. Also written by hand, a codex was a bound book generally containing medical, legal, or theological text. Libraries of codices were found first in monasteries, and later in universities.

Although the Chinese invented block type five hundred years before Gutenberg's day, Europe gets the credit for speeding up the printing process, opening the world of literature to you and me. Publishing as we know it today grew out of the printers' guilds, which developed into competitive printing firms, which moved to a proliferation of booksellers marketing their own products. As common people learned to read, creative word lovers (most of them university-educated) found a market for their thoughts. They obliged by writing novels, short stories, drama, and poetry. Like the final peck that breaks the shell allowing a chick to emerge and peep, the English Copyright Law of 1710 cracked the shell of restrictions, freeing authors and publishers to negotiate royalties and terms of payment. Modern day publishing had hatched.

That important writing from those primitive scrolls and codices should be preserved for twentieth century readers seems somewhat of a miracle to me. It proves, among other things, that people have always revered the written word and that there have always been keen minds able to organize captivating thoughts on paper. There has also always been a select group of individuals who recognized durable manuscripts, gambled on their salability, and poured their lives into getting them published. Editors, we call them today.

Many early editors were writers whose main goal was to carry their own opinions abroad. Daniel Defoe, author of *Robinson Crusoe*, has been called the father of modern journalism. Like many editors, his opinions were important enough to him that he wanted the world to know about them. His first writings appeared in pamphlet form, but he wrote continuously and was, over the years, connected with some twenty-six periodicals.

Because of his poison pen, Defoe's life teeter-tottered between success and failure, depending upon who was in political power. A Britisher, he was for nine years editor of *The Review*, the government's main periodical during his era, but he also suffered lengthy stints in prison when his political enemies were on top. He was nearly sixty when he paused during his fascinating life to write about Crusoe, turning out, in the process, one of the world's bestsellers of all time. Most editors can relate to the setting Defoe chose, for it is the paradise of their dreams. Being stranded on a desert island alone, far from phones, dwells in the fantasies of a good many people locked into frenetic activity. In reality, half a day alone in such a setting would leave them pacing the beach, because editors are people of action.

Benjamin Harris, another man of high goals, hoped to establish America's first newspaper. In 1690 he put out a newsletter which he expected to publish "once a moneth (or if any Glut of occurrences happen, oftener)." The next major occurrence involved him. The government slapped him down just a few days after his first issue rolled off the press. A Boston newsletter published fourteen years later became the first paper to endure.

Benjamin Franklin was apprenticed at his brother's print shop when he was only thirteen. He took over when his brother ran into political harassment, and throughout his life he kept returning to his trade as printer, writer, and editor. Franklin, who regretted having been born too soon because scientific advance tantalized him, nevertheless was a true writer: He failed in mathematics; he rewrote essays by memory to increase his vocabulary and improve his style; he admitted that his personal life was full of "errata"; and he spent half of his earnings to buy books!

The Pulitzer Prize is a continuing ovation for the Hungarian immigrant who started his newspaper career in 1868 as a reporter, emerged as an editor, and made his fortune buying and selling newspapers. Joseph Pulitzer is only one in a long line of famous writer/editors. Among them are Charles Dickens, William Makepeace Thackeray, Samuel Clemens, Samuel Johnson, Jonathan Swift, Rudyard Kipling (whose first job as a teenager was editing), Ralph Waldo Emerson (whose periodical was a platform for controversial opinions), and Edgar Allan Poe (who edited to support his insatiable writing habit).

THE EDITOR'S HABITAT

The publisher generally refers to the owner(s) of a publishing firm, or the corporation that operates it. Often one thinks of the editor of a newspaper or magazine as the head boss, either of the company or of a department. This may well be the case. How much clout such an individual has depends upon how large his organization or department may be. However, editors range from the top of the ladder down to the flunky who may double as secretary or messenger. A good many "editors" are in fact administrative assistants able to cope with whatever situation arises. Truman's "the buck stops here" usually rests on the desk of **the editor** who, in the final crunch, must answer to **the boss**, but, depending upon the size of the company, editors with expertise in a variety of areas shoulder a huge part of the load.

Since some of your first writing attempts will probably be

offered to newspapers, you may find a glance at their power structure interesting. It varies immensely from paper to paper, but the basic format is this:

Few large city newspapers are privately owned today, so the editor-in-chief is himself answerable to his colleagues who represent the national chain. Under the chief editor are the feature editor, the sports editor, the Sunday editor, the travel editor, the lifestyle editor, the religious editor, the economics editor, and others. In some regions there may be a farm editor, an oil editor, an energy editor, or a specialist in some other local area of interest.

Activity pertaining to daily news-gathering revolves around the city desk, where the city editor directs traffic. Reporters, departmental editors, and photographers receive assignments and turn in material to him, material which either closely resembles the finished product or is phoned in to be slapped into shape by expert rewriters. Final copy goes to copyeditors whose skill lies in checking the details: spelling, punctuation, accuracy of facts and figures, and names. Immense reference source libraries are at their disposal, as well as their own morgue, where back copies of their paper can be drawn from microfilm. A really big news story coming in the last minute will pull rank on the rest of the copy, and in the process, some stories may be killed, never to appear.

The whole crew on a top daily paper is hired to find news, to focus on facts, to avoid errors, to prepare tight copy, and to deliver on time. Those who can't get the job done before **deadline** will soon find their press cars have turned back into pumpkins and they are back wearing rags.

At the other end of the spectrum is the smallest weekly run by the owner, who may also be editor-in-chief, reporter, typesetter, printer, and business manager in charge of circulation. While the task at the big-city daily is to sift through a mountain of material to decide what is newsworthy, the pressure on a small-paper editor may well be to locate enough clubs, anniversaries, weddings, and birthday parties to fill the "inside news holes"—which in this case might be space left over between national, statewide, and county news of widespread interest, and the sports page which covers local school activities. If you are fortunate enough to find such an editor, you might become an instant success simply by turning your column in on time.

In between, naturally, stands the medium-sized paper whose editor-in-chief has a journalism degree and years of successful editing experience behind him. He or she is probably qualified to rule over almost any major publishing effort. Such editors have chosen to do what they do best while serving in a casual hometown atmosphere where they can scratch the earth and rub shoulders with readers day after day. Because of the editor's expertise, the whole editorial staff on such papers is required to be competent and versatile, able to handle a variety of jobs that would be specialized positions at any mammoth twice-daily paper.

While the pace at a newspaper is hectic because of the volume of words published daily, or even weekly, editors at a magazine or book publishing firm run back and forth tripping over the panic button, too. Most publishing companies of any size are divided into five basic departments: Administrative, Business, Marketing, Production, and, at the heart of things, Editorial. A great deal of time is consumed by interaction between these departments (which translated means meetings, memos, and minutes).

Publishers, perhaps more than any other business people, work by a system of time slots. Meticulous planning goes into arranging of a schedule that will allow ample time to beat the deadline with ease. While newspapers deal with the here and now, publishing news while it is hot, book and magazine publishers are forced to work well in advance. For months (in the case of magazines) or years (in the case of books), selected manuscripts move from slot to slot. The editor-in-chief (whatever title he or she may actually have) coordinates the whole operation, always with an eye on the schedule, always responsible to know who has a given manuscript, what is happening to it, where it is to go for the next stage, and what will happen to it there. Manuscripts may gather dust while waiting in line for their turn, but only rarely are they even temporarily forgotten. As a rule, the editor babysitting them knows exactly where they are, and why.

The schedule in publishing is so important that the rarest occurrence in any operation is to walk through the deadline relaxed. One small hitch seems to plague every operation; for the schedule to work as planned, everyone on the team must fall into line doing everything right the first time, turning his completed contribution in when it is due. Somewhere along the line, somebody always fumbles the ball.

The Administrative Department, for example, has among its responsibilities the hiring, firing, and pacifying of personnel. If it were not for personnel, everyone's day would go better, but Administration seems incapable of hiring perfect people. Employees get sick, have babies, retire, quit, or get promoted. Any of these changes weakens the team.

The star quarterback is the writer. Sometimes the writer's contribution may be relatively small, but it must be there, ready to run when its time comes. Writers bungle up the schedule by missing their deadline, by sending in copy requiring excessive editing, by forgetting the photos, and by numerous goofs. Among them the most unforgivable are sitting on the galley or page proofs beyond the deadline, or making copy changes after the type has been set.

The Business Department handles such mundane matters as reimbursing writers. On the busiest day in the life of the editor, someone from Business intrudes to ask why the list of last month's writers to be paid was sent to them without the writers' addresses (and late, incidentally). Or, they may make some other ignoble demand that brings important business in the editor's office to a halt until the information requested is located, typed, photocopied, and turned in.

The Marketing Department is concerned with one very routine duty. All they are required to do is sell the product, once it has been prepared. Just the same, they seem to break in to the editor's office during the moments of extreme pressure just to ask for coming titles, the authors' backgrounds, and enough information to produce advertising, catalog copy, or blurbs (due last week, of course, but delayed by Administrative and Business Department interruptions).

The Production Department handles all actual printing. In a

few print shops, relics out of antiquity remain in operation, because some old-time **letterpress** shops (which set type in hot lead) have hung on to the equipment either for sentimentality's sake, or because certain routine jobs (such as printed cards or business forms) could be done economically on available old presses, freeing new equipment for specialized jobs.

Because of its economical versatility, the **offset press** pushed letterpress into obsolesence. Offset, which is based on photographic processes, allows tremendous flexibiity in the use of art and color, and simply put, anything that can be photographed for the offset process, can be printed. Offset printing brought on the publishing explosion of our day, with amazing capability ranging from mammoth web presses which suck a roll of paper through an intricate web of mechanism which both prints and folds at incredible speed, to tiny, highspeed presses that can be operated efficiently in offices or print-while-you-wait shops.

Production people are of necessity precise. All aspects of the work in every area of the department require concentration, mechanical and mathematical skill, sharp eyes, and a mind attuned to perfection in detail.

Composition refers to the process of getting words set into type, a procedure which goes through several people. Detail editors carefully comb manuscripts and mark the copy with coded directions. Speedy typesetters with a high degree of accuracy pound out line after line precisely following the coded directions. Concentration in typesetting has become easier with today's equipment, which is quiet as a cat's paw on carpet—quite a contrast to the clanking of old-time equipment.

Proofreading (done in the **proofroom**) refers to detail checking, first on manuscripts (copyediting and **mark-up**), then on **galley proofs** (long strips of typeset copy that has not been divided into pages), and finally on **page proofs** (the finished copy pasted up as it will appear in the publication, artwork and all). Poor proofroom bears the brunt of all blame, because regardless of who made the error, the proofreaders should have caught it.

Thanks to offset printing, artists no longer need go hungry. Every publisher either *is* an artist, or hires one or more, and most printing firms have a large staff of **commercial artists**. Their work includes creating art concepts to embellish the printed page; planning layout of each page; deciding upon size and style of type; doing the actual drawing, lettering, and design; preparing all artwork according to specifications for the photographing process; and pasting the finished typeset copy, titles, and design into place. Word processors allow typing errors to be corrected on the screen and editorial and author changes to be inserted on a disc without retyping. This relieves artists of part of the tedious task of pasting on tiny typed corrections. However, many composing rooms still use photo typesetting, which requires either a costly reset or a precise pasteup of corrections—the artists' job. Fur can fly as careful-detail personalities tussle with creative writers who love to make changes. **The editor** must be concerned with both detail and overall content, and the cost involved.

Up to this point, Editorial has kept close tabs on the entire process. Once their final okay is given, however, the presses roll. Editors must keep hands off until Production delivers the finished product. (Typically, a cheer goes up in Editorial and Marketing when the first hot-off-the-press copies arrive.)

Production, however, has only begun. The publication is still in the embryo stage. It must be photographed, printed, folded, bound, trimmed, counted, and packaged for delivery. Whether the printing is done **in-house** (on the premises with company-owned equipment) or is **farmed out** (sent to another firm for printing and binding), Production is responsible to see that the job is done Right, and On Time.

The Production Department works so closely with Editorial that when one takes a breath, the other automatically exhales. Editorial, while plagued by all of the aforementioned demands, is responsible for only about ten duties:

1. Selecting/rejecting material.
2. Communicating with writers.
3. Coordinating purchases with Administration for final approval.
4. Communicating with writers.

5. Coordinating writers' payments with the business office.
6. Communicating with writers.
7. Combing manuscripts for libelous statements, mixed-up facts, plagiarism, and copyrighted material requiring permission to reprint.
8. Communicating with writers.
9. Editing, correcting, rewriting, retyping, rearranging, checking, and marking up manuscripts for typesetting; proofreading, cutting, okaying, or killing of material already typeset; and providing advertising information to Marketing.
10. Communicating with writers.

All this time, of course, machines and people in Production hum right along, never skipping a single beat.

What a wildly fictitious thought that is! Machines, like people, tend to break down just when you need them most.

With a magazine or book, a major crisis can develop at any minor deadline along the rocky road to completion. The final deadline brings the editor face to face with the boss. As you know, if you miss one flight in a tightly planned trip, you have messed up all other connections down the line. Facing this kind of frustration, when one deadline slips out of its time slot everyone with any clout at all rushes to the scene to get it back into place. Seldom is such code-blue action truly successful, but company loyalty and immense team spirit bring up the adrenaline. Following the adventure the whole team collapses into a celebration as the editor-in-chief heads off to report to the boss that the schedule is more or less back on track.

The whole publishing world revolves around the deadline. Every stage of production fits into the ever-present calendar. The clock on the wall stands guard over final procedures, tattling to the boss with every tick. No matter where you submit your manuscripts, you can envision them arriving at an office where busy people seem to be running to and fro, where phones never stop ringing, and where desks, files, tables, and cabinets (intended to hide some of the mess) are laden with paper: correspondence, galley proofs, page proofs, and manuscripts at various stages of production. Hidden somewhere behind the heap, probably talking on the phone, is the editor you hope to impress. The warmth of his or her greeting will depend upon how close the next deadline may be.

If it is very close, he may not hear a word you say. As the zero hour approaches, the lions begin to pace and roar, the bears growl, the birds increase their chattering, and the monkeys swing by their tails in a desperate effort to stay relaxed and sane in a mad, mad zoo.

EDITORS UNDERSTAND WRITERS

Surviving in such a high-pressured atmosphere takes a special kind of person. Thus, the first thing you need to know about feeding material to inhabitants of such a zoo is that they have chosen a life ruled by the monster, the Deadline. Unlike risk-fearing people who feel trapped by jobs they dislike, most editors are strongly motivated people, well qualified in varied fields, quite possibly multi-talented people who are addicted to adrenaline highs. They do what they're doing because they love it. As soon as they recover from one tough bout with the deadline, they turn to the next, raring to go.

Editors of past centuries had the option of writing their own material if they chose to do so, with self-publishing often their first goal. Modern-day madness has turned publishing into such a high-stress occupation that few editors have time or mental energy for personal writing projects on the job or off. At home the briefcase of leftover duties from the office must be dealt with. Thus, most editors are not author-competitors you must face. Although many editors *can* write creatively, writing is not one of the talents they have chosen to use. Writing and editing simultaneously is like eating your ice cream right along with the goulash: You don't fully enjoy either one. On the job, therefore, the writing urge is often satisfied by the joy of rewriting. Any editor will tell you tearing someone else's work apart is far more fun than writing your own.

Aha! So editors *do* revise the carefully penned words of writers!

Yes, they do. As a rule, editorial changes don't bother me. As I've told you, I never stop correcting or improving my copy until they slap my hands and tell me to go away, so if a kind-hearted editor sees something that could be made better, that's okay with me.

How much changing you should allow raises a few questions. A beginner doesn't have a lot of voice. Once you've sold the item, it belongs to the buyer. It should be some comfort to know that they wouldn't buy it if they didn't like it as it is. Certainly no significant manuscript is going to undergo drastic changes without consent from the author. But mini-manuscripts are purchased and processed without further contact with the writer. Beginners may lament the editorial changes, but they might not learn about them until the complimentary copies of the finished product arrive in the mail. Then complaining is too late.

The general rule is that editors can make any changes needed to bring the writing into line with the quality their publication demands. This might include altering the beginner's style to some extent, but it is considered unethical to change the author's intent and general message.

Does that happen very often? I've dealt with only one publication that changed my intent. The anecdotes and illustrations (all original) remained intact. What irritated me was that they put on a different punch line. Since I got no credit line, it amounted to stealing my stuff. I was so unhappy about it, I quit writing for them.

As you begin submitting material successfully, you will need to come to a decision on some of these matters. You probably will have to give some material away to get started. Check the samples to see if bylines are used. If they aren't, maybe you'll decide, as I first did, that it doesn't matter. If you don't like what is done to your material, don't send it there again. I decided you can't fight city hall, but you can spit on the steps as you walk by.

For the first few months after we obtained our Old English Sheepdogs, we had grand ideas about breeding them. Brandy ruined our get-rich-quick scheme by refusing to cooperate, which gave us time to rethink the whole matter. There are, we decided after the second rainy spring, too many big muddy feet in the world already, too many sloppy chins, and all too few human beings who appreciate them. Perhaps for similar reasons, a surprising number of highly regarded editors have never published a line. Too many words are already flooding the market. Good editors spend their lives sighing over muddy thoughts and sloppy presentations. Even if time permitted, many of them would be hesitant to write because 1) they don't want to add to the slush pile, believing there are already too many manuscripts in the world; and 2) their own high standards for quality writing deter them. Anything they write would have to top Hemingway, or they would burn it up.

The second helpful insight into understanding editors is that most of them are empathic, sensitive to writers' feelings. In some cases, printed reject slips are a cop-out, allowing the editor "no comment," instead of forcing him or her into a corner where the truth would have to be told. The Boss often makes the "printed reject" decision after seeing highly paid help staring at the ceiling searching for words with which to say a kind and understanding "No!"

IT'S YOU AND ME, BABY!

This brings you and the editor face to face. Interesting as it may be to talk about those awesome editors, the only thing that really matters in your upward climb as a writer is your approach to them and their response.

We've already discussed the matter of studying the markets, but the need to do so comes back to centerstage here. To win friends and influence editors, you *must* know your markets. Editors from coast to coast insist that most freelancers fail this test miserably. A composite of responses given me by various editors indicates that one book manuscript worth considering out of a hundred would be a generous estimate, while magazine editors claim they are inundated with thousands of queries and manuscripts each year, most of which are rejected. Certainly among these efforts are hundreds of poorly written pieces, but all too many have simply been sent to the wrong place.

To fight back, most companies have:

1. Closed the door on completed manuscripts, preferring to receive queries only.
2. Quit returning manuscripts without a self-addressed envelope, or started returning unsolicited manuscripts unopened. (They simply circle the author's return address, jot in bold print "**Return to Sender**,"and drop the package back in the mail.)
3. Turned to form letters and printed reject letters.

Smothered by rejection, writers feel frustration akin to the agony of reasoning with a computer. Writing teachers, friends, and writing club colleagues encourage them to "keep writing and keep trying," but the people who seem to matter most—the editors who claim to buy manuscripts—take one look and stuff a printed reject form into their SASE, shooting their efforts right back to them every time they try!

If a person *is* a good writer and his material is proclaimed as salable even by editors who reject it, why don't his manuscripts sell? They don't sell because

1. They are good, but not so startling in quality or content that they stand up head and shoulders in the stack.

2. They *are* unusual in quality (well above average writing), but something in the approach, style, content, or message to the readers is unsuitable for the publications to which they've been submitted.

3. The whole slush pile is being rejected because all the slots for weeks, months, or (in the case of book publishers) years ahead are already filled.

4. The writing is "good." That is, the writer shows unusual creative talent and could develop into an excellent contributor, but his inexperience is evident. Either his lack of general knowledge is apparent, or his writing is sloppy, filled with poor sentence construction, bad grammar, careless punctuation and spelling, or "all of the above."

The editor's habitat is not conducive to running a sideline editing service for beginners. Pat Perry, assistant editor of *Saturday Evening Post*, tells of being verbally assaulted by someone who phoned to say he *was* a writer but had just received a reject slip from the *Post*. "What do I say? His article wasn't for us," relates Perry. "Although a courteous personal reply might have been nice, deadlines are a reality to us here, and the article just wasn't for us. Unfortunately, the sheer number of manuscripts that a major publishing concern receives prohibits detailed comment. If I find an outstanding manuscript, I do take my time to jot down a few comments. Two manuscripts I singled out in this way were later published by other magazines."

Small kindnesses like Perry's comments have put many writers on the road to success. A wise writer takes such comments to heart and follows the advice whether it hurts or not. Now and then I get brave and tell a rejected writer that a character's traits spoil a story, or an article needs more anecdotes, or the writing needs tightening. It's risky. Most writers asking for criticism are really hoping for praise. They're counting on a check: Their Social Security number is written in bold print, they haven't enclosed a self-addressed envelope, and they've passed along their phone number so the editor can call and give then the good news.

Editors answering a simple survey I sent out shared some interesting pet peeves with me. One single theme surfaced regarding the offering of advice to writers. Many editors asked not to be quoted, but Daniel Clark, then an editorial intern at the *Post*, said it well: "The problem is that after getting the advice the writer will continue to correspond, asking for more and more advice to the point of becoming a nuisance." To the question "Do you appreciate pen pals?" the editors replied a resounding "NO!" They are glad to pass along a tip now and then, but running a correspondence course in writing is not one of their favorite hobbies. What they *did* appreciate was writers who took their small words of advice seriously, whipped the writing into shape, submitted it elsewhere, and wrote back to the first editor to say thank you for putting them on the road to success. It's nice to know one is appreciated, and nicer still to be told one is right!

Knowing how swamped editors can be with correspondence, I rarely pen-pal them (though on occasion I'm as guilty of that as anyone). Sometimes I really want to know something, such as, "Do you see any chance this manuscript will be accepted? I have a nibble from another publisher, but I told him to hang on until you had ample time to consider it." Or, "I plan to be in Cincinnati October 15. Will you be in the office that day, and would you have time for lunch?" (In the first case, you'll probably get the manuscript back, unless it's *really* exceptional, or already accepted. In the second case, depending on who you are and what you what to talk about, the answer would probably be, "I don't have time for lunch, but drop by and take a tour, and I'll squeeze in time for you to visit in my office a while.") To get a quick reply to such questions, I send an addressed postcard and ask the editor to jot a note on it.

Victor Hugo probably didn't use a postcard, but he is said to have written his publisher to find out how his book was selling. Both letters were straightforward:

> Dear Paul,
> ?
> Victor
> Dear Victor,
> !
> Paul

Allowing an editor to bypass the secretarial pool saves the company time and money, and a postcard allows a busy person to answer before the question cools off. One can post-card an editor to death, however. My favorite writers are those who submit top-quality manuscripts, wait patiently until I'm good and ready to read them, and then expect only big, fat checks in reply.

Newspapers dealing with local people and currently hot material (unusable a day or two later) prefer phone inquiries. Among magazine and book editors opinions vary, but most seem to prefer written communication. Phoning to alert an editor that a manuscript is coming does get an affirmative nod (or a negative response, which saves the author the trouble of sending it in). However, the reviewing process will churn along as usual. An author or a topic must be outstanding to receive red carpet treatment among reviewers. The quality of the manuscript pulls rank on the writer almost every time.

Phoning to trace a manuscript in hopes of learning the outcome can be futile. Manuscripts being circulated travel far and wide, so a spur-of-the-moment answer usually ends up to be, "We'll drop you a line and let you know." That in itself may take weeks. A brief, courteous letter with a postcard enclosed will get better results, in many cases.

I was talking with Paul Miller, program materials editor of Lillenas Publishing Company, when he was told that the call on his line was from a writer inquiring about a long-lost manuscript. "Now you can hear my pleasant bedside manner," he quipped. I listened as he diplomatically skirted the issue. After reassuring the writer and promising she would hear from him soon, he hung up the phone, turned to me, and in a mournful voice cried, "She'll hear all too soon! I think her mansucript was in a stack I rejected last night!" He didn't have the heart to tell her.

I couldn't say those nasty words on the phone, either, but writing reject letters is my favorite hobby. If I can't say something nice about your writing, I'll tell you how neatly you type. If that bombs out, I'll tell you the subject you have chosen is timely. And if it isn't, I'll praise you for your effort or your persistence and point out a few flaws as carefully as I can. Sometimes I explain that in the sifting process some excellent manuscripts must be rejected along with those that are less expertly written. You can draw your own conclusion as to which category you're in. An editor-friend located the best reject letter yet: "Thank you for writing. Please don't write again."

There is no easy way to hurt a person. Removing a manuscript from the slush pile to send it back home can be so painful that procrastination sets in. Most editors hate it.

So do writers. You never get used to rejection. We have one of those big mailboxes up on the street, an invigorating, mind-dusting walk from my front door. If I happen to be home when the mailman passes by, I run up there with eager anticipation. A quick glance is all it takes to spot a reject. Checks never come in SASE. How the sight of a brown manila ruins my day!

Hating to admit it's really there, I tuck the reject at the bottom of the pile under the junk mail, which suddenly looks very good. Back in the house I open the desk and without even looking to see who the reject is from, poke it into a corner. It always takes me about a week to build up courage to open the return envelope. Sometimes I never do.

One day I went through the depressing routine, this time placing the ugly SASE under a pile of papers on my table. A couple of weeks later in a burst of energy I cleaned off the table. For a long time I held the reject in my hand. Finally I took the plunge. Bracing myself for the worst, I squinted at the article. It was a fat epistle from my sister Ethel! She had written such a long letter she had to use her writer's supplies to send it to me.

Writers face rejection all the time. Successful writers are those who have learned to cope with it. Thank heaven for all publications still open to freelance submissions. Their number is diminishing rapidly, but you can still get your foot in someone's door. Practice on them.

Just because your manuscript is accepted doesn't mean it's good. Sometimes a slush pile gets so deep that stuff molds. I've been known to accept material because I had kept it so long I was too embarrassed to return it. A fairly good check was sent to a writer because I spilled coffee on her manuscript. One editor haggled with a sensitive author over a lost mansucript for weeks. According to reliable records, it had been rejected and returned, but she never got it. Weary of reasoning with an unreasonable woman, he accepted her carbon copy to get her off his back. Not all editors would give in that easily! You are responsible to keep a copy of material you submit. The publisher accepts no responsibility for manuscripts that he did not request.

CREATING A COVER LETTER

Martin Luther is said to have known a preacher who, when he had nothing to say, stomped around and shouted all the louder. Some covering letters seem to serve this purpose; they appear to be cover-ups, trying to make up for all the manuscript lacks.

The shorter the manuscript, the less you ought to say. I prefer no covering letter on mini-articles and short stories, and even on long manuscripts I usually read the covering letter after I have scanned the content of the article or book. Only one editor I surveyed underlined the importance of the covering letter. Her company is large, swamped with three thousand to four thousand freelance book manuscripts a year. By reading an adequate covering letter she can decide if the manuscript has any potential for her company, and if it has none she returns it unread.

In most cases, the better the writing is, the less need there will be to sell yourself. The day you drop a bestseller on an editor's desk, be it poem, article, short story, drama, or book, you will need to include only a SASE, because it bears all the information they need to find you: your name and address.

Most editors want a covering letter to be brief. Biographical material is needed only if it is pertinent to the manuscript. Post graduate degrees, significant published works, and job data or other information that qualifies you to write on the subject is worth mentioning. A list of mini-markets that have purchased your material probably is not. Your grade school, high school, wedding anniversary, and the names of your wife and children do nothing to enhance the sale of most manuscripts you submit.

Samples of how-not-to-do-it covering letters are as easy to find as violets in spring. Pompous and wordy, most of them overrate the writer, the subject, and the manuscript attached. More often than not they are addressed to the wrong person, because such writers rely on outdated market listings for their information instead of reading up-to-date issues of the periodical.

SEND A MILLION QUERIES

Sondra Forsyth Enos, articles editor at *Ladies' Home Journal*, advises, "send a million queries; don't give up, and don't harass editors that don't respond in two seconds."

A most interesting printed query landed on my desk. It was a loser in spite of its brilliant approach because

1. It was printed, addressed to: "To whom it may concern."
2. No SASE was enclosed, so no reply was expected.
3. It was arrogant, promising a bestseller.
4. The writer did not know his markets. It was totally unsuited to us.

The letter was memorable because the writer stated that any publisher wishing to review his manuscript would be required to pay a five-hundred-dollar fee for the privilege!

Sending a million queries does not mean printing a form letter to offer your wares. It means writing a million personal letters elucidating your idea and proving your ability to write the quality of material the periodical demands. The following are minimal prerequisites for writing an adequate query letter:

1. You read the periodical regularly and you know who is in charge. Address the letter to the proper person.
2. You have read enough back issues to be able to say, "I've noticed that you haven't covered [name the subject] duing the past two years."
3. You have specific material in mind, a unique focus and slant, valid reasons for wanting to submit it to the periodical you're addressing, and (if applicable) you have photographs or access to them.

Querying is to the writer's advantage. It saves wear and tear on a manuscript as well as time and postage. If a subject proves to be unsalable the writer can turn his attention to something else. Queries can be sent simultaneously to several publishers. (When they are, however, write a *personal letter* to the proper editor at each firm, and mention that you've sent it several places. A photocopied "Dear Editor" letter puts the first negative check on the slush editor's list. Subconscious vibes begin to murmur "dump-it, dump-it, dump-it!") Outlines and proposals can be photocopied, a timesaver and certainly less costly than photocopying the entire manuscript.

SASE must be enclosed if you expect a reply. Don't send a little envelope for the return of your big manuscript. Affix a properly addressed label to the proper-sized envelope and put the correct amount of postage on the envelope. The practice of enclosing stamps, a dollar bill, or—heaven forbid—a personal check is disliked by editors. One of the reasons for the self-addressed envelope is to save time addressing the label. In some companies this would amount to sixty or eighty labels a week on *unsolicited* manuscripts.

Apparently many post office employees are not alert when they give writers a dated stamp label for the return envelope. Six weeks later (or six months), the publisher will have to pay postage on those returns. Take control! Lick the stamps yourself!

Personally I use first class mail for both outgoing and return envelopes. In many cases I use priority mail, not because I feel a need for rushing the manuscript to its destination, but because something within me is acknowledging the importance of the material over which I have slaved. Priority mail is simply airmail, but seeing "Priority—Priority—Priority" stamped all over the package makes me feel very, very good.

I'm not personally a lover of query letters. As an editor I object because writers (whom I hate to disappoint) put too much stock in my affirmative reply. A green light means only that you can drive one more block. The timing and all other factors being perfect, you might sail clear through town, but chances of doing that are very slim. In speculative writing, anywhere along the way your manuscript is apt to hit a cul-de-sac, come upon a dead-end, hit a red light, or run out of gas. When the editor says he likes the idea and wants to see more, most writers (myself included) jump up and down elated over the big success. All the editor has offered is a chance to gamble two more envelopes and postage on another try.

I object, too, because query letters, outlines, and resumes don't tell the whole story. All too many writers produce beautiful query letters. This is why so many green lights are given. The project sounds good, the subject is pertinent, and the writer knows enough to write a decent letter. But the manuscript that follows is a total flop. The only way to tell if a manuscript is decent enough to buy is to see it. The whole thing.

I stand almost alone in my opinions. "Query only" proponents (and their tribe is increasing) are sick and tired of wading through complete manuscripts. Forcing writers to discipline themselves to producing strong proposals separates the amateurs from the professionals. And, as economic pressure forces publishers to tighten their belts, among the first to go are the slush editors.

The reasoning is sound. Paying someone to read what you consider junk mail hardly makes sense. Most of us who do it love it so much we're surprised to be paid. Perhaps we are at fault, working the pile too slowly. Oscar Wilde said you don't need to drink a whole cask of wine to know its vintage. Joe Bayly is quoted as saying "You don't have to eat all of an egg to know if it's bad." Being a good Swede, I insist one sip of coffee is all I need to decide if it's time to make a new pot. Bookaholics have plunged in and read to their heart's delight, wading through manuscripts they knew from the first page were rejects. The boss, trying to balance the budget, has made them get back to work. "Query only" is the result. Readers unable to give up their vice become agents.

The only manuscripts worth reading in detail are those chosen as holding sales potential. Cass Canfield, Senior Editor at Harper and Row, points out that "any intelligent, well-educated person can tell if a book has quality. What's hard to tell is if a book is going to sell."

That's the big question. Will the product sell?

We've said that editors love their stress-filled jobs and the writers, who make publishing possible. We've pointed out that most of them are empathic, sensitive to the writer's feelings. The third point I want to make is this: In the publishing world, *sales* is the name of the game. No matter how much an editor enjoys a manuscript or likes its author, no matter how intriguing the subject matter may be, its sales appeal is the deciding factor. That is what an editor means when he replies, "We didn't see anyplace it would fit." "Not suitable" means "not enough sales appeal."

Caught between the writer and Marketing, a seasoned editor sides with his colleagues who are responsible for knowing the readers. Marketing experts feel the pulse of their audiences through complex market tests and surveys, reader feedback, and constant study of future trends. There is no reason to purchase a manuscript unless it has widespread sales appeal. Personal opinion plays only a small part in editorial choices. Final decisions require an educated, objective viewpoint, which is based upon the sales potential. Will the manuscript please subscribers? Will it bring reader response? Would its title and photos grab browsers at a magazine stand, causing them to buy? Is it a winner?

Once you grasp the full significance of that facet of publishing, you will understand how important it is for you to study every aspect of writing, including the markets. Either apply yourself to becoming a top quality writer or drop out.

How do I dare say that? Because I know this: If writing is burning in your soul, you'll write! To make the sacrifices necessary to stick to it takes only one thing. You have to want to succeed more than almost anything else in the world.

If you've got the "want to," you can do it. Tune in to the minds of your own projected audience and come up with appealing material properly timed and skillfully planned. You'll soon begin to taste success. If you persist toward that goal, you will find those awesome editors ready to make friends!

ASSIGNMENT 8

WARM-UP: Call a local editor, reporter, author, or printer and invite him or her to lunch. Identifying yourself as a beginning writer (be candid about your writing level), say: "I'm trying to learn all I can about the publishing business, and I wondered if I could take you to lunch someday soon." If that isn't possible (for you to ask or the busy person to grant), say: "How about at your office? Could I drop by for fifteen minutes this afternoon?" (Ask for half an hour, if that's how long you plan to stay.) If he says, "I have to be at the airport at four," say, "Oh, could I drive you out there? We could visit in the car!" Make your call brief; let the person choose the day and the hour. Be there when he walks in, ask how much time he has, and watch the clock. (Just think; someday some budding writer might be giving you that red-carpet respect!)

Do not take along samples of your work. Tell the person *briefly* what you are doing as a writer, but spend most of the time he gives you listening to him. "How did you get started in this business" should get the conversation rolling.

Repeat this procedure now and then if several prospective guests are available.

In light of what you have learned about slush piles, editors, and deadlines, look over any material you have written. Ponder ways to bring it up to professional standards.

Using what you know about studying the market, begin to scribble sample query letters. Nobody needs to see them. You can create imaginary proposed articles or stories, but for best learning results you should aim the samples to actual editors at existing publications you like. Create a QUERIES file, building it from the periodicals the addresses of which you noted at the library, and from other publications you read regularly.

FINALLY: Do you need to enroll in a typing class?

9 Now the Sweat Begins

Well, you've come a long way.

You've decided that you have what it takes to become a professional writer: the talent, the burning desire, the patience, and enough basic skills to bravely begin.

You've learned to relax, freeing your mind to explore the past, the present, and the future; to unearth ideas and destroy hang-ups that might hinder you; to sort out thoughts and discover who you are and what you love, hate, or fear. You've gotten in touch with your emotional feelings and you understand why certain things please, anger, unnerve, or frustrate you, as well as why you agree or disagree on major issues that confront you. You've let your creativity out of the cage, granting it permission to explore, examine, and use secrets from your life to slant and brighten what you write.

You've learned the value of fresh anecdotes, and you've begun to see them, collect them, and organize them for future use.

You've acknowledged the need to broaden your base of general knowledge through use of the library and through reading perodicals and newspapers outside of your usual scope of interest. You plan to take advantage of events on the community calendar whenever possible to keep in touch with the world beyond your home.

You have a good idea of what is meant by "style," and although your own may not have surfaced, you've learned enough to recognize and try various uses of style.

You've torn down the fences that boxed you in to one type of writing, so you plan to experiment with various forms.

You see the value of knowing your market before submitting queries or finished manuscripts.

You've learned to appreciate the editor's job. You understand that editors are potential customers for your wares, rather than enemies to be conquered.

NOW THE SWEAT BEGINS

Join me as together we tackle nonfiction article writing. Let's begin with . . .

But what a gorgeous fall day! Bright sun and azure skies are beckoning me! Enough leaves have fallen so that the neighbors' houses can be seen from my dining room window, and I know Judy, at least, is home, because her car is in the driveway. Dorothy probably is, too—more than likely raking leaves. Days like this are all too rare, and I do believe I ought to lay aside writing, make some sandwiches, and hike up to surprise the girls with lunch. There will be plenty of time for writing after the cold front moves through.

Or shall I make one last trip to Englewood Park to feed the ducks and roam the wooded paths one last time before Winter blows her icy breath across the pond, wraps her chilling arms around the trees, and blocks the woodland trails with snow and ice?

Ah, no! I shall do neither. I promised myself I would write

today, and I plan to do it. I'm going to write. Knowing my truancy tendencies, I planned ahead. Early this morning, to get the call of the wild out of my system, I hitched up the dogs and hiked to the mailbox a mile away. This took care of the urge to rake leaves, as well. That certainly needs to be done, but not after racing up and down Avondale hills. The dishes and dusting are done; the dry cleaning went out yesterday, when I also made the rounds to service the car, buy groceries, and do other errands that so conveniently come to mind when it is time to write. The plants have been watered. Lunch and supper are both almost ready, because I've learned the value of cooking ahead, using leftovers or freezing a few meals in advance to avoid cooking on writing days.

You will not succeed in professional writing until you consider your writing important. It's a job: a commitment. The more advance planning you do to make sticking to writing possible, the better you will work. The sweat begins by beginning, not by beating around the bush. I understand the difficulty of setting a schedule and sticking to it. Fortunately, one doesn't have to set a schedule—every evening at eight I will write one hour—*yuk!* But one *does* have to say "today I plan to write" and then do it.

Do you have all your equipment ready? Paper and other tools are scattered all over my apartment, so where I end up writing doesn't matter. Since I write my first draft in longhand, usually on lined yellow pads, I need only decide which room to sit in, or I can carry my equipment to the yard, the library, the park, or the beach, and keep on writing. Some of my best thoughts have come while I was speeding bumper to bumper across the freeway bridge, so I'm prepared to write in a moving vehicle without looking at the scratch pad. I often scribble a few lines when lights turn red; and traffic jams can become delightful interludes in my life.

Even if I had a word processor, I believe I would stick to pen and scratch pad. My thoughts flow through the pen. Years of secretarial obedience probably hinder my flow of thoughts at the typewriter. Without my pen I stare vacantly into space as if waiting for some dictatorial authoritative voice from above.

As I told you earlier, I write best in the silence of my dining room, feet propped up in the windowsill, alone. I'm in good company. Thoreau, who has been described as "a freakish original," did some of his best writing out of his cabin in the woods where he lived alone. His essay "Solitude" begins, "This is a delicious evening . . . " and he remarks in the essay, "I have as it were my own sun and moon and stars, and a little world all to myself." He admits to having been lonely once, shortly after moving to the woods, when for an hour he mused that "the near neighborhood of man" was necessary to a serene and healthy life. "To be alone was something unpleasant," he says. "But I was at the same time conscious of a slight insanity in my mood . . ." Later he learned to love spring and fall rainstorms (as I do), finding "their ceaseless roar and pelting. . . ." soothing. When friends were concerned that he must get lonesome and ought to be closer to people "rainy and snowy days and nights especially," Thoreau replied that "no exertion of the legs can bring two minds together."

Dark "rainy and snowy days and nights" are my favorites and are extremely creative times for me. How I hate to be at work (for someone else) during a storm, realizing I could be home writing! But Thoreau and I differ on one point: the "black kernel of the night" is dreadful to me when I *am* alone, but sense I am not. I tend to listen for "things that go bump in the night," falling into that class of people Thoreau describes as "a little afraid of the dark, though the witches are all hung and Christianity and candles have been introduced."

No, I'm not a recluse. I like people and need them. But not when I write. When I write I have to be alone. The hum of the refrigerator just stopped. All I hear is a distant bark, which reminds me that Barney is lying on the floor beside my chair scarcely breathing, like a big bear rug. Thoreau would describe this sunny morning as "delicious." It's a perfect time to write!

WHAT DO YOU PLAN TO WRITE ABOUT?

Wherever you are—perhaps in a busy library with ghostlike figures silently brushing past you—you must decide what to write about. An article needs, first of all, a subject. Thoreau chose

"Solitude" at a time when he felt "no more lonely than the first spider in a new house." He often wrote, as did his friend and contemporary, Emerson, on nature, which he knew so well: the trump of the bullfrog, the note of the whippoorwill, the fluttering alder and poplar leaves, the fox, the skunk, the rabbit, and "every little pine needle." But the scope of his subjects reached beyond the quiet forest where he lived. He philosophized about man, society, government, art, and literature, as his keen mind reflected on the fast-paced world he chose to leave.

Another of Thoreau's contemporaries, Margaret Fuller, championed women's rights as early as 1839. At that time colleges were closed to women. If you were denied a college education for whatever reason, you would be encouraged by a study of this brilliant woman's short but successful life. She was born into a world where women were decorative and entertaining, their place somewhere between the theatre and the embroidery hoop, rather than the kitchen. She was twenty-five when her father died; but until then, he taught her and encouraged her. After his death she pressed on, teaching school and writing critical essays, finally winning a place as editor of a quarterly magazine. She ventured into adult education in 1839, teaching Bostonian women literature, education, mythology, and philosophy—all subjects stolen from the male world. Her feminist discourse, "Women of the Nineteenth Century," won the attention of Horace Greeley, who published it in 1845.

Fuller's dream was to complete a biography of Goethe—a man-sized job—but meanwhile she went to Europe (becoming America's first female correspondent). She married an Italian marchese, Ossoli, and became involved in hospital volunteer work during the Italian Revolution. En route back to the States in 1850, the Ossolis' ship wrecked. Margaret, her husband, and her daughter all died, and her history of the Italian Revolution also went down with the ship.

There is no limit to one's choice of subjects. Possibilities lie all around us. Women's Rights, a study of frontier life, a biography of Goethe, interpretations of European literature, history of a revolution—these are some of the topics Margaret Fuller Ossoli chose to write about. It would be hard to decide which might have been her favorite, for her life seemed to burst with the ongoing enthusiasm of a radiant personality. She found much to write about, and time to write it. But for our purposes, let us say she chose Women's Rights, because "Women of the Nineteenth Century" is one of her best-known works:

> As to men's representing women fairly at present, . . . The father and the philosopher have some chance of liberality; the man of the world, the legislator for expediency, none. . . . What Woman needs is not as a woman to act or rule, but as a nature to grow, as an intellect to discern, as a soul to live freely, unimpeded. . . .

NARROWING YOUR SUBJECT

Combining Thoreau's thoughts on solitude and Fuller's on women has turned my mind to today's elderly. For many elderly, solitude is preferable to the hubbub and bickering of a nursing home. They cherish their thread of independence, so they hang on where they are, facing the four walls of small apartments or little old homes they simply can't bear to leave. Loneliness replaces solitude, as day piles upon day, night upon night.

The subject "The Elderly" is too broad to be covered in one article. The scope must be narrowed, the spotlight focusing on some small segment of elderly citizens: the poor, the rich, Chicanos, women in cold climates, men in nursing homes, the elderly in America's ghettos, California elderly, or old-timers of New England.

Any one of the above segments could become the theme of an article; but even so, if you began to dig for material, you would soon find mountains of facts, anecdotes, interesting profiles, and usable material of all kinds, far too much for your article. How does one narrow a subject down to workable size?

DEFINING YOUR PURPOSE

Allowing your mind to recall articles you have read recently, you will see that the subjects have been as broad as the world itself: crime, humor, how-to, discovery, travel, science, strikes, employment opportunities or lack of them, education, entertainment, animals (wild and domestic), abuse, rights, and even nature. What made them palatable and interesting was the writer's viewpoint.

In each case, the author made a decision before beginning, determining what it was he wanted to say. The questions you want to ask yourself are simple enough: "Why do I want to write about this?" "What is my purpose?"

The same issue can be treated in many ways, but your answer falls somewhere within the following reasons:

1. To inform
2. To persuade
3. To awaken thought
4. To convince
5. To rebuke
6. To entertain
7. To unload your own thoughts

If your subject is crime, you might **inform** the readers of a suburban newspaper that crime is moving closer by citing incidents such as burglaries, murder, and rape which occurred within your suburb the past six months.

On the other hand, your purpose might be to **persuade** readers to join a Neighborhood Watch, so you could include illustrations of such organized efforts in other areas of the city. The fact that crime is moving closer would be secondary—a motivating factor to assist you in your persuasion efforts.

If you had a special interest in crime as it affects youngsters, you could focus the article on high school, with interviews and illustrations pertaining to crime involving teens. Your purpose would be to **awaken thought,** to alert parents and teens to what is going on elsewhere, concluding with "Could it happen here?" or, "Is it happening here?" or, "Let's not let it happen here."

To convince people sometimes seems hopeless, but good writers do it successfully all the time, as we all know from both advertising and political campaigns. Convincing people that crime is moving closer, for the purpose of prodding them to action, can be done in a variety of ways, not the last of which is human interest profiles of people who have been hurt. I recall accompanying a fragile, china doll woman more than eighty years old to court so she could testify against a twenty-year-old man who not only took her purse, but also knocked her down and kicked her in the stomach before running away. If that had happened in a crime-free neighborhood, citizens would have been aroused to action when the story was released. (In inner city, such stories are hardly considered news.)

Rebuke is so difficult to do effectively that the average beginner should beware of tackling it. Satirical rebuke, well done, can turn defeat into victory, where preachy rebuke will probably fail. As with writing intended to convince, the best rebuke may be a heartrending story that proves the point.

A great deal of writing—even gory news reporting and certainly human interest stories—is done to **entertain.** Entertain means "to amuse; to provide diversions." We've already mentioned earlier in the book that people often appreciate morbid entertainment: following the fire truck, so to speak; enjoying the thrill of monster movies; watching fiery car crashes; and seeing people trapped or gunned down. Even the subject of crime, therefore, can be written up in a nonfiction article for the purpose of entertainment—and in fact readers pick newspapers and news magazines that have skilled reporters able to do this well.

Essays and editorials are two excellent platforms for the writer who simply wants **to unload his thoughts.** For the beginner, any soapbox will do. A "letter to the editor" is a good starting place for one who has never seen his name in print.

Here are some questions to help you identify your purpose and narrow your subject:

•What interests you?

After all, one of the key factors in successful writing is originality. Is the topic "Sleeping"? "Sleeping late," maybe, to narrow it down. How do you view sleeping late? As pleasure? Or as laziness?

If your subject is "Dogs," do you love them so much you hate the leash law, or hate them so much you wish other people had fenced yards, as you do? (I might write an essay on three little twerps that threatened with menacing growls to take on both Barney and Brandy this morning. Thank God my arm muscles are made of steel! And my dogs, although reluctant in such an aggravating situation, obey!)

Ah! I know what your topic is: Home! Donald Grant Mitchell, forty years a professional writer, said in *Reveries of a Bachelor* (1850): "From my soul I pity him whose soul does not leap at the mere utterance of that name!"

What do you think of when you hear the word "home"? Mom, homemade buns, and coffee with real cream! Viv's Saturday afternoon Metropolitan opera! That's what I think of. Games and popcorn. Holidays. Birthdays. Slumber parties. Company.

Perhaps you think of broken homes, of foster homes, one after another, of unhappy homes. Is your thought a pensive wish for a home of your own? Or a wish that you could escape from the home you know?

You can write about any one of these and many more. Mitchell focused on long evenings alone before the fire enjoying his reveries. "The warmth, the hour, the quiet, create a home feeling . . . about which my musings go on to drape themselves in luxurious reverie . . . —There she sits, by the corner of the fire, in a neat home dress . . . She repeats in a silver voice, a line that has attracted her fancy; and you listen . . . your eyes . . . on the finger, where glitters like a star, the marriage ring—that tells you, she is yours!"

The fire burns down by midnight. The room gets cold, and suddenly he realizes—"She is gone!" He throws himself across the bed thinking about the "cantankerous life" he will have to face again the next day, and falls asleep musing: "I wonder if a married man with his sentiment made actual is, after all, as happy as we poor fellows, in our dreams?"

Home! It's a worthwhile subject, so broad eveyone who reads this book might write on it with not one article duplicating the other!

- **How much do you know about the topic you've chosen?**

If you've chosen "Home," and you intend to write an essay about the kind of home you grew up in, you know quite a bit—almost enough to write a good article. If, however, you want to broaden your scope, your knowledge may be limited. Let us say you want to write about "Foster Homes." You may know about your own experience taking in foster children, or the home of a neighbor or relative, or the home of your foster grandchild. Perhaps your knowledge stretches to four or five homes you lived in as a foster child, but your viewpoint still is limited because included in your feelings toward the people who cared for you may be feelings of loss, separation, guilt, grief, anger, and insecurity, all subjective.

To write well about any issue beyond personal recollection (which, as we've repeatedly said, is not widely accepted by publishers), you need to increase your knowledge of the field. You accumulate detail through reading, interviews, and general research, learning all you can. Far too much material piles up on your desk, but you sift and sort, deciding "this fits, this doesn't; this may be usable later, but not now."

If you have been writing unsuccessfully, a clue to the reason for your collection of reject slips may be found here. Amateurs often shuffle memories and material they have on hand, hoping to come up with enough pages to create an article. That is like starting off on a race with a wad of gum on the botton of one shoe. While the amateur is struggling with limitations of his own memories and the material he has on hand, the creative professional is passing him by.

A good article does not begin with a heap of notes. It begins with an organized plan of action:

1. Identify what you're going to write about, and why . . .
2. Decide what you're going to focus on in your article . . .
3. Determine the points you want to be sure to cover . . .

4. Decide how you're going to approach the material . . .
5. Identify what you know now, and plan to include . . .
6. Find out what is lacking and what you need to know before writing . . .

You can see that if you begin at point "5," you will fail to develop your subject adequately. In fact, far too many articles considered well written by the tearful recipients of reject slips have overlooked the very first point. They have not chosen a subject. Material has been shuffled and typed and a title has been tacked on to it, thus creating a headless monster with a misshapen body and no feet.

Most amateur writers fail to observe point "6." What you have in your head and in your file is as valuable as I've indicated earlier that it is. However, your memories and experiences must be viewed as rich background material, not as meat to cover the skeletal structure of your article. As a general rule, some research is needed to create an article strong enough to face the competition. While it is *very, very* hard to lay aside your beautiful memories and fascinating experiences, you ought to do so. Consider them a hoard of gold coins to be invested carefully. Think of them as a box of chocolates to be doled out one at a time now and then, because if you munch them all up in one evening, you have nothing left the next day (except, maybe, an editor who feels nausea coming on when he looks at your sweet submission).

In the case of personal recollections—and this may be especially true concerning memories of one who has experienced loss, failure, disappointment, or trauma of any kind—the article becomes objective through use of outside material, with your own experience serving as the foundation upon which you can build.

Organize, then: Know what you plan to write about, where you plan to go with your subject, what you have as foundation knowledge, and what you need to go after, before writing. Research, then: Go after solid construction material. Don't try to build a mansion from scraps you pick up around home.

- **What kind of subject have you chosen?**

As you've already learned, the subject, as much as anything, determines the style. You need to ponder your focus (the small, specific segment of the subject you chose to write about) and your angle (the direction you plan to go with the subject) before you decide how you are going to approach it.

In "Reveries," for example, Mitchell focused on a lonely evening in the life of a single man. He slanted the essay for general readership pleasure, however. Anyone can enjoy an essay about the joys of an evening at home, the warmth of a fire, and a couple quietly reading, sharing a line or two now and then. That the woman was a reverie was somewhat incidental until she disappeared, and his conclusion left his readers feeling that his life was okay, maybe even better than their own.

Obviously Mitchell could have done as dozens of writers do today: He might have written about his lonely feelings, the disappointments of life, and the faults of women he has known. "Crying in the Night" articles come from the pen of every segment of society: "Life with an Alcoholic," "My Mother Doesn't Treat Me Right," "I Wish I Hadn't Retired," "My Child Got Sick," "Nobody Understands Widows," and on and on. Mitchell's skill as a writer precluded his turning out an unsuitable sob story, but the slant (rather than general) might have been to singles of his age group. This brings us to the next consideration:

- **Who is going to read your article?**

You could slant your dog article to kennel owners, to veterinarians, to senior citizens, to people who live alone, to suburban families, or to the general public.

I love query letters that assure me the whole world would be interested. That isn't true. Because it isn't, the clever writer puts his feet up on the windowsill to think about the readers he would like to reach. Of course he has studied the markets. Naturally! He knows exactly who reads what. His is no shotgun approach.

Is your intended readership a wide group of adults with many opinions? Your neighbors, perhaps? Think back to Chapter 7, where we created a restaurant scene with possible readers of a magazine such as *Sports Afield*. They had only two things in common that we were aware of: their choice of a restaurant and their love for fishing. Objectivity is important when ages, social levels, marital status, and varied backgrounds are blended together in one audience. You can't whine about singles' loneliness in a family paper, but you might write from the viewpoint of a family that "adopts" single friends, sharing with them special occasions of life (and reaping good returns). Objectivity means taking a middle road, softening your bitter blows and spending some space focusing on the opposite viewpoint.

To begin, it's not a bad idea to write to one person in particular. Let's say you want to write for a senior citizen's magazine. You place your dear old grandma in the center of your mind, or that elderly neighbor you love. What would you write to her?

I can see right away how she would react to some subjects. No one likes to be pitied, so that tack is ruled out. No one likes to be laughed at, so you wouldn't poke fun at the way she wears her hair or the crazy things she says. You wouldn't write *to* Grandma the same way you might write to your college kids *about* Grandma. You would write about things she remembers with pleasure: the pump and the potato patch; the horse and wagon—especially the time they ran away, dumping Grandpa in the ditch; or the old washtub you bought at an antique shop—the major part it once played in the life of the American family might make a good nostalgia article. You might write about a drive through the countryside in spring, re-creating for Grandma the winding, icy stream lined with cowslips, or about your visit to the little old schoolhouse where she once taught. Grandmothers travel so far and so frequently today that they have little time for such minor excursions. They'd as soon read whether the lilies still bloom on Aunt Sarah's grave as drive out there to see for themselves.

Here's a sample of how an article begins to take shape:

Subject: Dogs
Scope: The trouble neighborhood dogs cause

> *Angle:* Fences are for the dogs' own good
> *Slant:* To suburban woman
> *Approach:* Human interest (my son's puppy was hit by a car)
> *Conclusion:* The leash law will soon be on the ballot and we plan to vote "Yes." But we're ahead of the game. Jared's new puppy doesn't run out to meet the school bus. At 3:30 every afternoon, you'll see Blackie waiting behind a shiny new gate!

The body of the article is made up of thought-blocks: the sentence, the paragraph, and the section. Properly dividing these thoughts—matching them up and getting them in order—achieves unity. Basically there are two ways to arrange one's thoughts: in natural sequence (the family picked out a puppy, brought it home and named it, and began to train it; it ran out into the street when the school bus came and it was hit by a car); or the writer's choice, the order which best serves his purpose or suits his fancy (the puppy was hit by a car because it ran out to meet the school bus each day; flashback to picking out the puppy and training it, the grief over the little boy's loss, and going back to get another puppy).

Sequence is determined by what the writer considers important. In this case, since we plan to show mothers the importance of fencing in their children's pets, the dog's being hit by the car is the grabber—it hooks them—and the little boy's grief is the clincher—they don't want it to happen again.

DECIDING ON YOUR APPROACH

You've decided on a subject and your material is beginning to fall into place. It appears to have possibilities—too many, in fact. You could do quite a variety of things with what you have on hand, couldn't you?

Any written presentation can be organized in a variety of ways: topical, chronological, spatial, or logical. As you begin to think through your subject, your outline should develop within one of these categories:

1. *Topical*

The topical plan organizes according to kinds, types, or methods. For example, the subject "dogs" could be focused on lapdogs, watchdogs, and stray dogs. If one's topic is planting a garden, one might cover various vegetables to be included: radishes, lettuce, beans, corn, squash, and tomatoes. Travel options might include air travel, automobile trips, and traveling by motorcycle; an article about extermination could cover *types* of poison, *methods* of application, or the effectiveness of extermination against roaches, waterbugs, spiders, and mice: *kinds* of pests to be exterminated.

A topical outline always divides a larger class into smaller parts or genre. It's like cutting a pie into pieces.

2. *Chronological*

The chronological approach divides a segment of time into smaller periods of time: A day is divided into hours, hours into minutes, minutes into seconds. For example, morning is followed by afternoon, which is followed by evening. Mitchell's "Reveries" began early in the evening and continued until the coals burned down signaling bedtime.

The puppy article I suggested moved from picking the puppy out to its sad demise. For the writer's purpose the chronology might be disrupted by use of flashbacks or projections into the future; but properly done, the true chronology is as clear throughout the writing as if it were a silver thread shining in the sun, and woe to the writer who loses it along the way. Readers do not need to *see* the chronological pattern; they must *feel* its presence. But the writer must *plan it*, *see it*, and *never* lose track of it, no matter how much jumping back and forth he may do. The true chronology may be *interrupted*, but it cannot be *disrupted*, so the pattern, although broken, will be mended again.

As an example, when one provides an illustration within a chronological development, the major time pattern continues after the example has been presented through a "side trip." The illustration blends into the large time pattern:

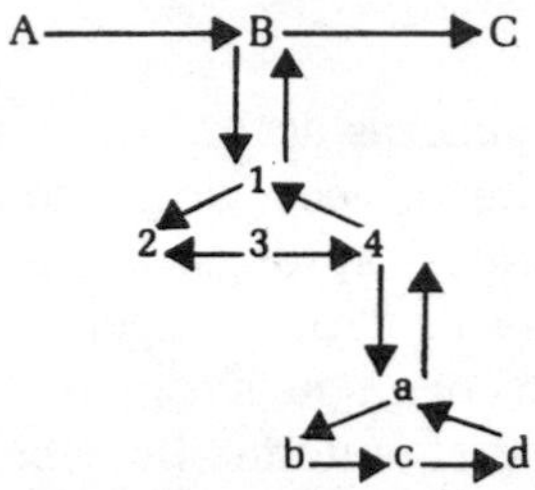

The A, B, C, is the major time pattern. B, however, includes a side trip, so the illustration drops down to 1, 2, 3, 4. At that point the writer could return to the major pattern, but I included another interruption under 4, before doing so.

How-to articles almost always are organized chronologically: first you do step one, then step two, then step three, and then step four. According to experts, fiction (which we will touch on later) has a chronological thread running through it, or it is not good fiction.

3. *Spatial*

The spatial approach (space order) organizes the subject geographically. Thus one might write about various areas of a factory, an office, a home, a town, or a tourist attraction in terms of their *space relationships*. Such a pattern of organization might be developed according to either the importance of the areas, the proximity of the areas, or the sequence in which one encounters them (a kind of chronological structure).

Many articles within the beginner's reach adapt beautifully to the spatial approach, including travel articles, factory tours, and descriptions of local attractions.

4. *Logical*

The logical approach is the most difficult type of writing. All of the foregoing patterns of organization have their own unique logical structures. However, certain subjects necessitate logical structures which go beyond time, space, and kind. Such an organization is usually necessary when one is attempting to be persuasive or when one is simply expressing an opinion, as in the essay. Since many beginning writers tackle these difficult subjects thinking they have chosen something easy, we need to take a good, hard look at logical organization.

At the base of the logical structure are two parts: the cause and the effect (what happened and what made it happen, to reverse them). One may argue from cause to effect; from effect to cause; or from effect to effect.

In practice, this pattern of organization is often seen in problem/solution form. For example, one might simply argue that a problem exists, providing evidence. Or, one might go beyond this point by indicating how that problem might be solved; or one might argue for some course of action because of desirable results that could be obtained.

One uses the logical structure when attempting to motivate the reader to respond in a particular way. The argument is defined (by explaining what one is talking about). The point might be to convince the writer something is true, not true, the way to go, or not the way to go. However, it might simply be to set the reader's mind to work—to make him think.

In articles of opinion, one gains more by awakening thoughtful consideration than by forcefeeding the readers. Shouting as one jumps up and down on one's soapbox might hold the audience's attention, but all they may remember and talk about is that some fool did it. To avoid this, use the following guidelines:

1. Present your facts in an orderly manner.
2. Be aware what is fact, and what is opinion.
3. Stick to the issue.
4. Use up-to-date evidence.
5. Avoid personal experience examples unless you back them up with several authoritative sources that agree.
6. Be logical in your reasoning.

7. Don't overlook issues on which you and the opposing side agree. They can be used to your benefit.

Informal essays are an expression of the writer's sentiment. He wonders, muses, reminisces, even argues, but not seriously and sometimes about trivial or amusing matters. Andy Rooney of CBS' *60 Minutes* excels at this.

Critical essays move from an objective overview of data to a measured critical response, allowing the writer to express his own ideas and make judgment on the implications or philosophy of the subject matter. The presentation may be very powerful even when it is low key or satirical. Columnist William F. Buckley, Jr. is one master of argumentation whose work you should examine. I read other choice columns with zest, as well, for others are also very skilled in this art, making persuasive or critical statements wrapped in satire or humor, with a strong punch line. You need to find your own favorite editorial columnists to read regularly, hoping by the process of osmosis to absorb some of the poison from their pens.

Critical essays are an expression of conviction. A person can be convinced of almost anything. On the shallowest level, skin-deep opinion fluctuates depending upon who is doing the convincing. Perhaps the best example of this is a couple out on their first date. She speaks, and he listens with rapt attention, nodding agreement with everything.

The second level deals with matters very important to a person. These opinions are much harder to change. On the second date our sample couple is more relaxed, so they begin to talk about more personal matters. Now when she speaks, he sometimes disagrees. She convinces him, however, because he weighs what she says and how he feels about her against his opinion. He decides in her favor.

The deepest level of a person's opinion gets at the core of the inner man, where built-in beliefs and value systems are guarded. Morals, politics, and religion are probably surrounded by the most impenetrable walls. She speaks, he disagrees, and he never calls her again.

Because of the difficulty of changing a person's opinion on

things that matter most, the expression of conviction can be as effective a literary tool as you can find. In the critical essay we express our opinions and show people how we got there. Opinionated articles which coerce the reader do not convince him; on the contrary, they alienate him, solidifying his own views.

To sum up the logical approach, let me give you some examples:

INFORMAL ESSAY
ELECT SNOOPY PRESIDENT

PROS

widely respected
been around awhile
loves children
kisses babies
immune to praise
wants no money
understands hardship
no prejudice
eager to please

CONS

he's a dog (but dogs are man's best friend)
can't talk (but that would go a long way toward keeping him out of trouble)
has some enemies (but by and large most people love him)

Conclusion: There may indeed be a few who might refuse to vote on grounds of incompatibility, but by and large the majority would agree a finer President could not be found. Yes! By all means, elect Snoopy President!

CRITICAL ESSAY
PROBLEM/SOLUTION OR DILEMMA/DECISION

You need a new car. Should you buy one?

PROS

1. Present car eleven years old
2. 114,000 miles on it
3. Rusting out
4. Seat covers torn
5. Only junky car at office
6. Upholstery needs repair
7. Ashamed of it sometimes
8. Big repair bills ahead
9. Might have some trade-in value if you act now

CONS

1. Old, but runs like a Cadillac
2. Trouble-free, repair bills small
3. But just one fender
4. Uses very little gas
5. Slant six engine has good reputation
6. New tires on it
7. Love the car and hate to change

Conclusion: It would appear that there are numerous reasons for buying a new car, but it seems wiser to run the old one until it falls apart. The reasons for keeping the old one are fewer but stronger. Here's how you would arrive at that conclusion:

If it has some trade-in value, it probably isn't much; a year from now it will be about the same. Many car dealers will make a deal with you if you have to *tow* your old one in. At 114,000 miles, a trouble-free slant six has at least 35,000 miles left in it. And it has new tires.

Numbers 3-7 can be remedied at a much lower cost than that of buying a new car. With those minor body and upholstery repairs it wouldn't look junky, so you wouldn't be ashamed of it. You could also wash the car now and then!

One of these days it *will* give out, but that might be a year or two away. When the big repair bills hit, tow it in and barter for a new one.

Using the method of reasoning to convince can be applied to almost everything you may choose to write about. In this type of an article, you become the salesman, and you could become quite good at it. There was the car salesman, you know, who suggested writing down the pros and cons on paper so his customer could see it in black and white. The salesman quickly jotted down fourteen reasons the customer should buy the car, and then with a winning smile he handed the paper to the customer. "Do you know any reason why you should not?" he asked.

Since almost every publisher you plan to approach with a query requests an outline, this chapter should be read and studied again and again, until you have thoroughly digested it. Haphazard outlines muddle up the writer's mind and nauseate busy editors. You must learn to present a strong outline. Once you have picked your approach (topical, chronological, spatial, or logical)—and you know *why* you have chosen it—creating the outline will be relatively easy.

CREATING THE OUTLINE

Are you ready to go? An outline is a skeletal form of the article you plan to write. It's the artist's rough sketch, the architect's design, the cook's recipe, the builder's plan. It's the picture on the cover of the puzzle box, except that the picture is in the writer's mind. Putting your thoughts down in order helps you to see that you have all the parts for a well-rounded article, and it helps you to decide what comes first, what fits together, where to put it, and what material you will use to conclude the article.

If you have your mental organization done properly, you should have notes, research results obtained thus far, and your own scribbled thoughts on the subject. When you sit down to begin, you may feel as if you are facing a puzzle, and all you can hope is that none of the pieces are missing. They might be! As you organize, and even later as you write and rewrite, new ideas worth pursuing may come to mind. To begin:

1. Turn all the pieces face up.
2. Separate into various piles those that match, using the outline as guide.
3. See how many seem to fit nicely together, as if that is where they belong.

In a puzzle, one usually searches for the corner pieces and builds on them. In an article, it's the beginning, the middle, and the end that count. Organizing (perhaps on scribble paper following your outline if not with heaps of notes) requires that you define your main points and look for your connecting links so that the transitions can be smoothly made. You begin in the middle. What is it you want to say?

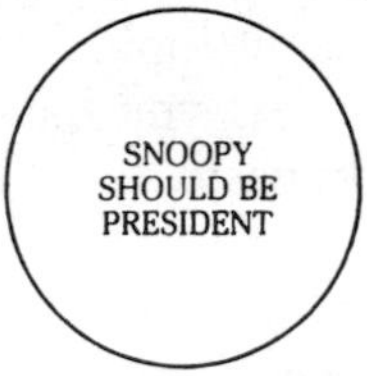
SNOOPY
SHOULD BE
PRESIDENT

To lead your audience to that central thought, you'll have to present certain arguments. For simplicity, let's think of three—but they must be three very strong reasons to elect him. Check back to my Snoopy essay notes to find these reasons. You, as the writer, decide for yourself what will be the focal points, and your decision must be made after thinking over what you can say about each point to build your convincing argument:

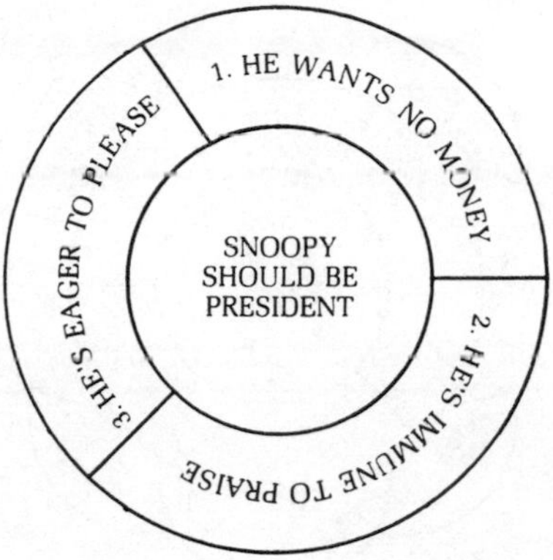

In the initial thinking stage of your outline, it's important to list the cons, as well as the pros. You will notice that I picked the three high points from my pro list, and we'll use the other factors to strengthen and embellish them.

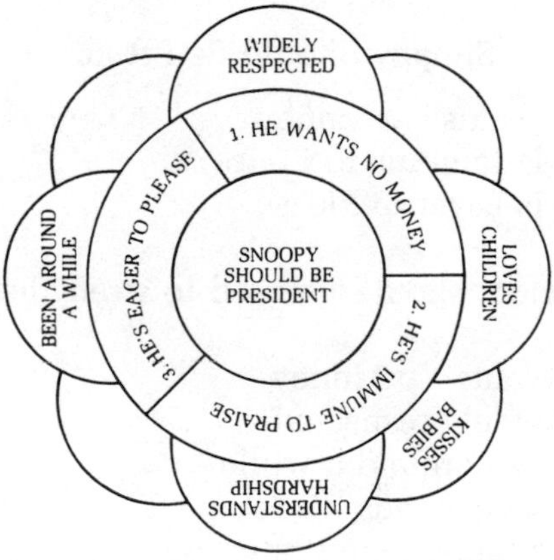

The three cons I had to admit when thinking through my proposed article appear to be dark blotches on Snoopy's record. 1) He's a dog (we've never had one for President before). 2) He can't talk (how could he make speeches?). 3) He has some enemies (a bad start, since he's bound to make more). The voting public knows dogs well, and they know Snoopy in particular, so we can't cover up these flaws. The only thing we can do is to admit them, then turn them into advantages:

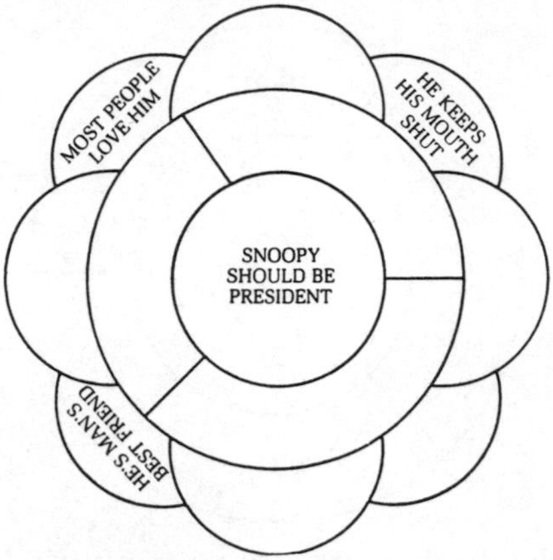

We're working our way out to the border, and we're about to start jotting down the highlights in outline form. Highlights to be considered:

Snoopy Should Be President

I. He Wants No Money
II. He Is Immune to Praise
III. He Is Eager to Please

Lesser factors should be used to strengthen the article or story:

- I. He Wants No Money
  - A. Widely respected
  - B. Been around a while
  - C. Understands hardship
- II. He Is Immune to Praise
  - A. Most people love him
    1. Man's best friend (anecdote—give an example)
    2. Can't talk, which keeps him out of trouble (anecdote—relate a prime example of his opponents' foot-in-mouth disease)
  - B. He Is Eager to Please
    1. Loves children
    2. Kisses babies (statistics could be used here)

The "outline and query letters" that arrive at any editor's desk are samples from which he will choose manuscripts he hopes to buy. Clarity is extremely important: What are you driving at? How do you plan to make this clear to your reader? Other deciding factors in the editor's mind are smooth, careful writing, proper sentence construction, good grammar and spelling, and reader appeal. Your outline cannot be a scribbled rough. By the time you have finished the successful outline, your article should be well in mind, and one glance at it by an expert eye should convince the buying editor that you can produce the kind of article he wants.

To round out the points of your outline and clarify your meaning, you need to ask yourself questions the editor will be asking:

1. Widely respected? By whom? How far from home? Why is he widely respected? What has he done to earn this respect?

2. Been around a while? What do you mean by that? Around where? And how long? Is he really old enough to have the experience needed to serve as President? On the other hand, perhaps he's too old? Is he old enough to make wise plans, and young enough to execute them?

3. Understands what kind of hardship? What advantage would that experience be in the Oval Office?

You probably get the picture. Answering questions of this nature as you build your outline will round out a nice, convincing paragraph under each main point; a paragraph which will in turn give you opportunity to display your writing talent and organizational ability. In addition, some of the anecdotes you might use will come to mind, and you can incorporate the gist of major anecdotes into the outline. The reader appeal comes in part from your focal points, and in part from the illustrations you plan to use to back up what you are saying. Anecdotes form a border around the piece, giving it a finished look. In this case, we want to create an "I feel good about Snoopy" atmosphere, so the anecdotes need to show his finest qualities, as well as back up the points they are meant to strengthen.

Snoopy won first prize at the dog show, but he let the children keep the prizes. The children meant more to him than money.

When a little girl dropped ice cream on her new shoes, Snoopy quickly licked it off before it had a chance to stain.

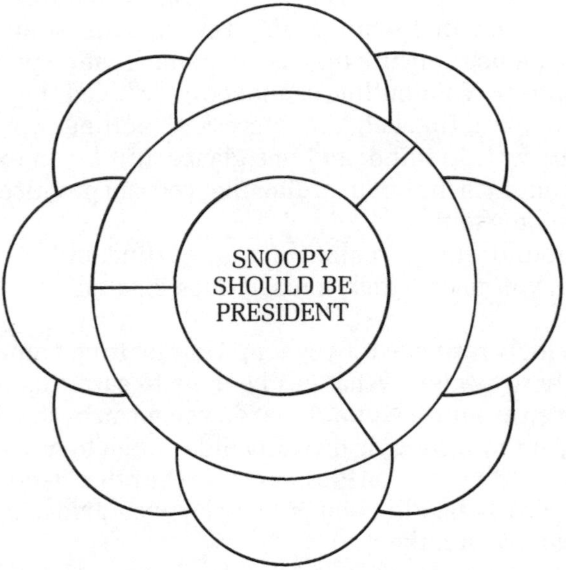
SNOOPY
SHOULD BE
PRESIDENT

When the boys needed a baseball glove, Snoopy ran and got one from the yard of a new kid on the block, so the kid got to play, too.

Snoopy barked for Lucy to get the child she was babysitting off the street. When she came to praise him, he was sound asleep.

The outline is your road map, and although you may want to take detours and sideline excursions along the way, a wise writer has thought the article through so carefully that he can follow the outline, sticking to it diligently, though not at all rigidly. Creativity is at work all the time, gathering anecdotes, preparing surveys, sparking ideas. The outline simply ropes it all in so the writer can put it on paper with coherence as he adds the colors to make it come alive.

WE'RE READY TO WRITE!

We've said that the first sentence must grab the attention of the first editor who reads your article. The lead paragraph is so often buried by amateurs that I like to say a person who finds it and puts it in place has turned professional. A pro knows the value of a good hook. The hook snares potential buyers of written material, as well as potential readers, and one that is dull or bent all out of shape just won't do the job. Worst of all, most beginners' hooks have been lost in the shuffle of material. You will find them hidden somewhere in the middle of the article as sharp and shiny as if they were brand-new.

What makes a good beginning?

1. A startling statement: a "zinger."

If you can come up with a humdinger of a zinger, you're in. Zingers, jolting statements practically guaranteed to catch the eye of anyone who glances at the page, are true hooks, because their concise, catchy, clever intrigue draws the reader into the article almost before he realizes it. The first sentence of this paragraph might work as a zinger. You do a double take when you see a good zinger. In this case, one might think: A zinger? What's a zinger? and be drawn into reading one. Begin looking for zingers in top magazines and newspapers, and you will see what I mean.

Not all zingers are clever plays on words; in fact one needs to be careful not to fall into the trap of being too cute. Other possible zingers would be:

> Children who visited the zoo last week were exposed to a rare virus—the contagious laughter of a newly acquired hyena from Australia.
>
> After midnight, one driver out of four is drunk.
>
> This year Santa is going to steal some of the gifts and keep them for himself. (Computer games are too much fun to give away.)

The zinger wakes up the reader, aggravates him, entices him, startles him, or makes him laugh. It grabs his attention by surprising him in some way.

2. Key information.

In newswriting, key information would include "the five W's and an H."

> **Who?** (senior citizens who used to eat their meals alone at home)
> **What?** (are now transported)
> **Where?** (to Community Hall)
> **When?** (every day at noon)
> **Why?** (to share a wholesome meal with a friendly group of peers)
> **How?** (thanks to the Federal Government's meals for the elderly program)

The five W's introduction works very well with many articles, for it helps the writer focus on the subject at hand while introducing the reader to the article's content. The same article might begin with a zinger: "Sometimes Van Baker feels more like somebody's grandson than the veteran taxi driver that he is. Van is one of ten cab drivers hired by the Federal Government to transport senior citizens to their daily dinners at Community Hall." (The Federal Government hires cab drivers for that? Hey, I've got to read this and find out more . . .)

3. Definition of the subject.

Sometimes this has been called the "summary lead approach," because it summarizes the subject in the first sentence:

> The laughing hyena purchased from the Sydney Zoo arrived from Australia last Thursday and is welcoming visitors at the main building of the Grand Old Zoo, where it is temporarily housed.

4. The question.

A question introducing an article is meant to entice readers to plunge in to discover the answer:

> How many middle-aged women reading this article will die of cancer in the next ten years?

5. The anecdote.

If one were to pursue the leash law article introduced earlier, the story of the puppy hit by a car would be a good place to start. As an introduction, this anecdote explains to the reader why the author feels as she does: "My son's puppy was hit by a car, and it needn't have happened."

KEEPING ON TRACK

A strong, well-formed outline makes writing a good article fairly easy. Following it keeps one from rambling, and—if the writer is at all like me—guards against leaving out choice thoughts which tend either to be drowned in the outpouring of ideas that flow when one begins to write, or to be buried and overlooked in the stacks of notes. Many times I have realized too late that my favorite illustration fell behind the desk or was lost in the shuffle of paper and never made it into the article.

To keep on track, asking oneself questions along the way is helpful.

1. What is this sentence about? Is this where it fits?
2. What is this paragraph about? Does it belong under this point in the outline?
3. What is this section about.? Why am I including this illustration? Does it fit?
4. What is the article about? Why am I saying this? Does it fit?

Coming at it from the other angle is important too.

1. There seems to be something missing here. What could I add to make it more complete?
2. This transition is too abrupt (or vague). How can I move more smoothly from here to there?
3. I wonder if a stranger reading this would know what I mean to say? How can I clarify this?

In the first instance, you will often find something to remove or switch to some other section or paragraph, while in the second, you will see things you might add to make the meaning more clear. Scissors and Scotch tape play an important part in my writing. When I say I whack out a paragraph, I often mean just that: I take the scissors and whack it out, scotch-taping small pieces onto larger sheets to keep them from getting lost, and cutting apart full pages to insert (by pasting in) paragraphs from some other page.

Transitions, extremely important, are connecting links determined by division of thought, sudden change of thought, or new thoughts being introduced or interjected. Transitional sentences decades and even centuries old are still acceptable:

—We've discussed________; now let's consider ________.
—This brings us to ________.
—But let us lay aside that problem and turn to ________.

Creative writers, however, can pull a huge variety of transitions from the air, moving from one thought to the next without announcing that they plan to do so. Smooth, unobtrusive transitions allow the flow of thought to go on uninterrupted. This is an important consideration, because every time a reader's mind has a chance, it tends to escape. The best transitions are more than well-oiled hinges that allow the door to open without a squeak; they are open arches with an intriguing view beyond, so inviting that the reader steps through and goes on reading, unaware of the enticement that compelled him to do so. A transition can be a word or two, just an inviting phrase, or even a paragraph or several paragraphs in a long article, which lead the reader along a path so pleasant he can't bear to stop, or so startling he is forced to continue.

For an example of switching gears within the article, let's go back to Snoopy. Let's imagine that we have been discussing in the paragraph at hand the fact that a dog is man's best friend—a good reason to elect him, since what we need in the White House is a Real Friend.

> Now I know what you're thinking. How can we elect a dog President? He can't talk.

> You are so right. A dog *can't* talk. Perhaps that's just the reason we ought to elect a dog. Heaven knows we've had Presidents who talked too much!

This puts you into the new subject, the problem of Presidents who put their foot in their mouth (which dogs do only when a flea gets between their toes).

Illustrations and anecdotes carefully chosen and strategically placed add interest, clarify, prove, and strengthen one's writing. One key value of the anecdote is its use in transitions, because most people can't resist reading a story, especially a clever, short vignette. Contrasts and comparisons also serve as transitional tools. Narrative is a sequence of connected actions. One must remember, though, that the reader was not around when the action took place, so the writer needs to draw word pictures to show how it really was. This is description, and without it one's writing lacks strength enough to hold on to the audience so cleverly captured.

How are good word pictures drawn? The best way I know is to imagine your readers as an audience given opportunity to ask questions. Whether you are addressing one person or one thousand, it's nice to stop talking long enough to check the response. Are their faces blank? Are they restless, looking at their watches, yawning? Are they snoring? Do you envision them closing the magazine on your precious article, laying it down, and reaching for the latest *TV Guide*? Heaven forbid!

As you read over what you have written, give your imaginary audience a chance to talk back a bit. If you could get a response from your readers, they might ask such questions as

> "How is that done?"
> "What did the people look like?"
> "Who is so and so?"
> "What do you mean by ________?"
> 'What is the truth about ________?
> "What sort of a place (or day) was it?"

As you imagine readers' questions, you will find yourself forced to answer them adequately, which might mean

1. clarifying statements
2. using more description
3. finding better illustrations
4. choosing more suitable vocabulary

None of these requires as much sweat as dealing with structural problems. To answer readers' questions properly, you may have to give more background, present more logical arguments, or prove what you have said. Tackling any of these problems is worth the trouble. It might change a weak article into one strong enough to sell.

Pomposity—ostentation—is one of the writer's worst enemies. As you write, keep in mind that the desire to impress people was not one of the accepted reasons for choosing your subject and writing about it. Eye level contact with the reader is the rule: If you know too little, learn more; if you know too much, use an approach and a vocabulary that appeals to the rest of us.

WHEN IT'S TIME TO STOP

Earlier I mentioned articles which had no head, a misshapen body, and no feet. The well-written article has healthy feet, not necessarily big ones, but feet adequate to do the job. The article stands or falls on the conclusion. It cannot leave the reader dangling, wondering what in the world was the point of all those fine words.

Coming to the end of an article is like coming to the end of a trip. I like a conclusion that leaves my readers hoping we will meet again. Any number of emotions may be created by the conclusion: excitement, gratification, nostalgia, fear, challenge, or surprise.

I shall never forget reaching the end of the line when I first crossed the Atlantic Ocean from New York to Casablanca. As I told you, I had nine days on board—days of adventure, but days of anticipation as well, for I was leaving our familiar shores to embark on a new life in a different world. We finally neared our destination, drawing close enough to shore to see the white-washed buildings of the city shining in the morning sun, but we were forced to drop anchor for hours, awaiting clearance from the port authority before moving in to dock. Meanwhile, Arab merchants in tiny boats paddled out to entice us with their wares, offering as well to help us down out of the freighter into their rowboats to paddle us back to shore.

Casablanca! How I wish I could adequately describe the ancient old Mediterranean seaport to you! First of all, Casablanca is an immense city, containing more than a million and a half people crammed into a relatively small area. Secondly, it is a beautiful, modern city. Spacious streets in the new downtown area are lined with department stores, businesses, and apartment buildings. Highrise apartments are replacing the shacky tin-towns on the outskirts of the city, and closer in, old French villas with walled-in yards are wrapped with bright fuchsia bougainvillea vines in bloom almost all year around. Villa neighborhoods are a photographer's dream world when poinsettia bushes six to eight feet tall are in bloom in almost every yard. Such a villa would be a writer's paradise!

But the real Casablanca is the kasbah, where huge cement homes are jammed together, joined wall to wall, their front doorsteps opening directly onto the damp, clammy city streets, dark and cool and even on the hottest days, for rarely a ray of sunshine reaches them. None of the homes have back doors, nor are there any windows, except for tiny peepholes from which one may peek at passersby or check to see who might be banging the great brass knockers.

Large modern stores are not nearly so picturesque as the antiquated cubbyhole shops where turbaned merchants haggle over prices with veiled housewives. On an average morning, crowds trundle along together, body to body, in a year-round Christmas shopping atmosphere, pushing their way goodnaturedly through narrow cobblestone streets in an easygoing effort to make purchases, conduct business, and arrive back at their homes in time for a leisurely lunch and siesta.

From the flat rooftops—ancient version of the patio—one

sees the skyline of mosques towering high above the homes; and one looks down on the jostling crowds trundling to and fro. I love the kasbah in any Middle-Eastern country, and I know what it is like.

That the set for the 1940s movie *Casablanca* was designed and created within a studio amazes me, for it is realistic enough to have been filmed on location in the grand old city itself. You see the coffee shops, hear the din of the bustling crowds, feel the intrigue—almost smell the blend of shishkabob smoke, mint tea, spices, new leather, and wood shavings.

That the old World War II love story lives on after forty years amazes many people. That the script was written piecemeal, often leaving the cast wondering what their lines might be the next day, amazes veteran writers, and yet it was, according to Harry Reasoner of CBS' *60 Minutes*. It is said no one was sure how the story would end, but three conclusions were written. The first one to be filmed was so beautiful the others were laid aside and not used.

Successful endings rarely happen that easily! You might compose several conclusions to your article before you finally mail it, but choosing your purpose and selecting your angle, focus, slant, approach, and transitions should have carried you along to a natural ending which probably surfaced as you were preparing your outline. Maybe you chose to follow the advice of the old writer who said you introduce your article by "telling them what you plan to tell them; then [in the body] you tell them." If so, you can conclude by telling them what you told them!

A satisfying conclusion lets the reader know you have finished. You've exhausted the subject, he understands your purpose, and he is winding down with you, expecting you to end.

While you probably don't want to say "The moral to the story is . . . ," a moral to the story, unannounced, is a fine conclusion. So is your opinion, which you can give without saying "I think so and so." One can also end with a question or with a challenge.

We need to move on to a discussion of fiction writing. I'm dying to do it, and if I don't watch out, I'll run out of time and space. I haven't mentioned the punch line conclusion as yet. It's sometimes abrupt, but fairly effective:

When the time has come to stop, stop.

ASSIGNMENT 9

Are you ready to rough out an article?
Your subject? ______________________
The purpose of your article? ______________________
The scope of your coverage? ______________________
Your angle? ______________________
Slanted to whom? ______________________
The approach? ______________________
Conclusion: your clincher? ______________________
If you did assignments 5-7, you probably have at least one article in mind. The purpose of this assignment is to practice planning articles; so choose a subject, think it through, and make a brief outline:

Purpose: ______________________
Pattern of organization: ______________________

Introduction:

I.
a.
b.
II.
a.
b.
III.
a.
b.

Conclusion: ______________________

Like practicing piano scales, making a new outline and polishing the old ones each time you settle down to spend time writing is a dandy habit. It enables you to improve your skills; and think of the wealth of article skeletons you'll be storing away. If you do enough of it, you'll need to add a third category to your GOOD and GARBAGE files—one labeled OUTLINES!

10 The Spinning of Yarns

To spin a good yarn, you have to like stories and something of the child within you must be set free. Interestingly enough, as we grow older, freeing the child becomes easier. It doesn't take much to test this phenomenon; just get together with buddies from your tour of military duty or a group of high school friends you haven't seen in a long time. The cool reserve of the parent/boss role you've assumed over the years can melt in a hurry as you giggle over silly jokes and recall foolish incidents dug up out of the past. I watched one group of happy people play "Pin the Tail on the Donkey," laughing and shouting like ten-year-olds at a birthday party, and I almost collapsed with laughter when one of them, a retired businessman, threw himself on the floor pretending to have a tantrum because he didn't win! He was the life of any party, never became senile, and was written up in the suburban paper when he remarried at the age of eighty!

The ability to revert to childhood works to the advantage of the writer, because as a child he must be capable of showing his emotions; view life objectively; accept people, creatures, and situations with candor; and spontaneously record, with the accuracy of candid camera, what he sees, hears, feels, smells, and experiences. This means living life to the fullest, as a child does, giving it all the gusto you've got.

If you'll join me mentally in the back hall of a country house, I'll show you what I mean. We're visiting from the city, decked out in fancy garb totally unsuited to the activity our hosts have planned for us, so we need, first of all, to borrow outfits. Let's share what we find: somebody's old wool socks, a couple of pairs each. When you slip one on, we discover it has a hole in the toe. We laugh hilariously over that. One of mine has, too. More loud laughter. The feet of the socks are long enough to fold the holes up across our toes and cover them with a second sock. No time to worry about how anything looks; that it feels good is what's important. Somebody hands us bib overalls way too big. We pull them on, trying to figure out how the buckles work. You look sober as a judge, lower lip sticking out and brow furrowed.

Khaki rubber boots (smelling slightly of both barn and feet) are pulled on. You've got to tuck the pantlegs in by folding the legs and holding them down as you put the boots on, the way we used to fold over our longjohns under our long, brown cotton stockings. Warm wool jackets (same homey odor)—one for me, one for you. They appear roomy enough to be comfortable. Nubby wool scarves for our heads, two each. It's about fifteen below out there, so wrap one of them around your chin and pull it up over your nose. More uproarious guffaws. Mittens—two pairs each.

Now! We're decked out like a couple of spacemen, toddling like snowsuited three-year-olds, legs apart, arms sticking out. Ready to go?

The toboggan we're towing behind us isn't empty. (How did we get stuck with pulling it?) Kids are rolling off and jumping back on; dogs barking with glee jump over it or on it for a short ride before being shoved off. A snowball hits me square in the back, so I drop the rope and give chase. Amid laughter and panting, I fall at last onto the toboggan. I'm trying to catch my breath when you yell some obscene remarks about my tonnage. I get up on my feet for another chase, but you stumble over your big boots and tumble into a heap in the soft, snowy path.

Writers must be participants instead of spectators. They must know what it feels like to pile on an eight-foot toboggan snug as berries in a jar of jam. How can they describe the exhilaration as the last one in line gives a shove before boarding with a loud whoop of joy, if they have never experienced it? They must know the sound of the slick, waxed wood whizzing down the steep hill. They must be able to re-create the scene as it was when, moments later, yelling like fools, the tobogganers—amid shouts, noses running—disentangled themselves to plod back up the hill to do it again.

If tobogganning is so foreign to you that an afternoon on a Wisconsin farm leaves you cranky and cold, you might try creating a happy experience of your own. You could join a gang of children as they take turns grabbing a rope swing, and thrill to the excitement churning in your stomach as you fly out over the swimming hole, let go, and plunge into the river. You might get up off the hot, sandy beach to join the surfers riding the mammoth waves, daring the ocean to shove you off your board to dunk you into her foamy wake.

Whatever it takes to shake you out of the confining mold encasing your soul, do it, at least mentally, because although your body may remain dignified and your facial expression may never change, to write publishable fiction, you must become emotionally involved. Your mind and soul must be set free, and the best way to do this is to free the child within.

One night my eyes popped open with that finality which told me in no uncertain terms that I was not going to go back to sleep. I knew it was pointless to lie on the bed tossing and turning, so I turned on the light, reached for my trusty scratch pad and pen, and started to write. A beautiful story poured out. The plot was clever, the characters had life, the descriptions put the reader right into the scene, the climax was surprising, and the conclusion was satisfying. When I was done I laid down the tablet and pen, turned out the light, and fell back into a sound sleep. In the morning I looked at my story with amazement. It was very good.

That's the beauty of writing fiction. What else can you do lying in bed propped up with pillows—no research, no interviews, no effort? The words pelt onto the paper like raindrops. You scribble out the plot, pull characters from the storehouse of your mind, step into their skin, move around in their world, think their thoughts, enjoy their happiness, experience their frustration, and cry their tears.

Stories are conceived in so many ways one can scarcely trace a pattern. It isn't at all uncommon for a good story to be born suddenly during the night, because fiction is fantasy. The elves of the mind arise out of the subconscious to play all sorts of games while a person is asleep, busily creating fascinating scenes, scooting back to their hidden caves when the alarm goes off. Now and then a person recalls activity of dreams and wakes up laughing, crying, screaming, sad, pensive, troubled, unaware of the elves who have been at work forming the mood. Often when the body has been put to bed at night the mind refuses to go to sleep because of busy, creative thoughts. Creativity may lie dormant during busy working hours, for the elves are too timid to come forth, afraid of being trampled, or they are told by the conscious to stay in the cave.

Civilizations go through cycles that deeply affect a nation's creativity. The minds of children are trained to think war, to think science, to think space, to think education, to think financial success. In the past few decades, well-meaning parents have so ordered the lives of their little ones with lessons, sports, clubs, and other planned activities, that the children have had no time to think for themselves—nor have the parents, harassed as they are, synchronizing the schedules. Even during "free time," minds are entertained and brainwashed. I bleed inside to see people dashing around shopping centers week after week, wanting this and that, absorbing false values so harmful to the aesthetic mind. Between stops, adults sigh that they are too, too busy, and teens pace the floor when there is nothing on TV worth watching. Children don't even spend their carefree preschool years with imaginative thoughts. They march off to organized group activities before they are potty-trained, not because their parents are at work, but to prepare their minds for twenty-first century survival.

Fortunately some minds rebel against community control. The majority will need to know how to operate twenty-first century computerized life, but some minds must remain free to dream, to plan, to invent, to paint, to compose, and to write. Letting one's rebellion get out of hand serves one's own purposes poorly, of course, so a certain amount of regulation in childhood is important to setting a good pattern for adult life and for learning valuable disciplines. Even the imagination must be corralled to be of any value. However, as we pointed out in Chapter 2, the writer, especially the fiction writer, must be allowed to dream. *You must relax!* Have fun, loaf in the sun, and still consider yourself hard at work!

I've always been a dreamer, creating situations in my mind with talkative people to populate them. The first story I had published brought me the huge prize of one dollar. I hadn't intended to become a writer, nor did I think of myself as one after the first-place story hit the front page of the high school paper. A sophomore in my first semester, I supposed no one else in the student body of 1,500 had been interested in entering the contest. The publicity of winning embarrassed me, but I was glad my story was good enough to fill the space in the paper, and I was delighted to get the dollar. No one in the family kept a copy of the story. After all, what's a story? All you do is find a paper and pencil, and spin a yarn.

Storytelling probably began around the world's first campfire. Storytellers in primitive cultures today are still the best in the world, and from them we learn the basic ingredients of a good story: suspense, excitement, humor, realism, variety, action, and surprise. Civilized readers, your audience, demand the same quality of entertainment.

Your idea of good fiction may be worlds apart from mine, but if we closely examined our differences of opinion, we would find our taste varying as to content, not quality. In spinning a yarn, content may go a million different directions. Quality good enough to spellbind an audience, however, is universal, regardless of content or length. Because of this, I hope as a result of reading this chapter you will do three things:

1. Become an avid reader of the type of fiction you want to write—mainstream, mystery, romance, western, science fiction, didactic, fantasy, allegorical, propagandist—whatever interests you.
2. Apply the principles of quality writing explained in this chapter.
3. Keep writing. Don't stop with one story, waiting for it to sell before starting another. Churn out the stories one after the other, finding some kind of audience to test them on. Always keep another plot waiting in the wings.

If you have all the ingredients, writing a story is easy:

1. An idea, a small one, perhaps, but strong enough to build on.
2. A plot, strong, clearly defined.
3. A theme which runs through the story, creating unity.
4. Characters that live and interact.
5. An environment that others can envision.
6. Action to keep the story moving, and suspense to liven it up.
7. A distinctive mood that satisfies the emotions.

Mix the ingredients, blending them with an ample measurement of narrative. Decorate with vivid description and spicy dialogue—*et voila*! You've spun a yarn!

THE IDEA

Speaking of timidity in Chapter 1, I referred to Charles Dickens' "The Holly Tree," and I suggested that he might have begun the story musing about his own bashfullness. Whether this is so or not, I do not know, but ideas spring from such simple sources. One could think things through, instead, as Poe claimed he did, scientifically weighing all factors until the perfect foundation for a story has been found and the skeletal structure has been set in place. Nathaniel Hawthorne excelled in structure building (and Poe praised his craftsmanship). Throughout Hawthorne's writing one can follow the unity of his outline, the interweaving of characters' lives, and the action which traces his plan and develops his plot.

While Dickens was extremely skillful at creating fictitious characters by piece-mealing people, Hawthorne's stories contained recognizable characters with events good and bad from his own life. His stories were didactic, meant to teach something (his opinions showed through); they were moralistic (his religious beliefs were more orthodox than those of his friends Emerson and Thoreau); and they were allegorical (he cleverly created symbols to disguise the meaning, making his moralistic lessons more palatable). One might assume from reading between the lines that Hawthorne's ideas germinated, at least in part, from a desire to make his opinions known, hoping to convince others to mend their ways. Doing so is not always bad. Teaching and admonishing through fiction can be done so cleverly that the reader sees no reason to object. Hawthorne, preaching on paper, wrote some of the greatest American fiction of his era.

Kipling, born a lover of words, seems to have bubbled over with ideas which pelted onto the paper in whatever literary form suited his mood. His idea well never ran dry. Perhaps his early exposure to storytellers of India gave him an edge on the rest of us. Although Kipling's parents sent him to England for some of his education, he was back in India by age seventeen, and as an editor, at that. His story ideas were fresh, his stories full of life, his narrative rich, his dialogue down to earth, and his stories exuded the atmosphere of their settings as few stories can do.

Children can spark ideas. In discussing our writing options (Chapter 6), I mentioned both Longfellow's and Stevenson's ability to switch from adult writing to verse for and about little children. Stevenson's *Treasure Island* began as a game for his stepson, developed into a magazine serial, and eventually became the superb novel we know today.

It's rarely a setting that sparks a story idea for me. A good friend of mine in Morocco lived with her elderly husband in a natural cave on an isolated hillside overlooking a town, a cave so deep she had never explored beyond the first bend. Dope smugglers wanted the cave, so one dark night they sneaked up the hill and set fire to combustible belongings at the entrance. Fortunately, the old man knew of a tunnel, through which they could escape.

An incident is more apt to spark an idea for me than a setting. In my mind, a cave is a cave. Back streets of Naples, Genoa, and Marseille; beaches of the Mediterranean; the Riviera, Palma de Majorca, the Canary Islands; a night train speeding through France; Mexican villages, cathedrals of Spain; castles of Germany: none of these exotic settings have helped me one iota as a hook to hang a story on. Similarly, I view people simply as potential characters; but what happends to a person—an incident—lights the fire. "Eureka! I've got it!" I think, as I carefully fold up the idea and tuck it away in my mind.

Even as I wrote that thought, I recalled one exception. In 1966 I was asked to write ten or twelve stories about Morocco which would be suitable for telling to children. A deadline was set for the booklet to be released, so it was not possible for me to wait for inspiration. Most of the stories were based on children I knew, using their environments as the settings. I had only to create fictitious incidents to round out the stories, somewhat of a backwards approach for me.

Often a setting does spark an idea, of course. My children's story "The Lonely Dragon" is a good example of this. An incident might have been a contributing factor, but the story is so far removed from the actual event that no one could see the connection.

One evening as I drove into our small town, a basset hound stepped out into the highway just as I rounded the bend. I brake for bassets, so tragedy was avoided. However, as I drove away I realized the dog was a stray and would surely be killed before the evening was over if it were left to wander around the center of town where traffic is heavy. I went back to get the dog, took it home, ran an ad in the paper, and after a few days, located the owners.

You can imagine that a short-legged, long-eared hound, added to my team of sheepdogs, caused some comment in the town. Various people told me they had seen the dog on a busier highway early in the day on which I found her. Apparently she made her way into town and wandered from home to home looking for someone to take her in. Since all the residents of Avondale have all the dogs they need, no one had room for "Dreamer."

Several days after the basset was back in its own home, one foggy morning I sat with my feet on the windowsil sipping coffee. Slowly, dawn crept over the hill and trees wrapped in gray mist began to take on eerie forms. I began to think that surely some fictional character ought to rise up out of that spooky setting.

Something did take shape. I saw it arise, and I said to it, "Hang on; don't go away! let me find a pencil and paper, so I can get this down in black and white."

It was a dragon, not a dog, lost and lonely. No morning mist surrounded it, because by the time Mary Ann and her cat found it in the woods, it was almost noon. They spent the rest of the day trying to find a home for it, and finally they did.

Words, very simple ones are excellent sources of ideas. What do you think of when you hear the word "snake?" Incidents come to mind—snake stories I would love to tell when you have more time. But you—what do you think? Do you think of more words?

snake
Texas
rattlesnake
knife
camp
fear
courage
scream
torture
rescue
revenge
woman

One can play any word game long enough to come up with a story idea.

> books, loves books, ideas intrigue
> read, can't read well, wants to
> pages, turns them, flips them, fondles them
> words, blurred words, angry words, puzzling words
> teacher, young, nervous, caring, kind

I have a friend (an honest man, fortunately) who by putting his ear to a locked safe can "hear" the combination, and open it. Doing the word exercise is something like that. The words are only words scribbled on paper until suddenly you hear a vague "plunk" few others can hear. Excited, you go on turning over words until—presto!—the safe flies open revealing a beautiful story idea.

Ideas abound. Newspapers, magazines, comments by friends or passersby, letters in the mail (or no letters in the mail), memories of the past, thoughts about the future, advertisements, photos, purchases, places, experiences, mysteries, sounds, inventions, dreams—all these and many more tantalize the fiction writer, who never needs to wonder long what to write about.

A serious writer contemplates his immense source of story possibilities and jots down idea nuggets, along with any thoughts that accompany it. For example, one might hear on TV about an inner city bill collector. "*Hmmm,*" one thinks. "Bill collector." For a moment your mind recalls your bills and a feeling of panic sweeps over you. What would it be like to have a bill collector after you? Suddenly the elves of fantasy jump out of their cave. A bill collector! Good character for a story! The telecast becomes a blur as the mind goes to work:

1. Thought of using him in a story.
2. This led to thinking about what it would be like to have him stalking you, which . . .
3. Led to wondering what he was like, which . . .
4. Made you wonder what his job was like and . . .

5. What kind of neighborhoods he worked in, as well as . . .
6. What kinds of clients he had.
Then the question arises, "Was there some special client who would become a heroine?" Before you know it, you have a story!

Or do you? What is happening? What emotions are being shown? And by whom?

The newscast that provided the idea is still drumming on, although you quit listening five minutes ago. You have your story idea, and now you need a framework to build on.

THE PLOT

The bill collector rings the bell; he's overwhelmed by the charming widow who comes to the door, and . . .

Horrors, no! Originality means coming up with a new angle! Certainly someone could appear at a stranger's door. You might let it be a bill collector. But make it different; let's say, a homely young woman, instead of a macho man. She gets involved—but not with a man—with a lonely old lady. After overcoming immense obstacles the bill collector finds out the old lady is wealthy. However (an obstacle to the hoped-for inheritance), a grand-nephew turns up unexpectedly. Luckily he falls in love wih the heroine, who marries him. All is set for a happily-ever-after ending the truth comes out: The old lady is a pauper, the nephew is a fraud, and the bill collector is stuck with the two of them, responsible for all the bills.

A story can be as simple as one in which two characters who do not get along with each other are placed in a situation where their differences must be reconciled. They must learn to live together. The *plot* is people in conflict and resolution of that conflict. In the absence of struggle, there is no plot. There is only a plan, an idea which must be developed further.

Two questions must be answered as one plans a plot: What is the story about, and whom is it about? Let me give you some steps I used to prepare a close-to-deadline story (the kind I usually seem to write!).

1. Who will be in the spotlight? Whom is the story about?
2. What other characters will there be?
3. What kind of environment are they in? Where are they?

At this point, one needs to stop and get acquainted with the characters and setting, because the next step is to pick out from their humdrum everyday life something worth writing about. Fictional characters are people (or animals, or creatures); you must get to know them well.

4. The situation: What is happening?
5. The villain: Who or what is causing trouble?
6. The suspense: How can you blindfold the reader to make him wonder how things are going to turn out?
7. The responses: How do the characters handle the obstacles and how do they react to one another?
8. The surprise: How should the story end?

Developing such questions, you can build a story from whatever you have. You do not necessarily have to start with the characters, for as I've told you, I often start with an incident as my idea, but I place it wherever it belongs in my series of steps, filling in the answers to the questions above it.

I see someone raising her hand to tell me she doesn't intend to write stories containing villians. Ah, but you're wrong. Every good story has a villain. The black cloak may be billowing dark clouds; the hidden knife, the lightning that flashes out to frighten the heroine.

Tolstoi's "Master and Man" will serve as an example through which we can trace back through our suggested planning steps to find the plot. Among the characters introduced, two emerge as primary: Master (Vassili: church sexton, landowner, merchant) and Man (Nikita, the servant). These two characters travel through the story side by side, but as the story progresses the reader realizes it is Nikita's story. One is led to believe his wife and "the cooper" who lives with her will be the villains. Nikita no longer has a home, but his wife gets what pitiful wages he earns.

Several environments are introduced, but the story does not take place in Nikita's wife's home, at Vassili's home, or the warm places en route to buy timber. The environment is a blizzard, which sets up the situation. They never should have left home, nor would they have done so, but for Vassili's greed. They are lost, a situation not to be envied, considering their surroundings.

One might consider the blizzard the villain, but it is not. The blizzard hurt no one who had sense enough to stay at home. Nikita's struggle with alcoholism is woven throughout the preliminary pages of the story, leading one to believe liquor was the villain. Not so. He had "suddenly forsworn liquor altogether" and was the only one of Vassili's servants sober and able to make the trip. At one resting place along the way he trembled at the smell of his master's vodka, but (after a struggle) he took tea.

The master appears from the start to be the villain. As the story progresses, one realizes this is not so. But wait: Vassili *is* the villain, not because he mistreats Nikita, "the cob" (pony), and everyone else, but because he is greedy. Vassili's greed is the true villain, for it drives him out into the late winter afternoon to make a needless trip through the forest to a distant landowner's home, hoping to buy some timber before someone else had a chance to get it. And who would get it? Everyone the cold, miserable men met along the way told them they were foolish to continue the trip. Both times after getting hopelessly lost it was Vasilli's greed that made them get into the sledge and try again. Finally, as they settled down to wait out the storm in the wilds, knowing they would probably die of exposure, Vassili lies in the sledge wide awake recalling his good fortune and recounting his wealth.

The suspense is created not by blindfolding the reader, but by the blinding late-night snowstorm. The men have lost their way again; the forest and posts are gone; Nikita has fallen down into one ravine, and they know the pony is pulling the sledge along another precipice. If they go on, they will perish; if they stop, they will freeze to death. The deep snow makes the decision. They stop. And as they wait out the night, a wolf howls. (Surely it will get them!) Vassili, unable to sleep, unhitches the pony and takes off alone. He will perish, and Nikita, left asleep with insufficient covering, will freeze to death. The pony circles and comes back, and Vassili, with a changed heart after having faced death and relieved at finding the sledge in the dark, lonely forest, chokes up with tears. But Nikita?

The master, overcome with grief, opens his big fur coat and enfolds the frozen servant to his breast. Life comes back to the stiffened man; the pony, also stiff and suffering from extreme cold following the sweat caused by dreadful exertion all night long, hits the sledge with his hoof. We know they are all three still alive.

The surprise: How should the story end?

I can't tell you how Tolstoi's ended. You must go to the library, find the story, and learn for yourself. But what is the plot?

PEOPLE	CONFLICT	RESOLUTION
Two men	battle a snowstorm in a dark forest	to survive

What about the chronology? The story is so intriguing (Tolstoi, after all) one is unaware of either when the story is taking place, or how much time has elapsed. Once, while lying in the sledge wide awake, Vassili finds one sulfur match in his pocket which he lights to look at his watch. It is ten minutes past one. The story takes place "the day after the feast of St. Nicholas," late in the afternoon after the guests have gone home; the frozen men are found the following morning. (Are they dead or alive?)

While a novel has ample time to introduce many characters and allows room for a variety of settings as well as numerous situations leading up to a climax, a short story needs a sharp focus: one major character with a limited supporting cast; one key location, with other places being incidental; one conflict, with other problems being minor; and one important situation taking the spotlight, with other situations being used only as needed to strengthen it. As you plan your plot, you must keep this in mind.

If your character is in college, the story can be about one class, one professor, one experience, one weekend, one roommate, or one terrible day or night. If your story is about a vacation, you can focus on one hour of the vacation, or one morning, or one night. Fiction can cover any length of time you choose, and certainly with the use of flashbacks even a very short story can cover months and years. A good fiction writer steps into the skin of his primary characters and knows so well what is going on in their lives that he can pick out the most appropriate events and experiences and regardless of the time span, build a compelling story out of them.

Excellent stories can be written about a group of characters: a dozen jurors, for example, each at his breakfast table contemplating the experience ahead of him, but someone will have to rise above the others to take the blows or accept the applause. The first chapter of *Ben Hur* does this beautifully. Although it develops into a novel, I read the introduction every now and then because it stands as a story on its own. Three characters are introduced: the Egyptian, the Hindu, and the Greek, strangers traveling over the desert from countries far apart. Their common search binds them together, and the characters themselves fade into the background as The Star, representing the Christ Child, takes center stage.

I recently read a short story that seemed to have three different environments: a college dormitory, the heroine's home, and the new home of her father, who had remarried. The true setting, it seemed to me as I analyzed it, was the mind of the vacationing college student who, as she walked through the shifting sand to her childhood surroundings, discovered that the past was closed. She could never return to what had been. Although her childhood security was gone, what mattered was her own life, present and future. As she puzzled over the loss of her parents' familiar roles, her own values sorted themselves out in her mind, creating a solid foundation on which to build a life of her own. The conclusion was unspoken, but I was satisfied.

As you can see, planning your story plot is something like creating an outline. As with the outline, so thinking through the plot stimulates the mind, helping you rope in wayward thoughts, put them in order, or decide to put them back in file for later use. The plot is framework, so it needs to be strong enough to hold up the story, but the design must be flexible enough to allow you to bend it to suit your needs as the story progresses.

How does one get the plot on paper so the story can become reality? Primary thoughts must be written down. In the case of *The Lonely Dragon*, I thought of the dragon first:

I. A stray dragon. It is lost and needs a home.

A couple of little girls are my special friends: one seven, the other eight. They love animals and would respond to a dragon's plea for help, as I would. Both are town house dwellers. The story became *their* story.

II. A little girl

Summer was coming on, and I thought about my friends, Candi and Jenny. In both cases, their parents work. Babysitters keep an eye on them, but they are old enough to entertain themselves.

III. Has to entertain herself all day long.

CHARACTERS	CONFLICT	RESOLUTION
A dragon and a little girl	look for a home for the dragon	and find a good one!

You can do the same thing with any story idea you have. Under "Characters," add the names of supporting characters, along with the gist of what they are like or what they contribute. Under "Conflict," write brief notes about struggles your "good guys" are going to encounter, with notes about the villians who cause those conflicts. Under "Resolution," write down how the story is going to turn out, along with notes pertaining to things that will happen to bring about the conclusion.

To get an idea of the flexibility of my rough outline, think through how you could handle it yourself, if you were writing the story. To get you started, let me tell you I found a woman much like myself who had a big yard and was delighted to get a real, firespitting dragon. But—I *could* have located the dragon's mother, or might have solved the problem other ways.

THE THEME

Like any other artist, the creative writer develops his masterpiece through use of an artistic aim. Whether or not he sits down to ponder the matter, the completed work of an experienced writer will emerge bearing his mark. Through content, length, style, vocabulary choice, and general structure, the completed work is bound to reveal, at least subconsciously, the effect he hoped to achieve. His attitudes, if not his specific opinions, will run like colorful threads throughout the story, because fiction as an art form is transferred from one mind to another through impressions. In a captivating story (the kind of spellbinder you hope to write), an author in touch with his own feelings and emotions expresses so adequately what he is feeling and experiencing that the reader's temperament tunes in. Two minds are in touch.

The *theme* is the subject of the story, the track along which the artist's aim travels. It is the strong thread that keeps the color and design flowing in the intended direction. It is the boundary that keeps the writer from rambling. A themeless jumble of ideas might be considered a work of art in some circles, but most fiction judges would turn thumbs down on such a crazy-patchwork collection, preferring stories (however wild the content) to be artistically blended through use of a theme.

Sometimes the theme seems to be very clearly defined, as in my children's story, *Cathy of Canada*, where the goal (because of the assignment) was to introduce Canada to the readers. I stuck to the theme: Canada—What Is It Like? Letters from readers indicated I achieved my goal, because they said: "I feel like I have visited Canada!"

We've talked about Tolstoi's "Master and Man," in which greed was the villain, that drove them again and again into life-threatening situations. Greed was also the theme of the story, the thread that kept the story flowing in the intended direction.

James Brendan Connolly, a short story master of the early twentieth century, created dramatic, widely appealing stories full of adventure and humor. His stories (many of them about events at sea) so captivate the reader that all thought of the author or his views is lost. He explained in "Dan Magee: White Hope," that: "The first thing in telling a story is to tell it, not to stop to preach a sermon," and in "Hiker Joy" he advises the writer to "lay off too much talky-talky an' don't try to make yuhself out too wise a guy in tellin' your story." Writing strictly to entertain the reader, Connolly freed the artist within him to paint the surroundings in full color. Like few other writers, he could capture the crashing of the breakers against the rocky shoreline or describe a totally peaceful scene of a fishing boat gliding through still waters.

Basic themes of Connolly's stories were the love of rugged men for wives, children, and home; and the courage and loyalty of rugged men. He was the winner of *Collier's* $2,500 Short Story Contest, in 1914 and his story, "The Trawler," was judged by Mark Sullivan as "a sort of second sight about the springs of human emotion and human action." Teddy Roosevelt, who was one of the judges, acclaimed "the elevation of sentiment and rugged knowledge of rugged men"—indicating a blend of tenderness and strength in the story. The theme of "The Trawler" demanded powerful writing, because it was the story of a man who died so someone else could live.

O. Henry (William Sydney Porter) experienced a variety of cultures (the cowboy country of the Southwest, New Orleans, South America, Central America, and New York City) but wherever he went, he crossed paths with common people and he wrote about them. He was one of them, a middle-class man who worked at many ordinary jobs and suffered ordinary trials of the common man. A creative person, events of his life (including three years in a penitentiary for a bank embezzlement he claimed he did not commit) made him extremely empathic. It is a gross understatement to suggest that his stories merit careful reading by beginning writers.

O. Henry was especially skilled at evoking human emotions. His stories touched the funnybone or caused a lump in the throat because he lived with his readers and was able to put their own gut-level feelings on paper. His general theme was people: romance and adventure seen through their lives, their confrontations, their sorrows and their delights. Christopher Morley in the *Encyclopaedia Britannica* called O. Henry's empathy "tenderness for the unlucky," and it would probably be safe to say that the theme of many of his stories grew out of his camaraderie with people who lived commonplace and even bizarre underdog lives.

Jack London's themes touched always on the endurance of man: against wild animals, against typhoons of the South Seas or blizzards of the Arctic, against hunger, or against disease. The physical struggle was always evident in his stories and every event either caused the struggle, or resulted from it.

To recap, these are a few very basic themes:

—the love of rugged men for wives, children, and home
—the courage and loyalty of rugged men
—the endurance of man in touch situations

Such general themes narrow down to more specific ones and deal with specific cultures, locales, classes, or races (rugged Alaskan men; the courage of Chinese women and their loyalty to home; romance and adventure seen through a car dealer's eyes; the endurance of a night nurse . . .).

The theme often is elusive to the reader because when masterfully written, the story unfolds dramatically, masking it. The characters face contending forces outwardly while struggling inwardly with attitudes, moods, and emotions. The writer, on the other hand, knows the theme or sees it surface as he plans his story, so he uses it to achieve unity, create an atmosphere, establish a mood, reach a goal, or achieve a blend of all four.

Excellent stories are written without the writer realizing he has a theme. Words flow out in perfect formation. Forced into any mold, creative writing loses certain intangible qualities, irreplaceable depths of appeal which have come to life during rare moments of inspiration. Word artists exist whose mental elves turn out skillful stories with no apparent planning. Such stories are surprise events, but even they do not occur entirely by chance, because long before they "happen," the writers (perhaps unconsciously in early childhood) have freed their elves of fantasy to come and go as they wish; they feed those elves well and they encourage them to come out to play in the open anytime they wish, day or night. The elves are happily planning, even when the writers are not.

The theme may comprise the moral to the story. Sometimes the theme and moral are one and the same, whereas in other stories the theme leads up to the moral, which comes to focus at the climax or is woven into the conclusion. Fascinating discussions can arise as to whether every story needs to have a moral or has one hidden in its depths. I believe not, but my opponents continually point out morals to my stories I never knew were there. Such morals (if they exist) emerge through the artistic aim, arising out of the writer's temperament—from his attitudes' inadvertently rubbing off as he tells his story thinking it is purely entertainment. Moralistic stories are very rejectable, so if your moral is clearly apparent, your editing work is cut out for you. Tone it down.

Don't be surprised to find writing salable fiction tedious work, as well as fun. Any game overwhelms you until you learn to play it with ease, winning now and then. Organizing your stories with a plot and a theme starts you off with a sound structure, training you in necessary foundational skills. You need to do it consciously, at least for a while.

A PLACE, PEOPLE, AND THE THINGS THEY DO

Potential characters, settings, and action ideas ought to be added systematically to your i and i file so that when you are ready to write, you can flip through your file to find ideas from which to form readable stories.

I believe the best fiction writers use the piecemeal method

to build characters: one person's eyes; another's mouth; still another's size and attire, shape, or personality. Nor is this done consciously by artistic writers. Rather their minds operate behind the scenes, putting their characters together.

As I've told you before (and you already knew it, of course) you are surrounded by characters. Characters in fiction are the people, pets, animals, birds, creatures, and animated objects who inhabit your settings. One of the most important writing skills you can learn is to step into their minds and bodies (if they have bodies) "becoming them." The best way to do this is to study other people's feelings, which is done very simply by allowing yourself to talk to people about their feelings and emotions and to watch reactions during the times of crisis, stress, excitement, fear, happiness, boredom, or grief, imagining how you would feel if you were in their place. Getting in touch with your own feelings forms a base for studying other people. We have already talked about this, and as time goes on you will examine yourself over and over again, as you face various issues in life, to decide what memories, opinions, attitudes, and feelings to share with your readers.

You can start fascinating conversations about emotions you are particularly interested in. For example, you may wish to include a jealous person in a story, but you are not jealous; or perhaps you *are* a jealous person, easily incensed when someone invades territory you have marked as your own. You wonder if you are typical, or if your jealous character will immediately be identified as yourself.

The British are wonderful conversationalists. Among Britishers one need only ask: "What do you think of [pick any subject out of the hat] jealousy?" Your entire evening can be filled with conjecture and debate on that subject and others closely related to it. As the group banters back and forth—some serious conversation, some nonsense—someone may suddenly contradict himself deliberately in order to examine some new aspect of the subject. (For a good example of this, read Oscar Wilde's "The Critic as Artist.")

Your peers may not be as skilled in the art of conversation as are the British, but you can bet they will fill your hopper with more thoughts than you can digest every time you give them a chance. Imagine yourself at a party. During a moment of silence, you throw out the question: "What do you think of jealousy?"

After an hour of gathering gems from that question, you break in again, "But jealousy seems like such a malicious trait."

Another hour of mental note-taking, before you say, "Seems to me jealousy is pretty universal. It's normal to be jealous, isn't it?"

If you're smart and your partners fall into your trap, you'll stay up half the night getting your new views on jealousy down on paper. The next time you're in a long line at a post office, you say loudly to the restless person behind you, "At a party recently we had the most interesting discussion about jealousy." Time will whiz by for everybody in that line, as strangers express their views for your benefit.

In the best fiction, characters live because the author has embroidered their lives with the same kinds of complex personalities found in real people. Mixed feelings and a variety of opinions plague all human life. A description is much more than appearance. While a third grade composition might get a gold star for "The mother had black, curly hair," adult audiences demand a more complete view, a view that allows them to experience the character as a person, nasty or nice.

Interestingly enough, once you begin to analyze personalities, you find that most people are made up of Jekyll/Hyde characteristics. The more their personality flexes, the more interesting they become. The author's job is to bring out this variety, showing in elusive ways a character's reverse side. Going back to the old lady aided by the bill collector, her vulnerability appealed to the younger woman, but as the story progressed, the widow, fearful she might lose this new friend, cunningly planned the scheme of dangling before her a big inheritance. She might have been a sweet, helpless old thing, but she must have been deceitful and clever, too, to carry out her plan successfully.

Characterization is not black and white snapshots of people standing in a row on bleachers. Good characterization is fast-paced movement of real life in full color and sound. One doesn't point to a person in the group to say: "This is what he or she looked like." Rather, one announces, "John Doe just got off the train." What he looked like is incidental to who he is, what he is doing here, and how he feels about it. A satisfactory description encompasses appearance, actions, feelings, background and attitudes; and the picture is brought into focus through dialogue, as well as description, through what he says and thinks, and through what others say and think about him.

To learn the skill of description, you can practice describing the movement of television characters—or for that matter, any unspoken movement—to someone not watching. How would you describe the silent messages to a blind person hearing only the sound? Facial expression, body language, messages given through the eyes, wrinkling of the nose, frowning, touching, blushing, breezes ruffling the hair, perspiration, and other movement or visible emotions must be described to your readers because they can't see what you are seeing. Describing them aloud or on paper can become a routine learning tool for you. If your mate objects to being blindfolded or if you have no one to talk to, so much the better. Create a compatible character to sit with you, on whom you can practice each day.

You also need to take your unsighted companion with you to various locations. It's one thing for you to witness an accident or a murder, but quite another to adequately describe the details of activity and environment. It was reported that twelve witnesses saw a man shot to death in a Kansas City bar, but the police had no leads at all because all twelve witnesses described the murderer differently. A writer must be much more observant than that. It's the details that count. You must learn to view everything that goes on as possible evidence about which you may someday be questioned. You are the key witness. Everyone else will depend on you to set the stage.

Now you can see why it is important to be in touch with your feelings. How you feel about people and places sets the cornerstone for your fiction. You may admit you are fearful, but confidently build a character with courage or with weaknesses like your own. You may despise a certain characteristic, but create someone who bears it whom others love. Your own feelings give your fiction the kind of balance one finds in real life.

Amateur writers sometimes create characters too unusual to be true. I can hear you saying, "But I'm really talking about a real person! He *was* that unusual." Maybe he was. Of all the picturesque people I have seen in my life, none topped an old gentleman I spotted one morning at the taxi stand. His snow-white beard caught my attention first. It was quite long, perfectly combed, so straight it might have been ironed. He wore a cowboy hat pulled down to his white bushy eyebrows. Long white hair almost to his shoulders hung below the hat.

As if that sight were not enough for one day, when I drove by I noticed his walking stick. It was not a cane. It was a curved stick, dark brown, and polished until it sparkled. Moments later after I had parked, I walked past behind the man. He was as bowlegged as a fictional cowboy, and he wore skintight jeans.

Although the man I saw was really there (he hailed a cab and threw his bag in the back seat before climbing in himself), he was not a good candidate to become a storybook character. Truth is stranger than fiction. He was so unusual that if you put him in a story nobody would believe he was real. The burly cab driver wondering what kind of a nut he had picked up this time probably would serve a story purpose better as a lead character, because readers could understand a cab driver as an average man, and tune in to his thoughts. The cabbie's day might go wildly fictional, but the readers would have a base close to earth to stand on as they viewed the chain of unreal events his weird passenger might lead him into. The very next day I saw a hassled mother standing at the taxi stand, gripping a little girl tightly by the hand. Story ideas flooded my mind, ideas you would enjoy hearing about because at least a fragment of them rang true to life.

In creating characters, remember that everyone has a good side as well as a bad, a serious side as well as a comical. Every ruffian has a soft spot; every cruel person, a gentle touch. I will never forget many of the people I met at the inner city hospital where I worked. One tearful, fearful lady who clutched my hand pleading for reassurance because she faced surgery later revealed that she was a well-known nightclub comedienne. A shivering frightened lad for whom I bought a sandwich, a lad beaten up on the street, was a bold thief by day, six foot five and boisterous in normal life. And countless softspoken patients I talked with over the years were hardened prisoners under armed guard, handcuff locked around one ankle, chained to their beds. I saw their "other side," wiped away their tears, and heard their prayers.

Realistic characters in your stories will reveal their vulnerability as well as their boldness. Superman and Wonder Woman have endured because they have a human side, as well as being superpowerful, and it is their natural, vulnerable appearance that makes their feats so popular.

A good fiction writer lives with his characters, and they with him. I have a cubbyhole in my mind where I keep them. Now and then I feed them incidents from my life to brighten up their own. One story I've thought about for many years is based on an accident I was involved in during a Mexico trip. I have moved the story to a new location—but I don't want to tell the whole story here. As I drive through certain neighborhoods I view them through my heroine's eyes. Like an artist I note the shape of people's faces; the quality of their skin; the look in their eyes; the set of their chin; their hairstyles; and the things they do, say, laugh over, and cry over, and I muse: "Here, Mrs. Smudgin, add this to your story." Someday I'll invite this imaginary person to the front of my mind where she and I will talk things over. I'll give her a real name, and the whole story will fall into place with supporting cast built up over fifteen years.

THE VIEWPOINT

Who's telling your story? Are you?

The author's viewpoint used to be used regularly in short stories. The author was the storyteller, so here and there he would drop in remarks as a storyteller around a campfire might do, identifying himself through those remarks, and giving his opinion. The author could take any route with his viewpoint: divulging a great deal of information about all the characters, or withholding much of it to spring on the readers later, as a good storyteller often does.

The viewpoint of one of the characters in the story limits the reader's understanding of a situation, for the reader knows only what the character knows. The thoughts of other characters, for example, are a mystery, since the character telling the story doesn't know them.

The omniscient viewpoint, the author seeing everything as the Omniscient God sees a situation, allows the reader to know more than any one character knows, as much at a time as the writer chooses to divulge. This popular viewpoint allows the writer to expose the minds of various characters and reveal their plans.

Any viewpoint has its advantage. It would be well to study viewpoints in the stories you read to see how the writer has developed his plot through use of his viewpoint, how he has used it to introduce his characters, to spring surprises, to create suspense, and to build up a mood. Since you'll have to read "Master and Man" to find out if the men lived through the storm or not, Tolstoi's stories might be good ones to study, for a start.

TYING IT ALL TOGETHER

One of the most wearisome novels I ever read (a reject, of course) was made up entirely of dialogue, with not a word of narration in it. How tiring a person who never stops talking! I sat spellbound through the first few pages, amazed that one could create so rare a monster as a full length historical novel told entirely by four jabbering fools.

A decent balance between narrative and conversation is so utterly basic to good fiction that I wonder at the necessity of mentioning it. However, lest there be a second such genious as the one just mentioned, let me hasten to say that variety is one key to success. I turned thumbs down on a short story with *no* dialogue. It read like a book report.

Through reporting, description, and recounting of thoughts, narrative should give information pertinent to the story. A clever writer uses narrative to put ideas into the reader's mind, to arouse curiosity, and to create a mood. Narrative sets the stage, but until you have introduced conversation into your story, it is only a report. Dialogue should strengthen the narrative, making it come alive as characters are introduced; interact in places you have described; react according to the mood you have set for them; and carry to the plot. All of this is accomplished by weaving in conversation.

To practice this give and take, you might find a news report which adapts itself to conversation and rewrite it in story form. Here's one as a sample; "According to firemen arriving at the scene moments after the alarm sounded, neighbors insisted that a child was alone in the attic apartment, trapped." The following is what you could do with it:

> Joe Blair had ridden the back of the old red truck for seventeen years, so long he was prepared to face the confusion and angry shouts of neighbors always at the scene. As the truck rounded the corner, he saw them. And he saw, too, the black smoke curling out of a second floor window. Joe knew the house.
>
> "Apartment kitchen!" he shouted to his buddy, Jeff.
>
> "Hope they all got out!" responded Jeff. "That firetrap will burn up like a crackerbox!" Jeff was shouting, too, above the roar of the truck and the blaring siren.
>
> The truck eased through the crowded street and came to a stop surrounded by the angry mob. Too many people were talking at once, all of them angry, shouting. "Where you been? Took you all night to come!"
>
> As Joe jumped off the truck to begin his task, the crowd pressed closer. His heart sank when some of the words which were blended into one incoherent shout came into focus:
>
> "There's a baby up there! Third floor! Mrs. Green ain't home, but her baby am!"

Any news report can serve as a jumping off place for practice. Put action into the story and life into the people by putting appropriate words into their mouths.

Most lives are not lived happily ever after, but sooner or later, people find a way to cope. Before you come up with your coping device in stories (whatever it may be), put in hills to climb, rocks to stumble over, obstacles to surmount, and open wells into which your characters are bound to fall, with no escape evident. Even a low-keyed story should have the reader holding his breath a little while, wondering how in the world the hero will survive. No matter the age of your audience, appropriate levels of anguish, fear, surprise, and suspense are elements essential to your story. Fill the days and hours with action. Even though your character may be bored to death, the rain may beat upon a cement sidewalk, the wind may blow, a flower petal may drop, or a bird may sing. Even in a cemetery ants and beetles crawl to and fro. The weather forecast may predict a sunny day, offering a ray of hope. That's what life is all about. Your readers won't ask for more.

Analyzing the short story today is extremely difficult, because of the amazing variety in print. As I wound down in preparation for writing this chapter I read dozens of published stories ranging from O. Henry and Hemingway to those found in current magazines.

Subjectively I might say, "this I liked and this I did not." Objectively, however, I have to admit that most of the stories were delightfully entertaining in one way or another. Although one might close a magazine or a book, saying, "I don't care for that story," as a rule, stories printed by reputable publishers have been purchased because they present whatever the content may be in a quality manner. Winning stories have human interest appeal, they offer fresh new themes or approaches, and they are structurally sound.

I also studied page after page of markets listed in *Writer's Market*, all kinds of categories, and I talked to editors hoping to find some clue as to what publishers really want in fiction today. As to content, it varies far more than I ever dreamed it did. If you think, "I'm a man, so I can write for men's magazines," think again. Finding the right market is not that simple. That category, as all others, caters to a wide spectrum of readers. What one magazine flatly rejects, another may grab with glee as a hot sales item.

There is one common ground, however. The picture I formed from my study is that all editors are looking for

1. Originality
(a different twist, strong fresh insights, distinctive characters and plots, innovative ideas, inventive writing, fresh approach and style).
2. Ability to arouse emotions
(mentally exciting copy, emotionally satisfying, strong emotional impact, the hows and whys of daily living, coping with problems and solving them).
3. Technical mastery
(proper plots clearly defined, good organization, and good chronology, high quality writing, strong characterizations, structurally sound stories realistically told, convincing action, flesh and blood characters or convincing nonhuman beings, surprising climaxes, strong beginnings and strong endings).

I have become quite an avid reader of *The New Yorker*, because their short stories have broken away from the stereotype (which leaves one feeling the story has been told before, in a different disguise). For a fresh approach to today's readers, the fiction writer would do well to read *New Yorker* stories and others from top slick magazines. Short stories will sell. The problem causing discouragement among would-be fiction writers is that their stories are simply not good enough to buy. Editors do not want

1. Worn-out themes
(copied ideas with poorly disguised settings, characters, and action; themes used 10 million times, always approached from the same angle, following a predictable pattern).
2. Attitudes out of the past
(American-as-apple-pie characters and settings from the author's youth, not typical today; women portrayed strictly as homebodies and submissive helpers; minority races as inferior, as servants, and as poor; men as sole breadwinners—Prince Charmings who pay all the bills and Sugar Daddies

who shower their women with gifts; Victorian innocence in either adults or children).

3. Unrealistic plots, people, or action
(all of the above! Stories out of step with the times; unlikely events and reactions; extreme situations that do not fit the plot; characters ridiculous because they are too nice, too mean, too sweet, too stupid, too smart, too handsome, or too talkative to be true; excessive description; inaccurate recounting of facts or incorrect descriptions of known locales; overly vivid contrasts).
4. Impositions of morals
(head-in-sand approach to life which assumes everyone thinks exactly like you, or ought to; presenting a single viewpoint as a universal requirement; refusing to acknowledge as valid any opposing beliefs, customs, attitudes, or lifestyles, or actions; preaching about your own pet beliefs).
5. Depressing situations
(pessimistic, negative viewpoints; sad-sack, loser themes; moralistic condemnation imposed without a contrast of hope; overdoses of bickering; spirit-crushing trauma overridden with despair; unresolved conflicts or fears).

You can do the same market study I did, and as you do, certain periodicals may seem to be highlighted for your benefit. If so, and you are serious about writing fiction, I suggest that you rush out and buy current copies of those periodicals so you can read and dissect their stories.

My principles of good fiction writing are only a foundation for you to build upon. Your success is not guaranteed. It will depend upon whether you do your homework after you have read my book. Are you planning ways to fit reading good fiction into your schedule? Have you mentally made a list of magazines you'd like to study to see what kind of fiction they buy? Have you got a paper and pencil handy? Because you're going to need one, to do the assignment on the next page.

ASSIGNMENT 10

WARM-UP: Got a yarn to spin? Jot down the plot:

PEOPLE	CONFLICT	RESOLUTION
______________	______________	______________

Whose story is it (hero or heroine)?______________
Where is it taking place?______________
What is happening?______________
Who or what will cause a conflict?______________
How can you create suspense?______________
How will the characters react?______________
What surprise can you spring on the reader?______________

1. Listening to conversations, analyze them and write similar dialogue: parent to child; child to child; child to adult; adult to adult; adult to self; adult to inanimate object; child or adult to pet. Practice variety in dialogue: excitement, boredom, fear, happiness, curiosity, surprise. Find ways to describe the unspoken messages of facial expressions, body movements, breathing patterns, and vivid emotional outbursts that are part of conversation.

2. Write at least one 15-50-word description. Consider your readers as deaf and blindfolded, unable to hear or see what you are describing. Don't omit details experienced by any of your five senses or your emotions. Include texture, fragrance, movement, and signs of life (birds, insects, animals, and other creatures). If you can't think of what to write, imagine a blacktop highway winding through mountainous terrain in autumn.

3. Read over all you have written for this assignment. Are there more descriptive words you might have used? Has your dialogue contained unnecessary conversation? Is your description too colorful? After you have done all you can do to improve your writing, retype it (double or triple spaced) and lay it aside for a day or two. Come back to it later with a fresh viewpoint.

FINALLY: Don't forget to find out what happened to those two Russians lost in the blizzard!

11 Poetry: Pleasure or Problem?

You already know that Ralph Waldo Emerson is one of my favorite poets. (His "Goodbye, Proud World!" is one of my favorite poems.) We share a kinship for nature, for one thing. For another, I feel that if we were able to spend an afternoon together over a cup of tea (my place or his) we would discover that our thoughts on a number of subjects are similar. I feel terribly envious of Nathaniel Hawthorne, who was lucky enough to live in the old Emerson house in Concord, Massachusetts. There he was inspired to write his "Mosses from an Old Manse." Were I to dwell in the Emerson home, what inspired gems might come forth from my pen! The ghost of Emerson haunts me even now, as I ponder his wise words in "Set not thy foot on graves":

Life is too short to waste
In critic peep or cynic bark
Quarrel or reprimand;
'Twill soon be dark;
Up! mind thine own aim, and
God speed the mark!

In his essay "The Poet," Emerson refers to the poet as "the man of Beauty." He implies that great poets are "beautiful souls . . . their own acts like great pictures," that they have minds that "never cease to explore the double meaning . . . or the quadruple, or the centuple, or much more manifold meaning, of every fact [appealing to the senses]."

Emerson claims that poets write "primarily what will and must be spoken." They can "penetrate into the region where air is music," can hear "those primal warblings, and attempt to write them down." The good poet, he insists, is a person "of more delicate ear" whose "transcripts, though imperfect, become the songs of the nations."

Speaking of the average person "of poetical talents, or of industry or skill in metre," he complains that such poets "are men of talent who sing, and not the children of music."

Are you—or would you like to become—"a child of music?" Do beautiful thoughts waltz through your soul, sometimes pleading to be put on paper? Perhaps you are what Emerson calls a "true poet," one who

> announces that which no man foretold. He is the true and only doctor; he knows and tells; he is the only teller of news, for he was present and privy to the appearance of what he describes. He is a beholder of ideas, and an utterer of the necessary and casual. . . . The poet has a new thought. He has a whole new experience to unfold; he will tell us how it was with him, and all men will be richer in his fortune.

According to Emerson, when the poet sees ugly things, he views them "re-attached to nature and the Whole." To the poet, such mundane sights as the factory, the town, and [in his day] the railroad [rush hour traffic, in ours] are works of art. If he were writing today, he would say most of us are like commuters who stare vacantly out of bus windows; but the poet is like the immigrant who sees suburbia for the first time "and marvels at the fine houses."

The poet, with his "ulterior intellectual perception- . . . puts eyes and a tongue into every dumb and inanimate object . . . He turns the world to glass, and shows us all things. . . . The poet is the Namer, or language-maker!"

Oh, to be a poet! But for all his pleasant musings about the marvels of the poetic mind, Emerson's conclusion is depressng to someone like me:

1. "Notwithstanding this necessity to be published, adequate expression is rare." (We'd love to write good poetry, but the words don't come!)
2. "The great majority of men seem to be minors . . . who cannot report the conversation they have had with nature." (We're often deeply moved. The problem is that we can't communicate our thoughts well enough to move others.)
3. "The rays or appulses have sufficient force to arrive at the senses" (that is, the impact of what we see, hear, taste, smell, and feel gets to us), "but not enough to reach the quick and compel the reproduction of themselves in speech." (That is, we don't feel things quite deeply enough; nor can we find words to adequately express our feelings so others can tune in.)

That's the problem with poetry. What one has felt deeply may be poured out on paper, but the words chosen may fail to ignite a spark in some other soul. Many of us have poets' hearts, but the connections between the heart, the mind, and the pen seem to be loose. Our message doesn't always get through.

WHAT IS POETRY?

The creative mind sees mental pictures that an unimaginative or busy person may totally miss. Poetry is the ability to transfer those pictures into word images. When word images are successfully done, even the unimaginative can look at them and see what the poet saw.

Poetry can be a collection of well-placed, commonly used words, or it can be colorful figures of speech that require thought on the part of the reader to tune in to the poet's channel. Poetry is often expressive, employing unusual phrases and forceful word arrangements to achieve the "I wish I'd said that" effect. Tastes in poetry vary as widely as do tastes in food, but exceptional poetry generally has appeal, because it puts into words the emotions the reader is feeling.

The range of literature classified as poetry is very broad, from the simplest rhyming couplets we learn as children to the most complete aesthetic experiences which convey imagery with or without rhyme.

Primitive poetry probably evolved from a pleasant activity enjoyed by men, women, and children in daily life, who expressed their feelings through dance and deep emotional vocal outbursts at special moments in life, happy or sad. From this rhythmic expression came a variety of contemporary literary forms: comedy and tragedy, the reflective satirical lyric, the parody, the passionate song, and the religious hymn.

In early Greece, poetry seems to have developed hand-in-hand with drama. Homer is considered to be the earliest Greek poet, although the experts seem to disagree on when he lived and even on whether the works credited to him were written by one person or more than one. The greatness of his writing is indisputable, but trying to establish other pertinent data from 600 *B.C.* becomes futile.

Rome eventually produced poets, but they modeled their poems after the Greeks rather than creating original forms. Rome even borrowed the name for the writer of such literature: "poet."

In the Middle East, the poetry of the Israelites, which expressed their deepest feelings in worship through song and dance, predated Greek entertainment. Moses celebrated the Red Sea crossing with a song recorded in the fifteenth chapter of Exodus, and other poetry is recorded in early Jewish history as well. Several beautiful books of Hebrew literature are those designated as the poetic books of the Bible which are introduced by the Book of Job. The Psalms, many of them credited to King David, date back one thousand years before Christ, probably three or four hundred years before Homer.

Many readers of the Psalms fail to see how they can be called poetry. In an article entitled "Seesawing through the Psalms," *The Daily Walk* explains that in Hebrew poetry the *ideas* rhyme rather than the words:

> There are at least four different ways in which this "seesaw" effect (called parallelism) is used in the Book of Psalms . . . :
>
> *Synonymous* parallelism reinforces the thought of the first line by repeating it in the second line using similar words:
>
> *Run for your life,*
> *Jog for your health.*
>
> *Emblematic* parallelism uses a word picture in the first line to illustrate the thought contained in the second line. (Watch for the telltale words "like" or "as.")
>
> *"As the hart panteth after the water brooks, so panteth my soul after thee, O God."* (Psalm 42:1).
>
> *Synthetic* parallelism uses the second line to add to the thought of the first line or complete it in some way:
>
> *Hebrew poetry is fun,*
> *If you know about parallelism.*
>
> *Antithetic* parallelism takes the first thought of the first line and contrasts it with the thought of the second line. (Watch for the telltale word "but.")
>
> *"For thou wilt save the afflicted people;*
> *but wilt bring down high looks"*[1] (Psalm 18:27).

In the Psalms, one can easily see the patterns of these four forms of poetry emerge. A great many forms of poetry are in use today, recognized as such by the experts, although not always by the man on the street.

Although some of our finest verse during the Middle Ages came out of monasteries, during the early Christian era the church fathers frowned on the immorality and idolatry woven into the very fiber of pagan arts. They insisted on strict separation from earthy entertainment. During the Renaissance, poetry and drama joined hands with the church and surged once again throughout the everyday life. In Chapter 7, I suggested that you read Shakespeare for the sake of drama. Now you should study his poetry, for his plays were poems written in blank verse.

Did I just lose you? Blank verse has meter (you can consistently count the beats), but doesn't rhyme. If you want to go into a more extensive study of the mechanics of poetry, your librarian will help you find books on the subject. Judson Jerome is one of America's foremost poetry teachers today. He is accessible to you through his *Writer's Digest* column and I recommend his book *The Poet and the Poem*. Many of us draw back when faced with iambs, trochees, dactyls, and the like, but let me assure you that teachers like Jerome can safely guide you through the fearful maze of esoteric words.

A *pyrrhus* is not a snake—I'll tell you later what it is—but to me, an *iamb* conjures up a mental image of a caterpillar crawling through the verse: an unaccented syllable followed by one that is accented. Shakespearean blank verse has five *iambic feet* to the measure: down úp down úp down úp down úp down úp. You can visualize that caterpillar, can't you?

Here and there in well-known poetry of more recent vintage one runs across blank verse and it is well that we do; for reading it hones our minds, keeping us out of whatever poetic ruts we may tend to fall into. One of these is the continual use of our gift for writing rhymes, that is, the familiar three or four beats to the measure:

> Alás how éasily thíngs go wróng!
> A sígh too múch, or a kíss too lóng . . .
> (from George MacDonald's "Sweet Peril")

The famous hymn writer Isaac Watts apparently was born into this rut of rhyming! This amazing child started studying Latin when he was four, Greek when he was eight, French when he was eleven, and Hebrew when he was thirteen. However, the poetry form he used to revolutionize church music was simple.

As a teenager Watts rebelled against the tedious "lining out" of psalms. He complained to his father one time too many that "The singing of God's praise is the part of worship highest heaven, and its performance among us is the worst on earth!" He was probably right. The "clerk" would read a line of the psalm and the congregation would drone it after him. The elder Watts, father of nine children, was sick of griping. "Then find us something better, young man!" he challenged.

Before the evening service that Sunday, Isaac had written

his first hymn. Of the hundreds that followed and are known today, "Amazing Grace" is the most common.

Isaac Watts' childhood chatter had been a constant stream of rhymes. This got on his father's nerves so much we are told that one day his father threatened to whip him if he kept it up. Isaac pleaded:

> O, Fáther, dó some pí-ty táke
> And Í will nó more vérses máke!

Longfellow, too, was a prolific verse writer. (You recall "There was a little girl who had a little curl . . .") His mind on the Civil War, Longfellow wrote:

> And ín despáir I bówed my héad.
> "There ís no péace on éarth," I sáid . . .

Longfellow enjoyed much success during his lifetime, but after his death, critics called him "a hearthside rhymer." And that he was! You would do well, if you're a hearthside rhymer yourself, to compare your rhymes to his. Run through them and mark the beats. Practice until you can write rhymes as well as he did.

However, don't sit around forever jotting down rhymes! Some people tend to think:

> If yóu would like to wríte a póem,
> Go bórrow your néigh-bor's mét-ro-nóme.

The reasoning is not entirely faulty, but it is an immature approach to poetry. Rhythm is important, so setting a metronome in your mind to imbed in it proper rhythm is not a bad beginning. As you read over your rhymes, you should be able to tap a steady number of beats to the measure. Tons of poetry is rejected because the writer failed to do this.

But rhythm cannot be allowed to become monotonous. There are other poetic worlds to be discovered. You do not need a metronome to write poetry—in fact, if you speed it up you might churn out such quantity, quality would be buried. What you need to be a versatile poet is an understanding of stressed and unstressed syllables, which is rhythm.

Poetry does not always have to rhyme. Blank verse is unrhymed iambic pentamenter. *Pentameter* indicates how long the line is (five feet to the line, because *penta* means five). A poetic *foot* is composed of either two or three syllables, either stressed or unstressed. If the first syllable is stressed, the rhythm is said to be falling; if the last is stressed, it is said to be rising. The following identify the number of feet in a line from two to nine. Blank verse, such as Shakespeare's, consistently has five:

dimeter—two feet
trimeter—three feet
tetrameter—four feet
hexameter—six feet
septameter—seven feet
octameter—eight feet
nonameter—nine feet

There are four different kinds of two-beat feet: the iamb, the trochee, the spondee, and the pyrrhus.

1. The *iamb* has a rising beat, with accent on the second syllable:

   To bé or nót to bé
   (from Shakespeare's *Hamlet*)

2. The falling beat is the *trochee:*

   Ónce up-ón a míd-night dréa-ry, whíle I pón-dered wéak and wéa-ry . . .
   (from Poe's "The Raven")

3. The *spondaic* foot is comprised of two syllables, both of which are stressed.
4. The *pyrrhic* foot has two unstressed syllables.

The *spondee* and *pyrrhus* have neither rising nor falling rhythm. Although it is extremely rare a line of either spondees or phrhuses might show up, such feet will be found in complex poetic structures where iambs or trochees alone are inadequate to the poetic task. As a beginner, you may table thought of using the two, but you should be acquainted with them for use in Scrabble. And for *scansion*!

Scansion is the process of identifying the syllables. Many people are born with a feeling for rhythm, which is a good guide to writing poetry. A background of music or knowledge of dance can improve this natural rhythm and help one understand the basic principles of writing rhythmic verse. *Scansion* is an analytic tool developed to allow the poet to have control over what he is writing. As in learning anything else, a guideline to follow is an important help. Scansion is this guideline, a measuring stick which allows you to check your work to see if it fits the rhythm you believe you have created. As time goes on, you will confirm your natural feeling for proper rhythm often enough to be sure of yourself, but in the learning process, scanning your own poetry and the work of others is helpful.

Reading good poetry regularly (for pleasure) transmits proper rhythmic patterns into the mind. Reading to analyze good poetry (deliberate study) includes the absorption process, but in addition, one identifies syllabic patterns which can be followed as one launches out into new poetic ventures. Many "hearthside rhymers" have weaned themselves from the tedium of nursery rhyme mentality and clichéd rhythm by getting scansion down pat, and practicing new forms of poetry.

Let's move on to the three-syllable beat, since you will want to understand and use it. You have two words to learn (if you can't learn the words, learn the principles they describe):

1. The *anapestic* foot has two unstressed syllables followed by one stressed syllable:

   'Twas the níght be-fore Chríst-mas and áll through the
   hóuse
   Not a créature was stírring, not éven a móuse.

2. The *dactylic* foot is the reverse of the anapest. Instead of the third syllable being stressed, the first is stressed: óne two three, óne two three, óne two three, óne two three.

Húrry the báby as fást as you cán,
Húrry him, wórry him, máke him a mán.
Óff with his báby clothes, gét him in pánts,
Féed him on bráin foods and máke him advánce.
(From "Making A Man" by Nixon Waterman)

Let's imagine that you have an opportunity to write a poem for the office newsletter. Your thoughts might flow out in the pattern of the first example: one two thrée, one two thrée, one two thrée, one two thrée

one two thrée, one two thrée, one two thrée, one two thrée.
I was hó-ping to ásk for a ráise all day lóng
But the bóss was so bús-y the tím-ing was wróng!

Or you might use the second example: óne two three, óne two three, óne two three, óne two three.

Rún to the télephone, rún to the dóor,
Rún make some cóffee, and thén run some móre.
Rún to the máil desk, ánd while you're thére,
Rún for new nýlons—you've a rún in that páir!
(Stenbock)

BACK TO SHAKESPEARE!

This is not intended to be "all about poetry in one easy lesson," but a quick sticking the toe in the water to test it. Here is a brief recap:

TWO-BEAT FEET:
iamb—rising beat, accented on the second syllable
trochee—falling beat
spondee—two stressed syllables
pyrrhus—two unstressed syllables

THREE-BEAT FEET:
anapest—two unstressed syllables and one stressed syllable

dactyl—the reverse: one stressed syllable followed by two unstressed

THE PROCESS OF IDENTIFYING POETIC FEET:
scansion—the key to successful poetry writing

From *Romeo and Juliet*, here is an example using several different kinds of poetic feet. To get the flow of rhythm, read the sentence naturally, not in a sing-song fashion:

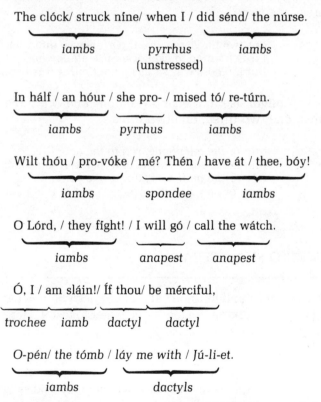

The clóck/ struck níne/ when I / did sénd/ the núrse.

iambs *pyrrhus* (unstressed) *iambs*

In hálf / an hóur / she pro- / mised tó/ re-túrn.

iambs *pyrrhus* *iambs*

Wilt thóu / pro-vóke / mé? Thén / have át / thee, bóy!

iambs *spondee* *iambs*

O Lórd, / they fíght! / I will gó / call the wátch.

iambs *anapest* *anapest*

Ó, I / am sláin!/ Íf thou/ be mérciful,

trochee *iamb* *dactyl* *dactyl*

O-pén/ the tómb / láy me with / Jú-li-et.

iambs *dactyls*

A fault of the amateur poet is to contrive a rhyme (cat with hat, mouse with house) in such a way as to lose the sense of rhythm. When you experiment with extra syllables or unusual arrangements of metric verse, you must weigh the words very carefully to see that they flow smoothly; that is, the structure is consistent so that the reader can feel the flow without being forced to wonder how you managed to fit the words in. Unexpected jolts in the rhythm ruin a verse, and you must learn to edit them out yourself.

Comments about metric verse wouldn't be complete without mention of limericks. What fun they are to write! And although they don't find a mention in the archives of great poetry, some periodicals think they're worth printing. And *I* do. This one has graced my dining room wall about nine years, for good reason:

If ḿy house stínks and my cómpany thínks
That I líve like a térrible hóg,
I hópe they remémber
from Ján. through Decémber
I've gót an odíferous dóg!

One can get into a free verse or prose poetry rut as well as into a rhyming rut. Thoughts jotted in a column a phrase at a time are not necessarily poetic. They may be meaningless and dull to all but the author, who of course loves his baby, overlooking all its flaws.

Prose poetry is poetry which, when put into paragraph form, has all the qualities of proper grammatical and sentence structure. Generally prose poems can be rewritten into prose form without losing any of the beauty or meaning of the content. The author has chosen to arrange his sentences artistically on the page with ample white space to set them off. The form is found in both books and magazines, and when properly done, is cleary distinguishable from free verse. Prose poetry is extremely controversial, rejected by many poets as lacking poetic rhythm, which makes it prose. Who knows?

Free verse is not "without rules." It generates its own rules. One can express himself poetically without rhyme or meter—sometimes without punctuation and often without regard to capitalization—allowing words and phrases to fall onto the page without military formation. Contrary to prose poetry, much free verse is tied to the form in which it is written, for it would become a jumble of words without meaning if put into paragraph form without using such basic rules as beginning the sentence with a capital letter and ending it with a period.

No one can tell you your free verse is not good. He can only express his opinion that he doesn't personally care for it. And who would be that cruel? Free verse is free of rules imposed by others. You make the decisions. If it's what you wanted to put on the page, it's okay.

But to sell free verse, you're going to have to sharpen your skills, whack a bit at your wording, think more about content, color up your vocabulary, work on your division breaks, and even bend a little; because to sell, you must consider the opinion of other people. You remain free: free to tell the editors "If you don't like it, send it back." Successful free verse is the pouring out of the heart and getting off the chest of whatever the writer wants to bring out into the open, to be shared or not. It is written down freely, as the author feels it. Like the enduring poetry we talked about earlier, however, the thoughts have to touch the heartstrings of other people for them to understand it, and the music of the soul must harmonize with the music of other souls in order for them to like it. In that sense, free verse, too, is bound by rules. Jan Markell's *Peace Amidst the Pieces* (Adventure Publications, Staples, Minn.) and Marianne Moore's free verse in *Collected Poems* (Macmillan Publishing Co., New York) are two good examples for free verse writers to examine. Helen Temple's *Come On In* (Beacon Hill Press of Kansas City) is a fine example of prose poetry.

Do I write free verse? No. I'm from the era that calls for punctuation properly placed, rhyming, and complete sentences. When I try I usually fall into Isaac Watts' habit of rhyming. If you'd like to see what I mean, here are some lines from a crazy poem born after I challenged a group of young female writers to come up with something pertaining to their thoughts on being drafted into military service:

Me?
A woman?
On the front lines?
    Out in the battle? The strife
    Holding a musket? Taking a life?
Me?

I'm a woman!
Name . . .
Age . . .
Height . . .
Weight . . . (even my weight?)
What's my fate?
Me?
On the front lines?
I'm a woman!
Sure me.
Why not me?
Why should I, cloistered 'mid carpet and pew
Sing quiet hymns, sharing joys with the few?
I'll care for the wounded, give hope to the dying,
Seek out the lonely, and comfort the crying.
Why not me?
Right is so right, and wrong is so wrong;
Nights in the war zone so terribly long;
War is so frightening—hate is so strong;
Out on the battlefront they need my song.
Why not me?
They need me.
Me.
A woman.
On the front lines.

—*Ev (1979)*

Times change. I suppose I've made some progress since writing, in 1945:

I think that I shall never see
A subject like Biology,
With creepy, crawly bugs and such
That I just cannot bear to touch . . .

POETRY IS PERSONAL!

But you're waiting for the answer to THE question. Where in the world do you sell poetry?

Get out your biggest box of Kleenex and sit down here beside me. It's hard for me to tell you this, but—

Poetry is extremely hard to sell. To succeed, you really must begin by submitting your very best poems to small publications (check your markets; study your samples). If you are successful in selling individual poems (and by successful I mean they are grabbed with glee almost every time you send them in) you *might* begin to think of gathering them into a book, but if you do, be prepared for disappointment. Only a few publishers accept poetry collections, so they are swamped, and very, very selective. (You know how to find these publishers. Check the market listings and go to the bookstores and libraries. Don't overlook greeting card publishers.)

You might end up tempted to pay a publisher to put out a pretty book of your poems, which will cost you plenty and not sell. We'll discuss that in more detail in Chapter 13, and until we do, don't.

Annie Johnson Flint got her start as a poet preparing inexpensive folders for people she loved. She really needed money, because she was an orphan with no relatives to care for her, and so crippled with arthritis that she was confined, finally, to a rest home. She sent her beautiful poetry out to friends in hand-lettered cards and gift books, decorating the verses herself. Her poems were so good that her personal cards were picked up by greeting card publishers. This serendipity got her some openings with magazines, and finally she managed to place her poems in three periodicals which carried them regularly. Only after letters from readers demanded a collection was a brochure published containing her poems, and eventually several brochures appeared. A century later, her poetry graces greeting cards![2]

Introducing myself in Chapter 1, I mentioned that one distressing experience in my life was my decision to leave missionary work (equivalent to leaving the convent). My family deserves applause for bringing me through the experience sane and happy, because they were loyal and supportive, always there when I needed them. Words my father penned, published in Swedish (a language I have yet to learn) about two decades before I was born, came to me in a letter from Ethel:

> Och sippan lyssnar til sin vän
> som sjunger i det höga,

och lyfter emot himmelen
med häpnad upp sitt öga.
Fast sangaren hon icke ser,
som sjunger i det blå,
en blick mot himlen verkar mer,
än du och jag förstå.[3]

—*Harald Stenbock*

The rough translation Ethel sent me is as follows:

The violet listened to his friend
Singing in the sky
And with hope,
He lifted his eyes toward heaven.
He didn't see the singer
Who was singing in the blue—
But one look toward heaven
Does more for the soul
Than you or I can understand.

—*translation by Ethel V. Leffel*

Twenty-five years after my father's death, that verse cheered me up, renewed my faith, strengthened my self-confidence, and put me back on my feet, and his hardbound book of poems will always accompany me wherever life may lead.

To me, one of the biggest challenges of writing is the knowledge that long after we are gone, our words live on. And whom would you rather delight, teach, or cheer more than your own descendants? Who would appreciate your humor more than they? Who would delight in the family history more than those who follow you in life? If no one else is privileged to enjoy your poetic expressions, at least, when you are gone, your heirs may find them in a box in some musty attic, read them, and be pleased.

Poetry is a very personal experience, often brought up from deeper recesses of the heart than in prose. Because of this scratching beneath the surface, because of this exposure of one's true self, well-spoken poetic thoughts reach from one heart to another in a way no other writing form does. Probably for this reason, more than any other, poetry endures.

Many people aspire to be poets recognized outside their own home. Many others feel certain they have arrived, needing only to be published to be appreciated. Slush piles always contain a few manuscripts of original poems, with an anthology or two buried somewhere in the heap as well. One editor, upon learning that I planned to include poetry in this book, pleaded with me to omit the chapter.

"I can't," I argued. "Too many writers are dabbling in poetry. They expect me to talk about it."

"No, I mean it! I feel like an ogre rejecting people's poetry. Poetry is so—so personal!"

Wouldn't it be fun to bury him in poems? For each of us to gather together all we have written, and on a given day drop it into the mail to arrive on his desk all at the same time?

The wicked gleam in my eye was my downfall. That plan was foiled. He made me promise not to tell you who he was!

You can write all the poems you want to write, but here are the ground rules for beginners:

1. You are not allowed to submit poems to a magazine until you have had ten local people tell you with tears how terrific they are and offer you postage to mail them in.
2. You cannot compile them into a book until twenty magazines have purchased them and are clamoring for more, or until you have won first place in *Writer's Digest* poetry contest ten years in a row.

I'm kidding, of course. But. . . .

IS POETRY PURE INSPIRATION?

Poetry requires a certain amount of "inspiration." That's the kind of thing Emerson spoke of in his essay, "The Poet." A poet can hear those "primal warblings," understand their meaning, and record them, translating them into words which others will comprehend. Inspiration is the ability to spot such choice thoughts in flight and capture them. Poets of the past as well as those whose names we know today possess this magical ability.

But poetry, to be well written, requires skill as well as magic. In Jerome's *The Poet and the Poem*, he compares "the hack" with the amateur. A hack writer hires himself out to write for pay, as opposed to writing purely for his own pleasure with the hope of someone's buying his work. The following points seem to me to surface in Jerome's comparison:

1. The first obligation of one hoping to publish poetry is to make oneself understood.
2. One needs to differentiate between carelessness and creativity.
3. To write publishable poetry, one must consider external factors as well as one's own internal desires.

HOW TO WRITE A POEM

Edgar Allan Poe was one of the greatest hacks of all time. On numerous occasions his ability to pound out copy decent enough to please some publisher saved him and his family (wife and mother-in-law) from starvation. Poe loved his booze and his freedom. Sooner or later, one or the other of these two vices cost him every good job he got; for if he didn't get into trouble because of heavy drinking, his nonconformist attitudes got him either thrown out or quietly replaced by some more sociable editor. His hack work included editing textbooks, writing book reviews and sports articles, and working at salaried jobs as an editor, a writer, a critic, and a poet. Hack work paid the rent and bought the spuds while the dreamer dreamed on.

Since many of us have a little of Poe's free spirit in our souls, he seems a likely person to turn to for advice on writing publishable poetry. It's not so much that we lack his natural creative ability—yours may even equal his—but more likely we fall short of his zeal, his burning desire to be recognized as a great writer.

I'm quite sure of one thing: Most of us do not build our poems with the precision of an engineer, as he claimed he did. We're more in the category of the poets Poe describes as preferring to have it understood "that they compose by a species of fine frenzy—an ecstatic intuition."

Good poetry is built by careful planning and precise, hard work, following a design as nearly as possible. I suppose few poets today do this as mathematically as did the intense, melancholy Poe. (But then, few poets will be remembered 150 years from now, either.) He could recall the progressive steps of any one of his compositions. In "The Philosophy of Composition" he reveals the process by which he wrote "The Raven." Following his general pattern, one can begin to construct worthwhile poetry—or prose, for that matter. It's a case of making a series of decisions *before* pulling the fantastic ideas out of the air, so that the finished product covers all the important points and comes up to the standards you have set.

How do you think Poe wrote "The Raven"? I'll tell you what I think. One day, while he was out pounding the streets of Baltimore looking for a decent job, he sat down on a wayside park bench to rest. He was totally discouraged.

"I quit!" he murmured, head down, chin resting on his knuckles.

"Nevermore!" cackled a strange voice nearby.

Poe, startled, looked up, half expecting to see some old witch, half hoping she would offer him a sandwich. Instead he saw a black crow perched on a fire hydrant. Jerking back and forth as he looked around, the hungry poet searched the area for some sign of a human being. "Who said that?" he whispered hoarsely at last.

"Nevermore!" squawked the crow a second time.

"Eureka! I have found the answer!" shouted Poe, jumping up. "I'm going home to write a poem about this squawking crow!"

As he went down the street toward his home, the crow flew onto his shoulder just as surely as the whole poem had popped into his head. And they dwelt together forevermore.

HOW IT REALLY HAPPENED

Poe by this time (1841-42) was recognized as a sensitive professional writer and highly skilled editor. In fact, during the two years he worked for the *Southern Literary Messenger*, subscriptions increased from seven hundred to three thousand, and in the year and a half he was editor at *Graham's Magazine* it was said the subscriptions there increased from five thousand to forty thousand. It isn't known just when he composed "The Raven." The poem was published in 1845, but a copy of it was known to be available in 1842, so possibly he was at *Graham's*. To beat the deadline, he had learned the importance of precision planning. So he leaned back, put his feet on the desk, and thought:

1. What shall I write?
   He decided to write a poem. Originality surfaced as the first requirement of the composition. It had to be new; something no one had ever done before. And, it had to be "universally appreciable," something everybody would love.
2. If a poem, how long a poem?
   The length seemed important to him. He decided on "about 108 lines," which it is, because that was the limit one might read at one sitting.
3. What effect should he create? And what should the tone be?
   The effect he decided on was beauty, and the tone, sadness, because beauty excites the sensitive soul to tears.
4. What should be the keynote?
   Poe's mind searched for a pivot on which the whole poem could turn, and the use of a refrain seemed like a good idea, because a refrain was often used successfully. People like refrains (universally appreciable). His mind came up with the

word "Nevermore!" (Inspiration entered, but only briefly. Back to the drawing board.)

5. If "Nevermore!" was to be repeated after every stanza, there had to be a reason for doing this. What might it be?
   A person repeating the word would sound stupid. Poe pondered the problem quite a while. A parrot! No, a parrot would be capable of repeating the word in a believable manner, but not in keeping with the sad tone. A raven! Able to speak, but black and somber! (Inspiration, but only after long, careful thought.)
6. What should the topic of the poem be?
   What is the most melancholy topic one can think of? Death, of course. When is death poetic? When allied with beauty. The most melancholy subject, then, would be the death of a beautiful woman.

At this point, Poe had two entirely different ideas. A raven was chirping "Nevermore!" into his mind, and a beautiful woman had died, leaving a mourning lover behind, he supposed. Somehow, he had to bind the two ideas together.

I wonder if you can feel the excitement at this point. The creative forces are at work. He feels it all beginning to fall into place. So far, he has written nothing but a few bare notes, but he is ready now. He writes only one stanza: the climax. (It turns out to be the sixteenth.) As if setting himself a goal on the mountainside to which he plans to climb, he writes these words:

"Prophet!" said I, "thing of evil— prophet still, if bird or devil!	(Establishes the character of the Raven)
By that Heaven that bends above us— by that God we both adore— Tell this soul with sorrow laden if, within the distant Aidenn,	(Establishes the mourner and his anger and frustration)
It shall clasp a sainted maiden whom— the angels named Lenore." Quoth the Raven, "Nevermore."	(Distinguishes that it was the woman he loved who died)

Writing this stanza did several things. It allowed the poet to establish the climax. He knew now what he had to build up to. He decided to make the first query to the Raven nonchalant curiosity, moving up to frenzied pleasure, into anger, concluding with sorrow and despair (which he did in two final verses). Writing the stanza also allowed him to decide on the woman, on rhythm, on meter and line length, and on arrangement.

The poem was still not written, nor was the planning complete. Inspiration was sent back to the cage for a while. There was the locale to consider. Poe didn't think of a park bench and fire hydrant (or he didn't tell us so, at any rate), but he did consider meeting the bird in its natural habitat: a forest or field. That was too big a stage. He decided to have the lover and the bird meet in a room, partly because it framed the incident well, and partly because it was an original idea. Birds don't commonly request entrance on stormy nights, do they? And the man alone in his chamber was a good setting with which to create the tone of sadness.

If you look back over his design, you will notice that the effect he wanted to create was beauty. The furnishings of the room were no accident. Even "the bust of Pallas" on which the bird settled was chosen for the beauty of the marble in contrast to the shiny black feathers of the bird.

The stormy night vividly set off the silence of the chamber. Contrast was evident, too, as the Raven burst into the quiet room "with many a flirt and flutter." Poe tells us he wanted the entrance to seem almost ludicrous. Not accidentally, the storm reflected the inner struggle of the mourning man.

To write a poem everyone would love, readers had to be considered. He decided to arouse their curiosity with the "tapping, tapping" on the window. He hoped the readers would think it was Lenore, which brings up his designed suggestiveness. He deliberately led his readers astray to complete his artistry, and he planned in metaphor to add poignant beauty to the poem—sad beauty, which would hit the reader's most tender spot: "Take thy beak from out my heart, and take thy form from off my door!"

The Raven, of course, refused, because Poe had it planned that way. As far as I know, it's still sitting there, "never flitting, still is sitting just above the chamber door"!

WHEN THE POEM IS FINISHED

Planning, for the professional writer, is a timesaver and a blockbuster. Poe knew that. His life, when he was employed, was filled with deadlines. He knew the importance of roping in his thoughts and organizing them for the sake of effective, tight writing.

An important poem (or prose) *can* just light on one's shoulder, but most winners at the poetry game do a certain amount of planning and have learned the art of self-discipline. James Dickey claims to write from subjects and situations, rather than just letting words go "wherever they want to take you."

Dickey's writing is just as tight as Poe's (and possibly will be just as enduring). According to a Bruce Hillman interview in *Writer's Yearbook 1981*, though, he works over a poem for a long time. He has three or four typewriters in the house, with various projects in them, and he keeps going back, changing, cutting, and perfecting, trying to get the poem "as close to what I think it ought to be as humanly possible."

"You never finish a poem; you abandon it," said Dickey in the interview. Most of us would probably do well to add his advice to Poe's planning procedure. If a tremendous poet like Dickey feels he needs to chop away beautiful words he has written, you and I probably ought to begin the editing process by scratching out half the poem!

I happen to like Tennyson. For one thing, he used exclamation marks freely long before they were in vogue. I overuse them! I love his remark in 1838 that "I require quiet, and myself to myself, more than any man when I write." He was also absent-minded, as I am: "apt to mislay objects." He lost the manuscript of *Poems, Chiefly Lyrical* and had to rewrite the whole thing "from scraps and memory." Another treasure, a collection he had worked on seventeen years, he left behind in a cupboard at a place where he stayed. The landlady overlooked it when she cleaned, so he got it back.

I like his willingness to "curb and prune" poems to improve them. He had the ability to whack out words or scramble up a whole page to begin again. In a collection reprinted in 1842, some think he chopped away too much; but from that day forward, he took his place as the leading poet in England, and I suspect there may be a connection there.

I don't intend to tell you to go to the library to practice scansion. Serious poets with the ability to make such an in-depth study will probably do it anyway. I've learned two things about poets: They don't appreciate criticism, and they don't really appreciate one another. Jerome in *The Poet and the Poem* best expressed the first: "Most of us have less desire to be instructed than to be recognized. . . . I pretend I am asking for help. But the only opinion I am listening for is one or another form of Wow!"[4]

The other thing I've learned about poets is expressed by Wilde in "The Critic as Artist":

> A really great artist can never judge of other people's work at all, and can hardly, in fact, judge of his own . . . The wheels of his chariot raise the dust as a cloud around him. The gods are hidden from each other. They can recognize their worshippers. That is all.

Wilde goes on to explain that Wordsworth considered Shelley's work "a pretty piece of paganism"; Shelley was "deaf to Wordsworth's message and repelled by its form"; the wonder of Keats was hidden from Byron; the "realism of Euripides was hateful to Sophocles": and Milton couldn't understand Shakespeare. He continued:

> Bad artists always admire each other's work. They call it being large-minded and free of prejudice. But a truly great artist cannot conceive of life being shown or beauty fashioned, under any conditions other than those he selected.

So there you have it. Love thyself, thou poet! But remember this:

The people who control the on/off buttons that operate the presses are probably poets, too—picky as well as sick of the stack of manuscripts staring them in the face. You'll have to be very, very good to sell your beautiful words to them. Your poetic passion will need to have the power to burn in other hearts as well as your own; your outlook on life will need to be transferable to other minds; your words will need to express the feelings of other people; and you will have to view life, as Emerson put it, "like a person who came out of a cave or cellar into the open air."

> O poet! [said Emerson] the conditions are hard but equal. . . . The world is full of renunciations and apprenticeships, and this is thine; thou must pass for a fool and a churl for a long season . . . and thou shalt be known only to thine own, and they shall console thee with tenderest love!

Back to Shakespeare!

A poet: "To be or not to be. *That* is the question!"

ASSIGNMENT 11

WARM-UP: You don't *have* to change a thing in your own poems, but in light of the lesson you might want to. Don't be afraid to cut, change, whack, or even kill those verses that will bring discredit to your longed-for reputation as the world's greatest poet. Spend some time reading any you have written.

1. This is a good time to begin a collection of poetry. Keep only what you consider the very best. Your sources will be magazines, books, newspapers and greeting cards. (Keep the publications in mind for later use. Someday you might want to query them.) In your search for good poems, go to the library, to friends, to used book shops, and to garage sales.
2. Examine poems you like, to see how they are constructed; and read poetry regularly to cultivate an

appreciation for rhythm, rhyming, and content. Reading poetry aloud, even memorizing poems, will also provide valuable input.

3. If you have never written poetry of any form, this would be a good time to try. Write a four-line jingle or a few lines of free verse. In the event that you absolutely fail in poetry, you ought to have enough back assignments to work on. It would be a good time to catch up.

FINALLY: Is performing surgery on your beautiful poems hard to do? You are allowed to cry a little.

12 The Art of Editing

Barney and Brandy were leading me up and down the hills of a quiet, shady street a few blocks from home, when a car pulled into a driveway and stopped. A meticulously dressed, grayhaired woman stepped out and waited, looking our way. I could see she wanted to say something to me, so with a tug on the two leashes, I signaled my team to slow to a stop.

Dashing down the street behind the dogs, I may appear to be younger than I feel. "Where do you live, dear?" called the woman in a motherly tone as we neared. I told her. "Your dogs are beautiful!" she went on.

That comment always amuses me. A person has to be crazy to own sheepdogs. They're very difficult to keep clean and they're notably droolers, all tongue and usually too warm. I gave her my standard reply: "They could use a bath."

"Where do you keep them?"

Had we the space for an essay on the joys of parenthood, a few choice suggestions as to where one's children sometimes deserve to be kept might have been in order. In a zoo, for example. One mother, not sadistic but harassed and busy, mused that she'd like to put hers in the deep freeze for a while, to be taken out alive and well when she had more time. Hairy, odiferious children the size of mine probably belong in a barn on the far side of the back forty, but mine happen to live with me. I can't imagine it any other way. Barney Bearpaw was tugging at the leash, ready to move on. The lovely matron and I had no time for reflecting on possibilities.

"I keep them in the house," I shouted as the dogs lurched foward. We took off, but as I glanced back I saw the woman totally disoriented by that terrible thought.

For a number of years it has been my good fortune to rent an apartment in a private home in an old town now completely surrounded by Kansas City. My landlord's daughter willed me one of her shaggy-dog pups, so (since they gave me the dog) Barney has a secure home, while I enjoy the peaceful, small-town atmosphere.

My landlady is a seamstress and uses heavy, professional machines. In place of hearing my father's typewriter late into the night, I now fall asleep to the buzz-buzz of her sewing machine. And I've learned to pick multicolored threads, cloth scraps, pins, and needles from the rug before running the sweeper. The hairy paws of an Old English are not only heavy enough to break a foot if they accidentally step on it, they're also magnetic. Everything they brush past sticks to them as they lumber through a seamstress shop.

Another interesting observation is this: My side of the ground floor is laden with valuable books and laboriously typed manuscripts; on the landlady's side there are expensive garments: lovely satin wedding gowns, silk blouses, and ultrasuede suits. When the inevitable great shake of a wet sheepdog comes, disaster results.

All that to say this: the art of editing and the art of alteration are very much alike. A tuck here and a tuck there changes an uncomfortable, baggy garment into a sleek costume. A custom-made look can be created by removing cuffs or straightening a hemline, by shortening or lengthening a skirt or sleeves, by narrowing a collar or lapels or widening them, or by letting out a seam. Sometimes the difference between homemade and hand-tailored is all in the final pressing.

The patience of a tailor amazes me. They spend endless hours sewing and ripping, sewing and ripping. Someone may bring in a cherished garment hoping the tailor will be able to copy it. My favorite tailor rips it apart to use it as a pattern, quickly sewing it back together before starting on the imitation.

As in tailoring, ripping is part of the process in professional writing. Many times I've seen Inez rip a beautifully finished garment to make one more tiny change; and many times I've retyped a page for what seems like the forty-ninth time, all for the sake of a word or two. A good writer may look at a project and see ways it might be improved. A professional takes the time to do it.

The more carefully you learn to edit your own work, the less butchering outsiders will have to do to it. This ought to spur you on to learn all you can about the process.

Every writer must get along with grammar. Don't let that scare you off. We're not going to delve into details. Maybe if you went back to high school now, you would find English to be your favorite subject; and maybe if the opportunity arises, you ought to study it. However, if you shudder at the thought, if you suppose a gerund is an unfriendly inhabitant of some obscure Soviet bloc nation, as I once did, you'll be pleased to know that one can learn to use the language correctly without studying grammatical terms. Children do this all the time. Their minds absorb whatever quality of language they hear, so in a home where proper English is spoken regularly, they grow up speaking well. English class is a breeze for them because they already practice the principles being taught. (The reverse is also true, as a sign in a Laundromat I once used indicates: "DON'T WASH NO RUGS IN THESE MACHINES.")

Adults lack the childlike ability to mimic, and let's face it—learning *is* harder after you become an adult. I believe part of the reason is that our minds are occupied with too many responsibilities. We become busy and as our minds become crammed with thoughts, little space is left for lessons. We relegate basic learning to childhood years, thinking we are done with it. In whatever way we have learned to talk, we continue to talk; and we never intend to change.

When an adult mind is reopened to learning, the interest factor makes absorbing proper English fairly easy; because as soon as something is fun, the child within takes over, making learning a game again. While I lived in Morocco, I learned Arabic this way. Morocco called for an elementary school teacher about the time I was ready to sail. I was given the assignment. (I can assure you that our school specialized in nature study hikes, drawing, and composition!) After three years of teaching in my one-room school, I entered Arabic language study. But three years in a community of Arabic-speaking people had me—to the consternation of my precise grammar teacher—chattering like the natives instead of going by the book.

The best writing gives the appearance of chattering like the natives. Good literature appears to be simply written. The truth is that every word has been scrutinized by several hard-nosed critics, clever editors to whom words are worth more than gold, who have teamed up with writers who invest words with the utmost care a few at a time in carefully chosen places. Rejects are usually full of excess words thrown out like chicken feed. To become a successful writer you must learn the art of loving words, learning words, using words properly, and removing words if they get in the way.

According to Philip Hamburger, S.J. Perelman was such a lover of words. Perelman, author of twenty books, Marx Brothers' movie scripts, and the Oscar-winning film *Around the World in Eighty Days*, recounted a near head-on crash experience. He was not so impressed with the danger, though, as he was with the new word he had learned as a result of it. The garageman told him his car had been "totaled." "Did you hear that?" Sid asked his friends. "An entirely new word for me—totaled."[1]

Perelman's word was colloquial, learned on the street from a guy with grease under his fingernails. "Totaled" brings to mind painful human feelings of despair, agony of financial loss, strain on the budget, frustration about how one might get from here to there without a car, and much more. It might result in feelings of elation—by a stroke of someone else's carelessness you've rid yourself of a lemon!

There may be a danger in using too many colloquial expressions, too many local idioms. Colorful writing, however, requires that we use words which throb with power and meaning. Such language is absorbed by sitting where people sit, listening to what they have to say. You learn it as a child learns to talk, as I learned Arabic and as Perelman learned "totaled"—by hearing words in their proper setting, and by starting to use them in appropriate and even surprising places.

COMBING YOUR WORK FOR CHANGES

One of the preliminary editing jobs you can do to improve your work is to read it with an eye for dull language, monotonous repetition of little words you remember from you days with Dick and Jane books:

> "Run, Spot, run. See Spot run. Oh, oh!" said Sally. "I see Dick. I see Jane. Dick and Jane see Spot run."

How could the same words be made more colorful? We aren't writing for first graders, although that's a wide-open field for those skilled enough to do it.

RUN	SEE	DICK
dash	look at	Chad
race	glance	Jared
tear down the street	glimpse	Jon
gallop	observe	Joey
hasten	peek at	Brahim
scoot	view	Chuckie
hurry	notice	Richard
sprint	watch	Zack
lope	peer	Andy

SALLY	SPOT	SAID
Ruthie	Whiskey	shouted
Amy	Princess	screamed
Clare	Magnet	exclaimed
Andrea	Chew-chew	whispered
Shirley	Puddles	cried
Beverly	Bowser	proclaimed

The "Run, Spot, run" paragraph becomes more interesting if rewritten, and you can also do this to your own work. Let's say that the boy's nickname is Sprinter and the girls are Karen and Sissy. The dog is Whiskey.

> "Scoot, Whiskey!" shouted Karen "Get going! Sprinter and Sissy are right behind you. If you don't watch out, they'll win the race!"

It isn't necessary to use big words. Search instead for interesting ones. Mark Twain figured if he could get paid seven cents for "city," why should he use "metropolis"? No one could call Mark Twain's writing dull. Sometimes "metropolis" would be a better choice—or today one might choose "megalopolis." (I don't happen to live in a truly megalopolitan area, but plenty of people do.)

If you happen to be plagued with the opposite problem, writing so colorfully that other people can hardly stand to look at it, you'll need to tone it down. One of the most delightful examples of this comes from Georgie Testorff, a talented friend of mine who would like to write but hasn't really plunged in as yet. At one writing class, she brought me a short essay so full of adjectives and innovative action verbs nothing was left in the dictionary! Colorful writing was definitely overdone, but I loved the "autumn wind swashbuckling down the street." "Swashbuckling" is a word one likes to roll around in the mouth like a chocolate-covered cherry. (But too many of either chocolates or swashbucklers makes one sick.)

You edit your work during the entire writing process. Even as I began this paragraph, I backed up and scratched out words I had written, starting over three times. At any point along the line, one steps back to look at the work objectively; that is, viewing it as an outsider, trying to imagine how it will be understood by readers who are unaware of the writer's feelings or background, and viewing it as one uninvolved in the thought process. One needs to look it over simply as an outsider checking for possible flaws.

As we learned earlier, there are a variety of editors who will handle the manuscripts you submit, some of whom will be forced to whip the material into publishable shape if indeed it is accepted. To perfect the art of editing your own work, you must step into their shoes, sit down at their desks, and put on their glasses. You look over your work as the first scanner; you criticize the content of what you have written; you check the grammar, sentence flow, verb sequence, punctuation, and spelling; you see that the paragraphs are glued together as one unit, and that the train of thought flows consistently from one paragraph to the next. When that is done, you go back to the beginning and eliminate unnecessary statements and excess words; you correct inconsistencies and vagaries; and you replace tedious thoughts with more colorful action. When you go back through it again to see what else might need to be done, you check for facts, to see that none have been mistyped or misquoted, you look for possible foggy areas that would be unclear to an outsider, and you keep combing until you are forced to quit.

EXCESS WORDS

To begin learning editing skills, it's more helpful to red-pencil the work of a stranger than it is to chop up your own. Adjoining a yellowed newspaper clipping of an article I wrote (which, strangely, has no red marks on it at all) is the following news item I apparently scribbled up with corrections years ago. It will give you an idea of what I mean by editing—or in this case, more appropriately, butchering. I've made the names fictitious, but nothing else is changed:

> The Square Community Club is sponsoring the "Happy Country Music Show" which has played in local areas several times. Susie is known as "Sweetheart of Country Music", and is 12 years old. A little gal with a terrific voice. She will be accompanied by her father, Jerry Jingle, that will be singing such songs as "All I Have to Offer" and many more. Danny, the youngest of the group and 9 years old will be singing "Shotgun Boogie" and other favorites. Chuck will be featured on the drums. A young man of great talent.
>
> You will enjoy the Brown sisters. These girls come from Knoxville. They started singing when they were eight years old . . .

• No quotations are needed in the first sentence.

• If the Happy Country Music Show has played in local areas several times, you don't need to say it. Scratch eight words: "which has played in local areas several times."

• Put a period after "show."

• If you say "Susie, age 12, is known as 'Sweetheart of Country Music,' " (comma before the quotation mark), you save four words.

• Words are saved as well by saying "Danny, 9, the youngest of the group . . . "

• "A little gal with a terrific voice" is not a complete sentence. "Gal" is slang. And what about the word "terrific"? It means "extraordinarily fine or intense, great, astounding, or awesome." Was she really that good? Or was she just talented? Scratch the whole phrase.

• Who knows, from the next sentence, who will be singing? In any case, the sentence should read, "accompanied by her father *who*," not "her father *that* . . . " He's a person, not an object. And I would rather say "Jerry Jingle, the director, *accompanies* the children," because the article is monotonous with "will be's." Circle them. There are several.

• When you say "Such songs as," you need not add "and many more." Scratch those three words.

• "A young man of great talent" is another example of wrong use of an incomplete sentence. And is it "great talent"? Great means "unusual excellence, remarkable, of outstanding ability." Chuck wasn't all that; he had a good teacher, a lot of energy, and loved to beat the drums. Scratch the "great talent" sentence.

• In the next paragraph seven words can be eliminated: "You will enjoy," "These girls come," and "They." Write instead, "The Brown sisters from Knoxville started singing when . . ."

This article is such a horrible example it could be improved several ways. If used at all by most newspapers, I think it would be rewritten. First of all, any decent newspaper item features the date, time, and location of such events:

> December 12, at 8:00 p.m., Jerry Jingle will present his Happy Country Music Show in a two-hour family program at Square Community Club. The show is open to the public. Tickets, at $3.50 each, will be sold at the door.
>
> Jerry Jingle, country western singer from Knoxville, Tenn., takes his show on the road several months each year. He began traveling 15 years ago with two friends still in the group: a guitarist and a banjo player. In time, his wife, Caroline, joined the show, and as the children came along, they, too, traveled. Today the Country Music Show requires a caravan of Airstream motor homes to get from place to place.
>
> Townspeople are expected to arrive early, quickly filling the Community Club. Arrangements for the overflow are being made with closed circuit television at Charlie's bar. Happy Country Music Show records will go on sale at 6:15 p.m. at the club.

One of the most revealing studies a writer can conduct is to check the meaning of words commonly thrown around by careless or uneducated writers. The flamboyant descriptions of the child with a "terrific" voice and her brother with "great" talent were totally out of place in the article, and many readers (excluding the editor who chose to print it, and possibly even wrote it!) probably laughed at the children, the writer, or the newspaper. Using a dictionary to check the true meaning of words you feel may be poorly chosen is doing yourself a triple favor: You check the spelling, you learn the proper meaning of a common word not considered before, and you increase your vocabulary. The synonym finder also becomes a useful tool in the search for the best possible word. A Roget's *Thesaurus* is a worthwhile investment, not to use as a crutch (which can kill your writing), but to discover words with various shades of meaning to depict exactly the picture you want to present.

What we've done to this very poorly written article can be done to anything you have on hand. You can correct your daily newspaper as you read it—or improve the writing one way or another. You can correct letters from friends without losing the joy of hearing from them (and don't tell them what you've done!). You can grab your children's compositions out of their hands when they come home from school and scrutinize them. In fact, you should; because seeing what their English teacher has done to them will give you insight into your own writing habits. (If you have no children, or you have woolly ones like mine, make a deal with somebody else's.)

You can make a game of looking for errors in spelling, typographical mistakes, and other boo-boo's in what you read. R.J. Reinmiller got us all looking for mistakes in *Reader's Digest*. In thirty-five years of searching, he never found one. But Clem Payne, a printer, had a collection of typos found in various Bibles; and the minute the *New International Version* came off the press, I found a typographical error in it. A friend lent me her copy of *Les Miserables*, and while I was caressing its crisp old pages in admiration, I read "see" went out into the street, instead of "she" went. . . . One day I showed Abe Goteiner the city "Wasington" in a magazine article, and within half an hour he had brought me—coincidentally—a novel one of the other employees had on her desk, with "Wasington, D.C." Betty Fuhrman found a mistake in the dictionary: "virture," instead of " virtue."

I pointed out the "will be's' in the Jerry Jingle article. Here's a partial list of other widely used excess words. Circle them wherever you find them, and if you're bravely editing your own work, find a better way to say the same thing:

It is my responsibility to . . .	My responsibility is to . . . My responsibilities include . . . Or, I am responsible . . .
There are many people *who* write well.	Many people write well . . .
It is obvious that . . .	Obviously . . .
It can be seen that these are . . .	These are . . .
These are beautiful books, aren't they?	Aren't these beautiful books? . . .
It is the right of the publisher . . .	(Blank) is the publisher's right.
Our friendship *was the result of* . . .	Our friendship resulted from . . .
As a result of our friendship . . .	Our friendship resulted in . . .
The house of the family . . .	The family's house; the home . . .
The preparation *of* . . .	Preparing . . .
Purchase *of*; use *of* . . .	Buying; using . . .
Writers *who are* busy . . .	Busy writers . . .
It is widely held that writers are funny people.	Writers are funny people.
There was a man named Dickenson who operated . . .	A man named Dickenson operated . . .
There is a woman in my neighborhood *who* . . .	A woman in my neighborhood . . . (Or, my neighbor . . .)
My manuscript *will be* focused on . . .	I've focused my manuscript on . . . (Or, My manuscript focuses on . . .) (In my manuscript I focus on . . .)
Next week's lesson will center . . . on . . .	Next week's lesson centers on . . . (Or, In next week's lesson we . . .)
Nutrition is *terribly* vital to . . .	Nutrition is vital . . .

I *will be forever* grateful . . .	I appreciate . . .
I'm *eternally* grateful for . . .	I'm grateful for . . .
It gives me immense pleasure . . .	I'm pleased . . .

"Forever" and "eternally" are both a very long time. To say you're eternally grateful, or to promise gratitude forever is overdoing it. This gushing belongs in the garbage bin. Someone may say spelling is crucial to good writing. Mind you, spelling is important—even *very* important—but it's not crucial. I've worked on excellent stories with delightful plots and on essays filled with interesting ideas, but with a few words misspelled. Spelling is not *crucial* to good writing. Copyeditors would be as sad as Maytag repairmen if there were no corrections to make at all! "Crucial is a harsh word, unforgiving, which comes from "cross."

"Catastrophe" is a similar word. The statement "It is a catastrophe to neglect discipline in the home" gives the impression all is lost. "Catastrophe" indicates "overwhelming disaster or failure." Neglecting discipline is a mistake; it's risky; it may one day be regretted, and it might lead to catastrophe. But you must weigh your words. "Catastrophe" is too harsh a word to use carelessly. Watch for other such words.

You need not qualify words like truth. Close to the truth is not truth, not even if it's *very* close to the truth. Truth is always honest; thus, to say "the honest truth" is to add a word that is unnecessary.

You might want to use such expressions (or whatever your pets are). I want to make you aware you *are* using them and to stimulate you to think of substituting for them or omitting them. The question should be, "Is this the best way I can express myself?" When you learn to weigh your words, you'll find many of the things you say tumble out of your head without thought. They look dumb on the page, and shouldn't be there at all. "Spank them all soundly and send them to bed!"

TROUBLEMAKING WORDS

Certain words seems to be universal troublemakers. Of these, some, when used wrongly, hit an editor as squarely in the eye as if the sun had struck a mirror which bounced its glare off in his face. We seem to think that everyone should know the difference between "accept" and "except," "their" and "there," and "whether" and "weather." On the other hand, if someone uses "who" in place of "whom" on the first page of his manuscript, he is forgiven. Woe to the foolish writer who dares to submit pages containing double negatives. That isn't double exposure, by the way. It's incorrect use of "not" and "no." One will suffice. No one gets by with saying "I don't have no education," because if that's true, "he ain't got no right to write!"

Writers make mistakes in number, as well, by following the bad habits of their childhood locale:

The dogs was chasing a squirrel. (Should be "The dogs *were* . . . ")

Many people was in the doctor's office. ("Many people *were* . . . ")

Many of us are very colloquial in our thinking: That is, we love to revert to our childhood lingo or we adapt regional speaking quickly. If one is adept at learning languages, the speech habits become such a natural part of thought that—good or bad—they flow freely both in conversation and in writing. Much creative writing is informal, but even so, glaring grammatical errors, even very common ones, are taboo except in actual quotations of regional speech. Only a Huck Finn can murder the Queen's English and get by with it.

Let's run through a few words that trip writers up. The list is incomplete, but it may serve to set you on guard:

WAS/WERE

"We" is plural, while "was" is singular; thus it is "We were," and "I was," and one should say "We weren't" rather than "We wasn't."

PRESENT	PAST
I am	I was
You are	You were
We are	We were
He/she is	He/she was
They are	They were

DOESN'T/DON'T

Mixing up "doesn't" and "don't" is a no-no. If I say "I *don't* look good," it's sad, but true. He *doesn't* look good, either. The weather *doesn't* look good. And they *don't* look good. *I don't,* he *doesn't;* they *don't,* but it *doesn't.*

ACCEPT/EXCEPT

I *accept* your invitation, *except* if it rains. Wouldn't it be nice to have a publisher *accept* your article—*except* if you had changed your mind about selling it.

THERE/THEIR

Wrong use of these two words is often a slip of the fingers on the typewriter—or at least it is in my case. "There" indicates the place (and it ends in "here"). "Their" indicates possession (and the word ends in "heir").

BARE/BEAR

The floors are *bare*; it's hard to *bear*. Bare means uncovered, but bear means to carry. (The fierce hairy animal is—go to the head of the class if you said *bear*!)

How about past, present, and future of the verb *to bear*?

You *bore*, you *bear*, you will *bear* . . .

Have you *borne* all you can *bear*? (I don't mean to "bore" you!)

GOOD/BETTER/BEST

I was slow; he was slower; she was slowest. (No sweat.)

I am attractive; she is more attractive; my sister is—attractivest?

No, she is the *most* attractive!

	few	fewer	fewest
	dumb	dumber	dumbest
	smart	smarter	smartest
	neat	neater	neatest
But:	slovenly	more slovenly	most slovenly

WEATHER/WHETHER

This introduces the pronunciation problem. Words like where, whence, while, wheel, and whether have a slight "H" sound. Ware, wince, wile, weal, and weather do not.

TO/TOO/TWO

I'm going *to* the store. Will you go, *too* (also)? That will make two (2) of us!

I/ME

You and *I* are going to the doctor together. To determine when to use "I" rather than "me," you ask the question, "Who?" Who is going to the doctor? You *are*, and I *am*. Nobody beyond age two says "Me am."

On the other hand, "The doctor didn't ask to see anybody but you and *me*," is correct, because (ask the question "Who?"): He didn't ask to see anybody but *me*. To test yourself, ponder the possibility of saying "He didn't ask to see I."

Wrong usage of "you and I" is becoming so common the best speakers are tripped up by it. The refrain of a popular song uses "you and I" incorrectly (when it should be "you and *me*") and all too many people think you and *I* are wrong when we say "you and me" where it really belongs! (Ask yourself the question: Who? Many people think "who" is wrong? You are and I *am*, thus it is you and *I*.)

For further study along this line, I recommend *Make Every Word Count*, by Gary Provost. Become a stickler in speaking correctly, and your writing will improve. It doesn't matter how many people are wrong. You and I can be right!

SPELLING TIPS

I'm told that one major company deals with its mountains of resumes by throwing out first of all every one that contains a misspelled word on the first page. I don't know about major employers, but I do know this: Writers who are careless about spelling sell their work less frequently than those who can spell. The issue, of course, is not spelling. Editors are digging through the heap to find the professional look. What I said in Chapter 4 bears repeating here. To get past the scanning crew the manuscript must have these basic qualities:

1. a professional look
2. a captivating first paragraph
3. smooth flow of words
4. a strong outline
5. professional quality photos (if used)

Numbers two through five can outweigh number one, but scanners have learned that a sloppy presentation probably comes from an amateur whose work is not worth paying more than one editor to read. Work which contains glaring grammatical errors or misspelled words that shout their presence to the keen editorial eye is sloppy, no matter how neatly it may be typed.

English spelling can be absolutely crazy, and we creative writers are apt to be careless. More than that, looking up words in the dictionary hinders the flow of writing. We can be very easily distracted, so much so that we might not get back to the project at hand for days, if at all.

I handle this problem by writing while the words are flowing. In fact, during one of those rare moments of great inspiration which will be lost if it isn't put on paper immediately, I step off the crazily spinning world, hole up, and scribble nonstop until I'm done. When I'm finished, I read, reread, and read again until I've almost memorized the manuscript and have it so badly marked up even I can scarcely tell what it says. This involves typing and retyping as often as necessary to keep the work fairly legible. I check some spelling during this retyping and editing period, rather than while I'm writing. In fact, while I'm writing I may scribble words I'm not sure even exist, which seem to fit. The final typing requires stopping for a last minute check on any words still doubtful in my mind.

Some words trick the majority of average spellers, while other misspellings are simply bloopers. Pronunciation is a large part of our problem (as in whether and weather). Since diction is so important to good spelling, you can improve your spelling by practicing oral reading. The following list, for example, can be read into a recorder as you would normally read it. When you play it back, you may be surprised at how many of the letters you've either omitted or slurred past. No wonder you spell those words wrong!

Accep(t), for example, has a "t" at the end of it. And it is *ak*´cept, not *ek*cept. You may call a little child "punkin," but the word is pump-kin.

*ani*mated	ane*c*dote	lan*d*lord
an*d*	gran*d*mother	promp*t*
ans*w*er	han*d*ful	recognize
brill*i*ant	iden*t*ical	asp*i*rin
civil*i*an	ki*t*chen	envir*on*ment
consum*p*tion	kep*t*	go*v*er*n*ment
congra*t*ulations	swep*t*	effectu*al*ly
temper*a*ment	tent*a*tive	

Many of the above words have an "i" in them which is pronounced as "y" or in some cases an almost silent "i." Others to watch for:

auxiliary	benefic*i*al	defic*i*ent
opinion	poinsett*i*a	famil*i*ar

By the way, the word is *fam*-iliar, not *farm*-iliar. I haven't seen it spelled that way (yet), but I hear it pronounced *farm*iliar all the time. On the other hand, I've seen responsible spelled with an "a" (responsi-*a*ble) although I have yet to hear it pronounced that way, except in jest. This serves as a reminder, too, that the "ible" and "able" endings give some people trouble.

Words ending in "ly" often give us trouble. As a Bing Crosby fan in the forties (of course, a *very young* one!), I loved his rendition of "Come out, come out wherever you are . . ." which we all concluded by singing lustily along with Bing, "Yes, and *incidently*, *mently*, I'm not up to par . . . " The songwriter didn't write that at all. He wrote "*incidentally*, ment*ally*." That discovery was a help to spell incidentally (and, incidentally, I still do struggle with it), the tune pops up out of the depths of my brain, and I think, "Yes, and incident*ally*, ment*ally*," The adjective is "mental," not "ment," and to make it into an adverb, you add "ly."

accidental/accidentally
grammatical/grammatically
temperamental/temperamentally

If the adjective ends in "e," you drop the "e" to add "ly":

Incompatible/incompati*bly*/incompatibility

Keep in mind that you are only adding "ly," not "ally." Thus it is

frequent/frequently
fretful/fretfully

IS IT "IE" OR "EI"?

It's still "*i* before *e*, except after *c*":

believe	receive	conceive
achieve	deceit	perceive

Complete the rhyme for further help: "or when sounded like *a*, as in neighbor and weigh. In the following words it is "ei," because it is still part of the exception in the couplet:

beige	freight	reign
skein	veil	vein

IZE, YZE, OR WHAT?

Words ending in the "ize" sound are another bugbear. It is *ize*? Or is it *ise*? Or might it be *yze*?

In American spelling it is most generally *ize*. You can memor*ize* anal*yze* and paral*yze* with no trouble at all. Get them down pat. You won't run across many others spelled with *yze*. As to *ise*, certain groups of words fall into this pattern:

—cise (such as exercise)
—wise (such as likewise)
—rise (such as sunrise)
—guise (such as disguise)
—mise (such as surmise)
—vise (such as revise)

Merchandise and advertise are *ise*; baptize is *ize* (but baptism may be spelled with an "s"). The "ize" category of words is the largest of the three, so categor*ize* the words and memor*ize* the exceptions.

We could go on and on. My simple dictionary has 158,000 definitions, which only scratch the surface of the English vocabulary. Spelling problems can arise at least that many times, to which may be added words personally created by the writer (which are not words at all), and words created by a community (idioms not widely known). No one knows how slang should be spelled until a widely accepted spelling surfaces. I recently tried to trace "glom" (to grab a handful; to swipe). I decided the spelling should be "glom" because I thought the word must come from "glomerate," which means something gathered into a cluster or mass. I might be all wrong. The *Dictionary of American*

Slang tells me that Perelman spelled the word "glom," so I'm in good company; but it also says Jack London (who isn't exactly shoddy company for a budding writer), chose to spell it "glahm," while "glaum" is also acceptable. Who knows? When in serious doubt, find another word. You get no special brownie points for using rare unknowns.

LET'S MOVE ON!

Editing your own writing must include taking a long, tough stand against clichés. Clichés are expressions so overused they have lost their sparkle. In the development of colloquial speech some expressions ignite and others don't. Not every spark that hits a California roadside sets the whole forest on fire, nor does every clever saying reach the whole earth. Everybody in the world does seem to use other expressions for a while, but finally even these popular expressions die. Clichés are cadavers dragged out of the graveyard of once-delightful phrases, ghosts out of the past, expressions strangled to death by overuse.

Some clichés are easily spotted. Even when they sparkle with new life, one can sense their rootlessness and know they are doomed to die. "Eyeball to eyeball," which was such a refreshing change from "eye to eye" or "looking one square in the eye," was one of these. "Quote, unquote," which required having both hands free to form a little curliques like horns over one's head, was another. Neither of them lasted very long (although the smelly carcasses are still dragged around by some people).

Other clichés last so long we begin to think they're okay. These are the tricky ones, and the only way you can guarantee that your manuscripts are free of their deathly pall is to march through page by page, pick them up, and throw them out. You'll soon begin to recognize a corpse when you see it. Generally a cliché consists of three or four words or more, is a cute saying everyone used to use, and even though it's "dear to my heart and yours" (a cliché), it's "so old it stinks" (another cliché)! You can find your own; here are a few I thought of:

hit the nail on the head	jump to a conclusion
busy as a bee	doing a great work
in the final anaylsis	strong as a horse
tired as a dog	on the outs
last by not least	more fun than a barrel of monkeys

I don't think "a cabin nestled in the woods" is a cliché. I like it too much, and I wish I had one. But you might see it as a ghost out of the past that needs to be replaced, and if you can find something I'll like even better (such as a shack on the beach), throw it out. Replace it!

PUNCTUATION—DO WE NEED IT?

We do need it, of course. Vocabulary changes constantly, but punctuation has remained fairly constant in spite of the innovative challenges to the establishment. The trend in popular writing has been to shorter sentences, doing away with some of the conjunctions and semicolons in the process. Good writing has always varied sentence lengths. Some will be five words long; some ten words; three words; seventeen words. One. Or two. Exclamation marks are so much more common now, they've been added to the typewriter keyboard! Just the same, if your problem is at all like mine, you'll need to go through the final typed copy and white them out. I *always* use too many. Everything seems so important! Or so exciting! Or so bad! Dots . . . and dashes—are commonly overused now. They should be used properly, and too many of either, no matter how modern they may appear to your eye, can become very tedious.

Studying punctuation in national magazines can bring you rewards. If you're good enough (or lucky enough) to have someone accept your work, the final editor to handle it will be a copyeditor in the proofroom. That's like having a tough English teacher correcting your paper; and as in school, the teacher has the last word. Getting a good mark is a nice feeling, and I like to imagine the "teacher" smiling when she sees my byline, knowing her day will be fairly pleasant because I happened to be a part of it. No proofroom expert will ever give me an A, of course. I leave enough flaws along the way to keep the job interesting, lest all those people, whom I desperately need, get bored and quit.

Tightening up your copy is the key to success. Once you have learned how to do this, you'll be on your way. The second stage is getting so particular the weak areas of your manuscript haunt you. The third stage is developing a willingness to retype a beautiful page; and in some ways, this is the biggest hurdle to cross. In the first few drafts you red-pencil the copy (correcting it, as a teacher would do); and you scribble it all up, rewriting and rearranging (as any professional writer would do). Finally, you feel satisfied, so you type it all up and get it ready to mail. It looks absolutely perfect, so beautiful your gizzard aches knowing you've created something really tremendous, sure to sell.

The next morning, just before mail time, you read it over ten more times. Here's a little change, there's a little mistake, here's another change, there's a terrible weakness, here's a flaw, and there's another flaw!

But it's ready to go! I can hear you as clearly as if I were sitting by your side: "Surely she's not telling me to scratch it all up and retype the whole thing!"

That's what I'm telling you. When you think your manuscript is ready to go, that's the time to start editing. Get out your red pencil, your blue pencil, your scissors and scotch tape, and your guts. To be a pro you must butcher your baby even if you have to grab it out of the postman's hand and bring it back into the house to do so. It's the final tucks, the little changes, and the whacking when it hurts so much it makes you cry that put your writing out in front, where the people who matter will notice it. Never allow a sentence to leave the privacy and security of your home to travel to distant places as long as you see one weak spot in it. You have to keep chopping, chopping, chopping.

I keep editing my writing as long as they let me. Finally, in the press room, somebody grabs my shirttail and says, "That's all, Ev." The presses start rolling; but even so, if I could, I would reach my hand in to change just one more thing.

Someday, I suppose, you'll hear that I was swallowed up by

a giant web press which spit me out the other end flatter than a photograph. You'll understand that I died in the line of duty, trying to make just one more little, ever so small but ever so important, improvement to an otherwise perfect book.

ASSIGNMENT 12

WARM-UP: To practice writing concise, colorful sentences, shorten long ones you wrote in the previous assignment; reword punctuation; cross out excess words; circle clichés. Change dull words to lively ones and gushy words to better choices. Keep working on everything you write until you are satisfied nothing more can be done to improve it.

1. Take out things you have written in the past, focusing on rejected material, if you have any. Look it over with a critical editor's eye. Do your own cruel editorial butchering. (Don't throw anything away. File it in GARBAGE, because later it may spark a winning idea.)
2. As of today, begin to analyze, correct, or improve the writing of other people. I hope you have seen things in this book you would have said differently. If your wording is better, go ahead and scratch mine out! (But don't you dare let me know about it!)
3. If spelling is your weakness, you can always write tough words on flashcards to memorize them. Never type dubious spelling. Look the word up in the dictionary.
4. Pick one or two of the best items you have written. Read them over one final time to be sure you have not overlooked some glaring flaw. Retype them (double spaced) as if you were preparing them for submission. But don't send them away. Put them in the drawer or file them for one week. Then, showing no mercy, edit them again.

FINALLY: Don't just sit there smiling at your ingenious writing. Come on! Tear it apart!

13 Everything You Always Wanted to Know About Writing a Book

In my pile of correspondence from hopeful authors, I found a letter that broke the camel's back—or bent it badly for that day, at least. A tediously familiar message was scribbled in pencil in childish scrawl on lined, three-ringed notebook paper, slightly soiled. Judging by the photo she enclosed the author must have been somebody's mother.

"I have this idea for a book," the letter proclaimed. "How do I write it? How much will it cost to get it printed? Where should I send it?"

How can anybody who rips the paper out of a notebook (as opposed to snapping the rings open to lift it out) have the patience, skill, time, and loving care required to write a book? On an ordinary day I might have gotten reckless enough to jot a note on her very own page. I could have sent it back, saying simply: "Not to us, Arabella, not to us."

But it was one letter too many. It blew my mind. A wicked gleam ignited in my tired eyes. I responded immediately, using up miles of carbon ribbon (which isn't cheap) and not a little lift-off tape.

"Dear Arabella," I began kindly. I put us on a first-name basis because I suspected I'd be a lifetime pen-pal anyway: "When we got your letter, we clapped our hands on our foreheads and shouted in unison, 'Oh no! Not another one!"

Too many people are writing books. Most of them end up in the trash barrel or, soggy from tears shed over them, are buried in some bottom drawer to be passed on to posterity in manuscript form. A few, of course, might be lost by disinterested editors who said in the first place they didn't want such garbage mailed to them.

With several book contracts in file and a few staff-written assignments of the same magnitude under my belt, I can assure you that writing a book is a Gargantuan job. The full impact of this fact hit me as I neared the end of my first full-length biography, "*Miss Terri!*"

In addition to the writing, the story required extensive research into files of the late 1800s. I had poured over yellowed pages and fine print of both public and private archival collections; had read handwritten diaries the subject kept up consistently during most of her fifty-four years in Morocco, and had bent my neck out of shape going through newspaper microfilm files. (Anyone who has tackled that job wearing bifocals will understand what I mean.)

As the conclusion came into view, I became totally wrapped up in the project, preoccupied and hyper to the point of either neglecting close friends and family, or being so garrulous they couldn't stand to have me around. At last I completed the book. I had said all I had to say. I laid my pen down, sighed deeply, and cried out through the four walls that had imprisoned me so long, "Now, God, just let me die!" The task had been so monumental I was sure it could never be topped.

Not many amateurs are ready to write a book. In the first place, until they have tested it, they don't know if they have talent of book stature. A top-selling author must have above-average writing gifts. In the second place the patience and skill to finish the job are rare commodities. In the third place, most would-be authors really have nothing to say. They dump out a basketful of words that are as unique as baby clothes at a Laundromat—meaningless words stacked into meaningless phrases, some carelessly stacked at that. Finally, after months of struggling furiously in this mad endeavor, people bundle up their baby, pretty little clothes and all, and ship it off prematurely to the wrong address to somebody who hates babies.

After explaining all this, I concluded: "We have some advice for you, all right, Arabella. Become a computer engineer, or the first woman on Mars—become anything else in the world. Any field you enter will welcome you more gladly than we will. However, if you insist, you may send your book to us. We will spill coffee on it, lose a few pages, and laugh ourselves silly reading it to each other during breaks. We can guarantee at least a nine-month delay in sending it back with a printed reject form. If we can do anything more to dissuade you, please call." (And I gave her a competitor's phone number.)

Well, the letter didn't get signed. My boss wouldn't let me send it. Publishers are funny about things like that. What good is the latest computerized typesetting equipment if you've got nothing to typeset? All the sophisticated printing equipment in the world would grind to a costly halt if we scared off all the budding writers!

So don't run off. Hang around a while. Anybody can see that some books *do* make it. New ones are rolling off the presses all the time. Popular authors are aging and dying; unpopular ones are giving up. So who's to take their place? Maybe you can.

How do you know if you ought to write a book? In this chapter we will sift through the myths and sort out the bits of information you have collected on the subject. The questions are

1. Why should I include writing a book in my writing goals?
2. Is the material I envision of book magnitude?
3. How does one get a book into print?

EXAMINING YOUR PURPOSE

To the question "Why do you want to write a book?" most of us would quickly answer, "Who wouldn't want to?"

Anyone who has read this far hankers to write for one or more of the following reasons:

1. For personal satisfaction
2. To tell the world something
3. for extra income
4. To gain prestige

There is nothing wrong with any of these reasons, but you can obtain these tantalizing rewards from almost any successful writing form. Perhaps you can remember the elation that accompanied your sight of a gold star on a childhood composition, or the heartwarming delight at seeing something you wrote published, even in the simplest form.

Personal satisfaction comes from two sources: the inward knowledge that you have done your best, and the gratifying awareness that someone else recognizes your accomplishment as worthy.

Nothing can top the first "gold star" of professional writing: the first check in the mail. Nor does one's heart ever swell with any more pride than it does the first time one is publicly acknowledged as a writer.

Between the terms *writer* and *author* the finest of lines exists. One can be the author of any "literary work," in which case the problem becomes distinguishing which writing can be classed as "literary." Length has nothing to do with it. A brief notice pertaining to a club meeting seems to fall short of that dignified label. However, even fewer words chosen and joined in some immortal phrase may later be labeled a literary classic:

> Four score and seven years ago our fathers brought forth on this continent a new nation, conceived in liberty, and dedi-

> cated to the proposition that all men are created equal. . . .
> —Abraham Lincoln

Is it the quality or endurability that gives writing class? Both, perhaps. But quality appears regularly in short-lived publications, dying at the end of the day. What great skill is required to produce topnotch material daily or weekly! Even *monthly*, top quality is a big order, with few writers being talented and disciplined to produce it year upon year. Consistent quality seems to me one of the most enviable attainments. Every writer must strive to reach that goal. Just the same, written material is not classed as literature just because of its quality.

It is the endurability of books that earns those who write them the title *author*. Almost all other published material dies young. No matter how clever copy may be, in this "Rush-Priority" era even the best magazines and the greatest newspapers are speed-read and laid down to be lost in a pile of paper. Magazines and newspapers serve an inestimable place of value in our society, but the fact remains: They are collectors' items when they are old because they are so rare. Almost no one keeps them.

But great books live on. Antiquated copies grace the shelves in many homes and libraries. Were the masters of early literature to walk through modern libraries and bookstores they probably would be amazed to see reprints of their work still drawing attention decades and even centuries after it was written.

As a professional writer, you will author a good many words which will bring you the rewards you seek. By popular usage, however, you will not become *an author* until you have published a book.

Now comes the question, "Is the author king of the castle?" If writing is an uphill climb (and it is), is writing a book at the very top?

As with almost every question in life, the answer must certainly be: "That depends." Many writing pursuits bring greater financial rewards than do books. Not only that, success on the job as a staff writer or editor can bring daily gratification, more fulfilling to many people than the frustration of freelance writing with its inevitable rejection and more enjoyable than the so-called lonely writing life. A successful article writer speaks to thousands, perhaps even hundreds of thousands once he begins to make good sales, while the author might hide his "important message" in a novel which fails to deliver it! One certainly can get great messages off one's chest in a bestselling nonfiction book, but only rarely does an author achieve such success that the book (which seemed so important) makes an impact equal to the steady input of a top syndicated column.

Writers who bombard the mini-market with thought-provoking articles achieve the same goal: unloading their thoughts on others. As to prestige, "Hints from Heloise," the quotable quips of the late Bill Vaughn of the *Kansas City Star*, and the cartoon characters of Charles Schultz with their whimsical style and words of wisdom have gained their creators prestige enough to satisfy anyone. Compilation in book form of the work of Schultz and Heloise is an outgrowth of their fame, not a deliberate creation. Think about that, Charlie Brown!

Decisions, decisions! So many upward paths tantalize the writer! One person's talent might lead up the rugged path of magazine writing, where reaching The Top could be obtaining a staff writing or editorial position at one of the better-known slick magazines. Another might choose to climb in political speech writing, with The Top being chief press secretary at the governor's mansion or the White House. Someone else may enter the field of advertising, moving ever upward, finally creating clever phrases which become household words.

The Top is as excitingly varied as any range of mountain peaks. Broadway plays, movie scripts, cartoon strips, TV soap operas, syndicated columns, and textbooks are only a few of the heights within the grasp of the hardworking writer. A writer may successfully scale several mountains in a lifetime, for skills and interests vary among writers, and there are opportunities to match them. Most people tackle one mountain at a time, often stopping there to relish the view, content with their achievement.

To author a book is to reach the top of only one mountain. If the project culminates a lifetime of writing success or if it is the one-in-a-million really big winner, that for the author may be

The Top. If, on the other hand, a book develops early in one's writing career, it may be the bottom. Writing a book sometimes seems like a mountainous task only because it was begun too soon. Far too often, books bomb out because the authors are amateur writers, tackling the job too soon. When they end in disaster, everyone—author, publisher, distributor—loses his shirt. Rarely, *rarely* does a truly successful book flow from the pen of an inexperienced writer.

Most books published today are not The Top. From my perspective as both editor and author, most books, my own included, have earned the writer a measure of personal satisfaction, they have allowed the writer to get something off his chest, they have provided a very small financial bonanza, and the writer has enjoyed some prestige. The glut of books on today's market, however, lacks endurability. We, the authors of today, have not reached The Top. We are still practicing.

Now. Why do you want to write a book? Before you do, sit back and think about this: Other very prestigious and rewarding mountaintops in professional writing are waiting for a genius to come along. Climb the mountain that is right for you.

While I was getting these very important words off my mind onto paper, the phone rang. After the conversation I leaned back, put my feet on the windowsill, and watched the birds peck away at their seeds. Did I hear the person correctly? Surely not. Let me reconstruct the gist of the conversation for you. He said, no, his book had not sold, but he had been studying at the library as I had suggested, and he was beginning to see his mistakes. I was pleased with his understanding and the improvements in his writing he told me about, and I told him so. Then I advised him to lay aside the book awhile to work on short stories and articles, practicing what he had learned and trying to sell short items to magazines.

"Oh, I can't write for magazines." (He said it in an I-don't-know-French tone of voice.)

"Why not?" I inquired.

"I'm not smart enough," he explained.

I took a long, deep breath. "Run that by me again."

"I'm not smart enough. I mean, you have to be *smart* to write for magazines."

Print a million copies of the message below! In bold, bright, shock-producing colors! Slap it up on billboards all over town! Help me spread the word around: To write a book you must be *very*, **very**, very "smart." One does not begin with a book, moving *up* to short items. It's the other way around.

The incident got me to laughing about a bearded fellow who waited with me for a driver's test in a foreign country. While we awaited our turns, he told us that he had failed the test given for automobiles, and had failed the test for trucks. He was waiting now to take the bus test.

Sometimes when slush editors dig through the heap of book manuscripts and proposals, they get the idea that kind of reasoning prevails among writers: "When all else fails, write a book."

GETTING YOUR ACT TOGETHER

The reason one begins with short stories and articles is that the basic rules of organization learned there apply to large projects. This is an overly simplified statement, but the longer a writing project is, the more complex it may become, because in a book-length production one has both time and space to expand. Whether writing 1,000 words or 100,000, the writer is dealing with the same kind of pattern, but there are expansion possibilities through flashbacks, sidetrips, additional character portrayals, shifting of scenes, and elaborate embellishment in the book.

The difference between a great book and a great big worthless manuscript lies in this complexity. There is a danger of seeing one's story idea expand into a monstrosity by filling pages with additional characters and events, with descriptions of new places and new situations, until the whole project becomes bogged down. The trouble with most book manuscripts is that they have grown like detergent suds, fluffing out in ever-increasing billows, threatening to drown the author and his idea in their worthless beauty. The book idea allowed to grow as it will to fill pages becomes a nightmare from which there seems no escape.

Whether you are cornered by such a monster or whether you are still safe, your idea locked in your heart, take courage.

Whether nonfiction or fiction, there is a pattern core around which a book is built. Getting the skills of the article and short story down pat is invaluable practice for the book. The most complex novel can be boiled down to a simple plot which becomes complex through weaving subplots into the story.

In most of the great books, central elements are few. *Les Miserables*, one of the most fascinating books ever, in my estimation, boils down to a simple plot:

PEOPLE	CONFLICT	RESOLUTION
A simple man /	struggles against a system /	to gain freedom.

Uncle Tom's Cabin, one of the greatest novels of all time, is a basic struggle for freedom, too: one of good against evil, if you will, for the freedom of a race. At a time when America needed her message, Harriet Beecher Stowe created a novel around it, saying "This is what is happening to blacks!"

Herman Melville, author of *Moby Dick*, was a self-taught man. His seafaring and imprisonment experiences provided him with rich background for writing, and he used it to good advantage, but when he got his hands on books, he read avidly. *Moby Dick*, like other nineteenth century novels, had a hidden message of good versus evil, a complicating factor in preparing the book. Added to this, the author gave his readers "a whale of an education" in whales and whaling. In spite of all the complexities, however, *Moby Dick* is the simple story of a man who hated a whale and pursued him, and the whale won.

As to nonfiction books, in Chapter 9 I gave you a simple diagram showing how side trips depart from the established pattern temporarily, *interrupting* the organized pattern, but returning to the basic outline so the pattern is *not disrupted*. The book (as opposed to short items) grows out of such side trips which can be extremely complicated, but which are deliberately planned into the package before the book is begun. Their purpose is to enlarge upon, explain, and in general enhance the basic plan.

Do not type up your garbage and submit it to anyone. Such collections are doomed to die. If you are a beginner with such a book as your long-term goal, you will have ample time to plan for it. If you have tried and failed, now you know why. Probably you should place the book in your file while you study and taste success, joining with the beginner in planning a book properly, from scratch.

Whether it is to be a novel or nonfiction, your book will begin with an idea; it will progress into a concrete plan; an outline showing continuity as well as content will develop; and you will begin to collect specific information to put meat on the bones. The satisfaction at producing a successful book of that stature is immense.

CHOOSING THE CONTENT

If you want to write a book, exceptional writing talent, above-average self-discipline, and substantial writing experience are necessary, but a fourth factor must be considered. Going back to Chapters 9 and 10, if you're "smart enough to write a book" you will spot it right away: What are you going to write about?

I'm reminded of the "Dah . . . I dunno" phase we went through in our household when I was growing up. Is that how you will respond to the question? Well, before you decide to write a book, you'd better find out what it's going to contain!

An editor wishing to remain anonymous told me she despairs of all the meaningless, unsalable autobiographies she receives. A few years ago, autobiographies were popular. Movie stars, TV personalities, musicians, evangelists, comedians—anyone who was well known—were quite likely to succeed in selling their life story. A certain number of autobiographies of common people also sold, especially when the story focused on trauma, disease, or drastic lifestyle change. The era passed as the market demanded fresh subjects. Almost every book editor welcoming mail today cries out the same plea: "Stop the flow of autobiographies!"

Market testing is fascinating. I would like to know more about it, and to do it. Precise skills have been developed to evaluate future trends in salable literature (as in everything else).

"Those awesome editors" know one thing for certain: The market has reached the saturation point in life stories. This is not the decade of autobiography. While one major event in your life might develop into a salable article (or you might find a variety of ways to tell bits of your life story), it is highly unlikely that the average person's life is outstanding enough to warrant writing a book about it. Too many awful details bog such a book down. As to trauma, think how many grief-stricken people have suffered a terrible loss as great as your own; think how many people suffer through cancer, chemotherapy treatments, and the threat of death; think how many people go through a hurricane, tornado, earthquake or flood. Even such drastic events are commonplace, because every disease and every natural disaster strikes many people.

Exceptional, fast-paced stories will always be in demand, but on the whole it is the lessons we learn from life's ups and downs that make for salable printed matter. To fill a whole book with the minute details of all that happened is to lose the ball game. I feel like a nagging mother saying this again, but I mean it: If recounting your life story or someone else's escape from disaster is what you have in mind, proceed very carefully. You're trying to enter an exit lane. That trend in books is on its way out.

This brings up the interesting possibility that writing trends may be like fashions. If you keep your rejected book proposal long enough, will it come back into vogue?

It might. If you suspect your rejected manuscript is simply a poorly timed winner, you could insert a PENDING file between your GOOD and GARBAGE files. If it really appears to be a potential winner, keep your eyes and ears open as you listen to the news and hang around bookstores and booksellers' conventions so you can be ready to jump the minute the trend reappears.

I had such an opportunity but lost it by losing interest at the wrong time. The subject was old China. I could have had a book on someone's desk the day the China trend came back, but I was asleep. By the time I woke up, China experts controlled the field. Never mind; that material is pending. When China experts have said all they have to say, "Pearl Buck the Second" will appear.

You will probably have to be younger than I am (or continue writing until you are very, very old) to see autobiography reappear. Biography depends more upon interest in the individual whose story is being told, than upon trends. Acceptable biography takes its place on the shelves of history. Good biography is always acceptable if the subject is well known. Autobiography has a fleeting time-span unless the writer has made a significant contribution of universal interest. If he times it right, a President can publish his memoirs; most others cannot.

If I were presenting this information in an article, I could be quite specific about current trends. However, I hope my book will outlive them, so I prefer to refrain from telling you what is in or out at the present time. Basically, however, the following list enumerates some rather risky categories from which to pick a book subject:

COMMON LOSER	REASON
1. Autobiography	a. narrow interest potential b. subjective viewpoint c. diary or letter form, rather than literary form
2. Personal Experience	a. passing interest; quickly outdated (tornado, flood, fire, hurricane, accident) b. subjective viewpoint, especially overemphasizing trauma common to mankind (cancer, loss of loved one, illness of child, loneliness, etc.)

(use both of the above as background to enrich other writing, or publish locally, or as articles. Or publish privately for family.)

3. Collections (of essays, devotionals, mini-articles, and local newspaper columns)	a. lack the thread of continuity needed for a book b. not enough thought given to the book's plan c. not book quality; lack literary quality and form d. lack endurability

(Remember that true literature endures, while other writing, no matter how good it may be, has a short life. Collections made up of the latter are doomed to die even when successfully bound in a book. For a book, total rewrite is needed, beginning with an idea, a purpose, and a plan.)

4. Novels	a. lack basic principles of good fiction b. tend to ramble, being poorly planned c. worn-out themes d. lack universal appeal and elements of suspense and surprise (See Chapter 10, "How to Spin a Yarn")

(The world is ripe for *good* novels. Outside trends affect their acceptance indirectly, by numbing the creativity of novelists. Until the writer breaks out of the social trends that bind him, frees his fantasy elves, and learns how to write successful short stories, the novel is a gamble.

5. Poetry	a. lacks universal appeal b. poorly written, with contrived rhyme and faulty rhythm c. rambling thoughts d. subjective (the "I" disease)

(If one poem doesn't set the town bells a-ringing, a collection of mediocre poems is certainly not going to do it. Study Chapter 11 thoroughly and sell individual poems, or study Chapter 6 to learn how to transform them into prose.)

PROVING THE EXPERTS WRONG

All of these risky ventures are accepted in manuscript form all the time. All you have to do to prove this is turn to current book reviews or look around a bookstore. The best venture in books is nonfiction (how-to/informational/technical/study books), but professional writers of author status are beating the odds and giving us good books in every category. All of these forms are accepted *if*

1. the content has widespread appeal
2. the book is organized with clearcut continuity and strong plot
3. the level of journalistic quality warrants consideration for a place on literature's shelves
4. the subject will still be alive when the book comes out
5. the book proposal, fresh, exciting, and professionally done, hits the editor's desk at the right time.

BUT I'VE BEEN ASKED TO WRITE A BOOK!

Lucky you! A bona fide assignment to write a book is the biggest bonanza any beginning writer could be handed. If you've been asked (or told) to write a book, acceptance all but guaranteed, any celebration that suits your lifestyle is in order.

Writing on assignment is much easier than writing to the wind, hoping somebody will like what you've done. As a rule, assignments go to professional writers with proven skills. But very often beginners get "in-house" projects: an organization or company needs someone to write a biography, a history, or a promotional book. Those assigning such a project may have gathered facts enough to launch the work and usually are enthusiastic enough to give excellent advice and moral support from beginning to end. (The opposite can also be true: zero help, which may be taken as a vote of confidence in the writer's ability.)

Assigned books also appear on the desk of a writer who is lucky enough to work for a firm that produces technical manuals, instruction manuals, and informational books either for employees or for the general public. Sometimes periodicals find a market demand for their information in book form, so they seek out a good writer to put it together. Book assignments can result from medical or technical advances, political events, theological debates, people or places in the news, and from public demand for reading material on any of these. Remuneration varies from a flat fee (if done outside regular duties) or a raise (if a good job is done in the line of duty) to top royalties and fame if the assignment leads the triumphant writer to pay dirt.

If you've been handed a book assignment, how should you, as a novice, proceed? Jubilantly! If you know you can handle it, accept it. Use the following advice to keep yourself from floundering:

1. Ask all the questions you need to ask.

Understand the assignment thoroughly. This is not freelance writing where you pull ideas out of the air and develop them. Others have the ideas and expect you to develop them in a certain way. They are looking for someone to step inside their minds, sort out their thoughts, and write them into the book they envision. Communication throughout the project is going to be extremely important, but an initial understanding of the projected book is vital to completing it successfully. How firmly developed are their ideas? How much flexibility are they allowing you?

2. Get the purpose for the book clearly in your mind.

They have a reason for wanting the book published, and all the creativity you pour into it will be in vain if the message is lost. Round up all previously written material (published and unpublished), photocopies, notes, diaries, memos, and minutes to meetings where the book was discussed. If applicable, get the names and phone numbers of people you might interview. One of the questions you'll want to ask is: When I need further information, approval, or someone to bounce my ideas on, whom do I turn to?

3. Decide on remuneration.

Perhaps it goes without saying, one vital question is: How much do I get paid, and when? It's wise to clarify what you are being paid for. Research, anecdotes from your own file, and final typing are some of the extras that deserve ample payment. Dawdling through interesting files for personal enjoyment does not.

4. Put yourself through a crash writing course.

Since almost all such book assignments will be nonfiction, reread the following chapters in this book and highlight sections that you will want to refer to later:

Chapter 3—Life is But an Anecdote
Chapter 5—Have I Got Style!
Chapter 6—Examining Your Writing Options
Chapter 7—To Market, To Market
Chapter 9—Now the Sweat Begins

You'll be looking primarily for

1. the most suitable approach to the subject (Ch. 5)
2. organization procedures for getting the material in order (Ch. 9)
3. an understanding of your future audience (Ch. 7)
4. ways to develop versatility in presenting your material (Ch. 6)
5. tricks to spotting good illustrations (Ch. 3)

Chapter 12, The Art of Editing, should be studied carefully after you have done some of your writing. At this point you'll be critically evaluating your spelling, grammar, punctuation, and basic sentence and paragraph structure. In addition, you'll be removing excess material, shuffling sentences and paragraphs around, and discovering more sparkling ways to express the facts you've recorded. Anecdotes sometimes come to mind in the primary editing process. If you're talented enough to be given the assignment, you can be confident enough to move ahead making decisions on your own. However, touch home base as often as necessary to see that you're on track. Depending on the project, this might include showing your superior (for lack of a better term) your outline with ideas roughed in; your first rough draft; and your last draft before final typing. These need not be lengthy discussions, but will give you and him an opportunity to add material or remove it, as needed. The powers that be will continue to think of things to be included, and quite possibly, so will you.

Many writing assignments are given out because the person(s) with the idea lack the ability to organize and write the book. You might be a novice when you accept the assignment, but by the time you are in knee deep, you're the professional writer. Never hesitate to pull rank on your "superiors" in matters which will affect the quality of the writing and reflect on your skills. Approach the project with an open mind, understand the purpose of the book, remain flexible throughout the entire project, but firmly squash ridiculous ideas they may present by relegating them to a company newsletter or the circular file. "That's really funny, but I don't think we have room for it," is one cop-out—which may or may not work! I've sometimes said, "We'll have to save that for your next book!"

Do assignments from publishers ever go to freelance writers? Sometimes they do, and on rare occasions a beginner will be taken on board because his or her skills are promising. Almost all book assignments, though, go to "insiders" who are well known for their writing skill, their knowledge of a subject, or their past sales record. You will be more apt to get an assignment by consistently writing salable material than by asking for one, and most writers land their first book contract by submitting a marketable manuscript "over the transom"—on speculation to a publisher who's never heard of them. You spin the wheel and pray your number will come up!

MASS MARKET POCKET BOOKS

Two of my books fell into the newest category of literature on today's market, and I have a hard time classing them as literature—contracts, royalties, and popularity notwithstanding. In several years of book reviewing (another business-related hobby many writers indulge in) I scanned scores of such publications. They never appear in hardbound editions, and they often have limited market value. They are much shorter than the true book, falling somewhere above the extended article in length: 66-144 pages. On today's market such books are usually copyrighted and listed with the Library of Congress. Sometimes they are even listed in *Books in Print*.

While a booklet is small enough to stitch or staple through the center-fold, the mass market pocket book is too thick for that. Perfect binding (glue) is common. The spine is broad enough to carry the author's name, title, and publisher's logo at least in small print, but the book seems too skinny to stand proudly on a library shelf. Manufacturers of library reinforcement tape love these books, since all paperbacks must be reinforced during the shelving process. Libraries often pass them by, as do catalog houses, because of their short life-span. Bookstores can carry only a small number of the total output. Reviewers are swamped with them.

New writers have the economy to thank for the small-book bonanza. This serendipity has come about through escalating paper, film, and labor costs. For economic reasons, many publishers have cut books to this short length while raising the price, and all over the country printers are becoming publishers, because the small book fits the small press, and can help subsidize the operational cost of the shop. Most printers love to print books. There's something about the feel of a book—no matter how small—the appearance of it, that makes a printer's heart swell with special pride.

The pocket book offers the writer the best opportunity to break into the field. Even though such books die young (as a rule), the small book gains the writer the title *author*, plus the background knowledge gained through the discipline of writing a book. Sales range from excellent down to zero, but compared with the cost of a full-sized, hardbound book, the publisher's risk is minimal. With a clever title, appealing cover art, and decent advertising (all handled by his marketing experts), he will recoup his cost. This guarantee opens the publisher's heart to writers whose book proposals hold promise. Only a few of the proposed books can be considered; fewer still can be chosen. But thanks to the tiny paperback's popularity, the new writer has a chance.

The author, whether receiving a flat fee or royalty, will be adequately reimbursed for his time, considering the side benefits of getting into print. Compared with the amount of work an author has poured into such a book, the finished product may appear disappointingly small, but a good writer who sticks to his business can turn out such a book in a short time, either in nonfiction, or as a novella. Often the inexperienced author hopes for a hardbound edition and national advertising, but that is not to be in most cases. With the proliferation of such books, the chances of one of them surfacing and attaining national attention are extremely slim. I know the feeling one has when faced with fans who want to find a copy in the major display of the biggest bookstore. The tiny book doesn't make it to that prestigious place.

On the plus side, however, the tiny paperback has opened up new possibilities. Anyone off the street can become an author by writing a short book, with a better chance of selling it than most gambles afford. You have as good a shot at it as anyone else, and better, in fact, since you now have some inside knowledge of organization and an understanding of how the system works.

If your pocket books proposal arrives the same day as a thousand others, how can you increase the chances of having it pass the battery of test and get accepted?

Most of my books were written because someone asked me to write them. All of them were published because they filled a need. For the same kind of success in this extremely competitive, but wide-open field, you need to (turn on the recording, Arabella)

1. learn how to write
2. become known as a good writer who can do the job
3. study the markets and find *the right* prospective outlet
4. produce *top quality* material *quickly*
5. deliver on time
6. be open to extensive editing

TRADE PAPERBACKS

Just above the pocket book stands the trade paperback: a full-sized, book-stature creation that holds its head up high, standing tall as literature.Such a book is suited to hardbound editions, but often appears in paperback first to accommodate mass sales demands. Most hardbound books come out later in paperback, losing none of their dignity in the process. Romances, westerns, science fiction, and many mainstream novels come out in paperback. Sales results are satisfying to the good author, and on top of that, a well-qualified, hardworking author can churn out such books in series or on new subjects one after the other, making a mint. The paperback rides on the popularity of key authors and key series. To get your foot in the door you must do your homework, but the rewards, if you win, will be worth all the work you put in.

COLLABORATION

Not all authors work alone. One of the best ways for an unknown author to emblazon his or her name in lights is to ride on the coattails of a famous person. During what I call "the decade of autobiography," when everybody who was anybody was telling his life story, famous people unable to write teamed up with ghostwriters to do the job for them. The bylines came out "as told to . . . " "with . . . ," or "and . . . ," followed by the ghostwriter's name. The subject provided the material through interviews and diaries. The upcoming author practiced on that material, learning how to write a book in the process!

The autobiography trend is fading, but ghostwriting will live on. Usually the arrangement is an even split of whatever financial reimbursement results, such as 50 percent of the flat fee for each, or 50 percent of the royalties. The ghostwriter is being reimbursed for his skill; the client for his knowledge, or his name.

Trouble brews when the writer knows more than the "author" and feels he is getting half the pay for all the work. Storms arise, too, when the writer is unable to do the job. Many ghostwriters are fired, sent off with a kill fee, or without a cent. As I explained earlier, writing a book (even with someone else's material) is too big a job for most amateurs. One ought to say a quick "yes," to grab such an opportunity, but think things through carefully before actually taking it, before it is too late to back out. If you think you can do it, try it. If you doubt that you can, don't try to bluff your way through.

Controversies arise, too, over how the byline should read, because to most writers, credit for their work is more important than cash. Ghostwriting with no credit or a small line of appreciation buried in the acknowledgement is commonly done. The remuneration must be adequate for the job and the deal must be signed and sealed before the work is begun. Feel good about doing it, or don't do it at all.

COAUTHORING

Coauthors usually work together providing the material. For a successful coauthorship the writer and the person he works with (writer or individual with well-organized salable knowledge) must be compatible and work as a team, trusting each other's judgment and reading each other's mind. When they disagree, they must do it agreeably, brainstorming until both are satisfied. Remuneration is divided equally because the work load is shared. (Sometimes an "expert" in some field has done his share of the load in advance; nevertheless, he has done it. The writer doesn't have to do his research for him.)

COMPILING OR EDITING A COMPILATION

One can make a name (and some money) by being named as editor or compiler, or as a contributor to a work. The editor of a collection is responsible to select and whip into shape the material sent in by contributors to the book. Sometimes he writes a portion of it, but not always. A byline on the front cover and a substantial flat fee are common rewards.

Some such collections are put together by a compiler, rather than editor. The difference is that the compiler begins one step sooner. He is responsible for soliciting material as well as selecting and organizing it. His remuneration should be substantial, and his name certainly should appear on the front cover. The contributor's portion to such a work is smaller. A flat fee based on space (number of words or finished pages) is common.

REWRITING

Finally, an author can do rewriting. I love to do it, but I hate to do it. Something within me rebels against such a task. A writer holding a contract ought to be able to write. If I'm going to do the work, then I ought to get the credit and the pay, *n'est-ce pas*?

No, not necessarily the credit. Like a ghostwriter, the rewriter fades into the background, allowing the originator of the idea or owner of the material to smile in the spotlight, taking the credit for what he has not done. For that tightlipped grace, if for no other reason, the pay should be very very good. I cannot ethically tell you the stories here that I would love to tell.

Rewriting and ghostwriting are fantastic hack work. One can find such jobs by moving in the right circles and by local advertising. As with anything else, starting small is a good idea. Rewriting articles, short stories, resumes, news items, and even theses, is a good place to begin. I warn you, rewriting a novel is a herculean task.

In either editing or rewriting, it is a good idea to work from a photo copy, to give the author's copy back intact and to arrange in advance for both adequate payment for a job well done, and a kill fee, in case you bomb out.

All the writing you can do for others is an education for yourself.

GETTING INTO PRINT

In these inflationary times, the one question commonly asked by budding authors is valid: How much is it going to cost to publish my book?

The bad news is: Plenty.

The good news is: You don't pay them; they pay you.

Most rank beginners—and a lot of professionals—donate time and writing skills to organizations, clubs, and churches. Nowhere is the free use of skill and talent offered more frequently than in the field of journalism. While Erma, Abby, and Ann pull their wagons to the bank each week laden with coins, Marietta Nobody smiles broadly just seeing her words in print.

There's nothing wrong with that. It's the best place in the world to begin, and many of us volunteer to write excellent professional copy for zero pay throughout our lives, to further causes we believe in.

Because of the personal investment of time and talent, my biography, "*Miss Terri!*" (which was an on-the-job assignment), could be considered a volunteer project. "*Miss Terri!*" had an initial printing of 85,000. I wrote it without contract and without remuneration. The first 60,000 copies were sent out worldwide to people who supported missionary work financially (with very good donations coming back in return for the free book). The remainder of the copies were sold through normal channels with proceeds going back into the work. For all my hours of labor, I gained an education in research and interviews, a study in book organization, many new friends in the publishing business, an international reputation as a bona fide author, and the satisfaction of a job well done.

BUT WHAT ABOUT THE BIG BUCKS?

When we think of book royalties, we think of Big Money. To donate time and skill is commendable and it's on-the-job training. However, there's nothing wrong with being paid for your book either, even if it is for a charitable cause or religious organization. And for most of us, making money is our prime reason for wanting to write a book. Look beyond your delightful hobby of volunteer writing and mini-markets to the future, where you will be paid Big Bucks because you write well enough to sell.

There are two basic ways to approach writing a book. First of all, you may come up with a terrific idea, get the plot down on paper, organize your thoughts, write the book, and send the entire manuscript to a publisher. I suppose most rejected manuscripts have been done this way, which is not a reflection on the method, but on the finished product, which—for whatever reasons—did not sell. Most first books were also done this way, and did sell. I have never seen a study on whether authors' first best-sellers were assigned, written after a query to some publisher brought an affirmative nod, or written off the top of the author's head and shipped off "on spec," hoping for an acceptance. I would venture to guess that most top-selling books came in "over the transom" (that is, through the slush pile either at a publisher's office, or an agent's) in full manuscript form.

Publishers and agents today are demanding book proposals. Whether or not you have written the entire book, all they want to see is a query letter, brief and to the point, an outline (a chapter listing with a short note under each chapter title capsulizing the content will do), a resume which gives the point of the book in a nutshell, and two finished chapters. The query letter should include your qualifications for writing the book and ways in which you believe your book is significantly different from what is already on the market. You don't know what manuscripts various publishers have "on the back burner" (under consideration, or in process), but you are well acquainted with what your library and various bookstores in your town have available, and you keep up with current book reviews. (Ahem. Don't you?) Don't send a query letter without the outline and sample chapters. And *always* enclose a self-addressed, stamped envelope for a reply. As to affirmative nods, you might get the green light from various publishers on the book proposal, but you will still have no promise of an acceptance. To get a contract and advance on a book not yet written is a rare occurrence for an unknown author. What you will get, which makes the "query/outlne" route the practical one to take, is enough rejection to let you know if your book proposal is not adequate. This allows you to start over, approaching a new subject or tackling the original one from a different angle before you've spent months writing the entire book.

To get to the gold at the end of the rainbow one must lay aside all else to pursue it. Writing a book falls into the class of building a fiber glassboat, restoring an antique car, handpainting a set of ceramic dishes, or planning and sewing all the garments for an elaborate wedding. You think about it for a long, long time before proceeding, because the investment is a good-sized chunk of your life. Once you have plunged in, you *must* do a good job, because to recoup your investment, you will have to sell the book and be paid.

How does one sell a book? There are many wonderful helps on the market to show you the specific steps for submitting manuscripts of any length. The basic rules are

1. typing the manuscript double-spaced on 8½x11 paper, leaving an inch or more for a margin. The writer's name as well as a page number should be on each page. (Envision the heaps of manuscripts, the busy activity, the numerous readings your manuscript will encounter, and the possibility that pages may be separated in the shufffle. Clever methods of paper-clipping sections together with

colored papers, or other unique forms of disorganization are unnerving to a harried individual with his eye on the clock.) Do not bind the manuscript or punch it for enclosure in a notebook.

2. enclosing a self-addressed, stamped envelope for the manuscript's return.
3. sending the manuscript to the proper place.

For further information about manuscript preparation, see *Writer's Market*. Step One is to send a query letter with outline and chapters; Step Two (if the publisher likes what he sees and invites you to do so) is to send the entire manuscript.

Your manuscript will be considered by either a select group of editors or by a committee of people. Unless the company is quite small, you can expect a delay of several weeks before getting a response. If you're lucky, your reply will come in the form of a letter announcing your acceptance as the newest author in the firm, or in the form of a contract, which spells out the terms of purchase. You have a right to jump up and down and shout for joy! When this happens, you have been selected from about four thousand competitors, all trying to get great books into print.

The terms of contracts vary a great deal. Many companies dealing in book contracts are long-established firms and can be fully trusted. You read the contract carefully and read about publishing contracts in some of the freelance writing books or writer's magazines. Then you call or write the editor you are dealing with to ask questions about things you do not understand, you sign the contract and mail it, and you keep on jumping up and down for joy!

WHAT IF YOU'RE NOT A WINNER?

Searching for a publisher is like falling down a mountainside. You start at the top (with the one you believe best fits your need), and you keep bouncing down the hill like a falling rock, stopping now and then to rest until someone bumps you off again.

On down you go, ever seeking for a niche where you can lodge permanently. I believe in starting at the top, because the goal of publishing is to get your books into as many hands as possible. There may be no difference at all in the appearance of the final product. Small companies turn out beautiful books with eyecatching dust jacket art, sturdy binding, and the author's name in bold print. The larger the company, however, the more prestigious it is and the wider will be the scope of advertising.

All prestigious firms are now requesting "query and outline." No completed manuscripts are considered at most of the major publishing firms. Some have closed the door on all freelance submissions, accepting books only as they are submitted by an agent. Agents can be located through "friends in the business," through writer's magazines and writer's clubs, and publishers, some of whom recommend those who serve them well. With the increase in the number of first-book authors, agents are also proliferating. Many of them can do no more than you can do yourself: Submit your manuscript here and there until the right home is found for it. An agent is needed to penetrate the top echelon of publishers. Publishing firms that still accept freelance submissions accept them directly from writers, and no go-between is needed, as a rule.

Because it is so difficult to sell a book manuscript, unscrupulous people do lie in wait, hoping to pounce upon vulnerable, disappointed authors. You ought to pick an agent carefully and understand in advance what services he offers. Many agents offer critique and editing services (and many beginning authors need these services!) I would like to know in advance such things as

—How much is it going to cost me if my manuscript doesn't sell?
—How many publishers is this agent going to contact for me?
—How well does this agent know my special field?

If my manuscript is too poorly written to submit as is, how much will it cost me

1. to get it back, no editing done on it?
2. to receive an evaluation that will show me how to rewrite it?
3. to have the agency bring it up to an acceptable standard? And if that is done, how much input will I have in revisions?

In the end, of course, even if the agency revises or rewrites your manuscript, no one can guarantee its acceptance. The term "on speculation" is used because freelance writing is a gamble, even for the pro.

Very good and reliable critique services are available—perhaps you have experts right in your own hometown. Before you look for an agent to *sell* your book manuscript, you need to look for competent help to *evaluate* it. *Writer's Digest* offers this service,[1] as does National Writers Club,[2] and advice concerning agents is also available through both of these organizations. I recommend joining National Writers Club to all my students, and of course no writer touches my life without hearing a long discourse on the value of *Writer's Market*, available at the reference desk of any library, or at your local bookstore.

Writer's seminars staffed by experts are the best places to learn the ins and outs of selling the manuscript. Rubbing shoulders with people in the know is one of the best features of attending such sessions. They are a good investment, and I recommend them highly.

Since you have learned to study the markets, you may know that your manuscript, although top quality in its class, is not suited to the major firms. Starting at the top for you may mean starting with a royalty publisher who specializes in your field, and circulating your manuscript to other publishers in that category until you have found it a home. Cookbooks, for example, are generally a specialized job; religious manuscripts go to religious publishers; poetry books go to publishers that publish poetry.

A few years ago, we used to say "when all else fails, self-publish." This has changed, however. Self-publishing now has "a top" of its own. Many writers now choose to seek out typesetters, artists, printers, and binders, and to foot the bill, in order to pocket the profits, instead of sharing them with a major publisher.

Self-publishing may be for writers who have the following:

1. The ability to edit their own work.
2. The artistic skill or the funds to hire an artist to produce a quality book.
3. The business ability to seek out the best printing price, getting cost bids and weighing them against quality and time schedule for delivery, and funds to pay the bill.
4. A ready market for a substantial number of copies.
5. Advertising ability, time to do it, and funds to cover it.
6. Marketability: the know-how to get the book into bookstores and catalogs (and funds to cover it).
7. Facilities and time to set up a shipping department.

Job printers may consent to handle printing the book, but the writer must handle locating a book binder if the printer does not deal in farming out that process, or have it under his own roof. Typesetting is one of the most costly aspects of self-publishing, so shopping around for the best price is advisable. One must also consider storage of both books and mailing supplies. And last—though perhaps it should be considered first, before entering a self-publishing venture—one must either *have* or *be* a good bookkeeper, because consistent and accurate records must be kept.

Vanity publishing differs from *self*-publishing in that the vanity publisher lifts the load of editing, artwork, printing, binding, some of the bookkeeping, and possibly even storage and mailing. A vanity publisher differs from a royalty publisher in that the writer foots the bill for printing, while a royalty publisher pays it, after the contract is signed. You don't pay a royalty publisher, they pay you.

The peril in vanity publishing lies in the fine print of the contract, which generally is not highlighted by the salesperson who approaches an author with encouragement and flowery promises. "Vanity" publishing it is! We writers are vain. We want to see our work in print—in hardcover and illustrated in full color, if possible! "Subsidy" publishing is another name for it: The author subsidizes the project.

I have seen beautiful—and even successful—books published by subsidy publishers. Zig Ziglar's *See You at the Top* is one good example. But horror stories abound. Most of us in the field have dried the tears of authors who didn't understand what they were paying for, who felt cheated in the number of bound copies delivered, the high price of a "cost-sharing" contract, the hidden costs of additional binding of printed copies not bound or delivered, the shipping costs born by the author, the lack of advertising on the part of the publisher, and the disappointing percentages of profit on copies the publisher might sell.

Many authors who go this route are not qualified to judge the editing or artwork, but bookstore managers and others who are presented with the finished book may hesitate to try to sell it, sensing its inferior quality. I cannot emphasize enough how important it is to your book to have it edited professionally, whether you pay for it, or the publisher does. Artwork, likewise, should be professionally done. With an expenditure possibly running into thousands of dollars, you are going to want to recoup at least the cost, and you ought to expect sales to provide a substantial profit, too. No matter who prints your book, even if you do it yourself on a press of your own in the basement, quality matters. To sell, every aspect of the publishing venture must be good.

In addition to vanity publishers who advertise widely for customers (often approaching writers disappointed by rejection), many other publishing firms use idle press time for vanity printing or self-publishing. The advantages, when weighed against the "all by myself" publishing route, is that one's manuscript is handled very much like one that has been selected for a royalty contract: It is edited; design and artwork are professionally done; the book is sometimes stored until needed; and in some cases the bill can be paid three months or six months after delivery, allowing the writer to recover costs before paying it.

I do not recommend vanity or self-publishing except in certain cases where either the writer has a guaranteed market (through national seminars, for example, or as a public speaker with a large following); or the writer is backed by an organization that has a substantial following. The average individual will lose his shirt publishing his own book. To succeed in going it alone you need above-average intelligence, creative zeal in all aspects of advertising and sales, a lot of stick-to-it-tiveness (because the bills won't go away if you lose interest), and a supportive family or friends. If you're a risk-taker, a little zany, and you know you can make it work, hop to it!

I am Gargantuan at heart. Even as I near the end of this major writing project, nearing the glassy-eyed maniac stage, I am thinking about the next one. Writing a book is a mammoth task which only a fool would undertake. If you're that kind of a hard-working, starry-eyed fool, welcome aboard. You probably are the author type, and that's what it takes!

ASSIGNMENT 13

WARM-UP: Why is writing a book called a Gargantuan task? Who was Gargantua, in what story did he appear, and when was it written? (Your dictionary will give you a hint, or you might check the *Reader's Encyclopedia*.)

Your assignment is to answer the questions asked in the chapter. Nothing in this book is stamped "RUSH-PRIORITY," so do the assignment at a meditatin', leisurely pace.

1. Why should I write a book?
2. Have I got the mental capacity and intestinal fortitude to do it? If not, can I obtain these qualities through study and self-discipline? Have I ever tackled such a big job and finished it? Have I ever tested my brainpower to see how much I do have? Do I *want* to work that hard?

3. If I do write a book, what publishing route shall I aim for?

FINALLY: When you finish the assignment, think through your writing goals and produce a short, personal essay. Title it whatever you want, but use what you have learned to identify your writing desires and to explain where you plan to begin.

Notice I said *where* not *when*. The "when" is *now*!

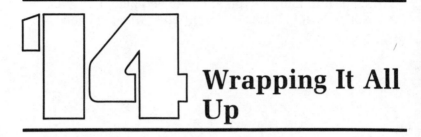

14 Wrapping It All Up

At the end of any course of study, an exam is inevitable. You are teaching yourself, of course, so I won't examine you. If you decide you want to know how much progress you've made since beginning to read this book, you will have to test yourself. I suggest you do it now, and return two years from now to do it again to see what progress you have made.

Before you begin, let me suggest that the purpose of your test will be to determine where you have been, to decide in light of what you have learned if it is advisable for you to take writing seriously, and to recall your writing options to decide where you want to go. At the end of this chapter are some suggested questions.

No one else need see the result of your final examination. You can be perfectly honest answering the questions, candidly evaluating your answers, and setting goals without revealing your secret desires to anyone. You can take all the time you need for the test: days, weeks, even months.

If you decide not to become a writer, you can admit that learning more about professional writing has been an invigorating mental adventure. You know now that good writing involves more than talent. Your new appreciation for other people's labor should make reading a greater pleasure. Even the smallest special interest publication you read will seem more valuable to you since you will understand the adrenaline expenditure necessary to getting it into print. You can get yourself an "I boost word lovers" bumper sticker and writing supplies, and barrage letters-to-editors columns with praise. Perhaps your gift lies in constructive criticism. Maybe your goal should be professional reviewing or editing instead of writing. Whatever your heart longs to do as a result of reading this book, go after it. A flame in a true writer's heart is always there. Time will only intensify it. Even deciding not to write won't put it out.

If, after examining yourself, you decide to pursue professional writing, welcome to the club! Undaunted by the mountainous task before you, you have decided to press on. You have passed the first test.

SHOOT FOR THE MOON

My father loved to teach. He once built a small observatory in the tamerack forest at Payne, Minnesota, and under the auspices of Science Clubs of America, gathered together a group of rough woodsmen, burly Swedes most of them, to lecture them about the distant wonders of that bright northern sky. Ruthie and I often went with him to the observatory on weekends. Our nook was the unfinished attic dome room where we threw heavy homemade quilts on the freshly sawed wooden planks near a hole in the floor. From that cozy perch we could look down on Pop and his pupils.

His professorial stance impressed his daughters, if no one else: solid pot belly, spine straight as a military man's, head held high, smooth, gray hair, glasses. My mind seems to recall, even in that crude setting, his dark suit, white shirt, and tie. The lumberjacks usually listened with respect, but discussions, which did not always center on astronomy, sometimes became heated. One night, for example, the whole crowd was for returning to the old country. Pop stood alone defending the U.S.A. In about 1939, he sprung on them his wild belief that men would someday walk on the moon. How those sweaty, whiskered fellows guffawed at him that night!

You *can* walk on the moon, you know. To get there, though, takes years of preparation, practice, consultation, experimentation, failure, new tries, and getting up to start all over again, investigating new angles. You don't take one giant step to success. You laboriously pull yourself up through blood, sweat, toil and tears. This means giving some writing away, selling to insignificant publications, proving yourself, disciplining yourself, and sometimes scolding yourself. You've got to start at the bottom, but you can't be content to stay there.

Youth of today make fairly elaborate plans with one-year, five-year, ten-year and lifetime goals. A certain head-in-the sand idealism has always kept youth's enthusiasm alive. We who have lived a while try to tell them that disappointment is only a heartbeat away, that nothing is forever, and that living today to the fullest is what counts. Somewhere between these two philosophies lies the balance a successful writer needs to find.

Sometimes early in the morning, when every joint in my body aches as I drag myself out of bed, even getting coffee made seems like a very long-range goal. I don't know that setting goals is terribly important, but moving ahead is. And it never hurts a thing to dream big dreams. If a dream a moon-distance away lurks in my heart, it will probably remain forever there: in my heart. My secret goal for years has been to write for a certain book publisher and two periodicals. Subject matter of their magnitude has yet to fall into my lap. If the subject matter appeared and the approach appealed to me, I'd tackle the job.

Aside from that, my writing goals have been simple: I've always wanted to please God, I've always hoped to produce the best quality possible, and I've always aimed to beat the deadline. I've offered my material for sale to test it, for the most part, to see if what I was doing as a staff writer was on target. I don't know that you can find more satisfaction than I have enjoyed but you can reach for broader coverage, more fame, and more money. If it's what you want, go for it.

I've stared into space pondering what motivational thoughts I might use to conclude the book. I believe I should elaborate on two things previously mentioned which seem very important to me: making friends in the industry, and learning to accept criticism.

MAKE FRIENDS IN THE FIELD

Success in writing is a combination of talent, practice, persistence, and lucky breaks. It is your talent, your grabbing opportunities, and your stubborn hanging on during periods of rejection and defeat that will win you friends in the magical field of publishing. Nine times out of ten, your lucky breaks will come through these friends.

We've already talked about one of the best ways to make such friends: through employment. A very talented artist I know has just recently decided to become a writer. When she was younger she worked as a proofreader and in other areas of newspaper production, but because of other interests, she never gave writing a serious thought. In the last few years, however, she has scribbled a line now and then, finally getting interested enough to sign up for night school writing classes at a community college. The more she studies, the more she knows her future holds a writing career, so she is taking the big risk of changing jobs, leaving a secure secretarial position to reenter the publishing world as a proofreader.

I feel in my bones she will succeed as a writer, because she means business. "I know I need to rub shoulders with writers and editors," she told me, "and the best way for me to do that is to go back to work at some printing plant."

Although you might eventally contemplate such a move, you don't have to upset your whole life to make friends in the field. If your world is a small town, your first objective should be the newspaper office, where you might be welcomed as a competent reporter, or as a proofreader or typist one afternoon or evening a week. If all else fails, the adrenaline-drained owner-editor might grab the first offer of a person willing to mop up after the job is done.

Not many small-town publishers will turn down an invitation to coffee or lunch, provided you allow *them* to set the day and the hour. Doubling as reporters, their eyes and ears are so trained to search for stories that they welcome people contact in any form. Add this to the fact that they are always listening to other people. If it fits into their schedule they will be glad for the opportunity to talk shop with another writer.

Nor is the coffee/lunch routine or mopping-up offer limited to small-town papers. Wherever printing presses are rolling, versatile writers can sniff out friends in these and other creative ways.

Large cities, of course, are filled with opportunity. For example, about sixty periodicals call Kansas City home; there are more than fifty newspaper offices in greater Kansas City, and a dozen book publishers. Since most of these firms are peopled with word lovers and almost all of their clients deal with the printed page, think of the potential education within listening range of a receptionist! You ought to gladly sweep floors or clean rest rooms in any one of those places just for the privilege of hanging around. Add to these firms the print shops, the quick-prints, the radio stations, the television stations, and the advertising agencies. One must not overlook college journalism personnel, high school creative writing teachers, English professors, and library employees, many of whom would qualify as "friends in the field." One could coffee a successful word artist every day of his life and never run out of people. (And perhaps one should.)

I have often thought I would like to open a boardinghouse for writers. We don't hear about boardinghouses much anymore, but perhaps they will come back into vogue. Of such a place, Oliver Wendell Holmes wrote:

> I am so well pleased with my boarding house that I intend to remain there, perhaps for years. Of course I shall have a

> great many conversations to report, and they will be of a different tone and on different subjects. The talks are like breakfasts—sometimes dipped toast, and sometimes dry. You must take them as they come.

Holmes' boardinghouse experiences formed the basis for an *Atlantic Monthly* series called "Autocrat of the Breakfast Table." They are considered to be his best work, but he also composed what he called some "sadly desponding poems," and a morbid theological essay, while suffering from indigestion. He ate too much pie! When he recovered, he labeled that writing "Piecrust" and laid the stack aside as "scarecrows and solemn warnings."

Any boardinghouse ought to provide enough material for a lifetime of writing for an observant writer. Mine, however, would be a boardinghouse exclusively *for* writers. I envision something like the lively discussions with students which developed into Martin Luther's *Table Talk*.

Actually, I suppose it would be well to include a few people other than writers. If all of us went into a creative trance at the same time, supper might become feeding ground for a clever cartoonist. One writer would stare into space without response, pour gravy into his coffee cup, and accidentally eat the jelly for dessert. Another might cause a conflict by neglecting to respond to an oft-repeated "please pass the salt." Someone else would be apt to eat the whole meal with his nose in a book, responding with an *ugh* if at all, and the fourth might gulp, swallow, and rush away to capture words before his brilliant thought escaped.

As to the cook, no problem. Long ago I learned to lift spaghetti from the boiling water, drain it, and set it on the platter with one hand, while using the other to keep on writing without missing a beat.

Many people are opening their homes to college students, and what better way to make "friends in the field"? If you are lucky enough to have a spare bedroom to rent, advertise for a journalism major. If you're a journalism student looking for such a home, run this ad: "WRITER SEEKS GOOD HOME: FREE ADVICE IN EXCHANGE FOR LAUNDRY AND MEALS." You'd get takers.

In my opinion, personal friendships and work contacts are the most valuable source of continuing encouragement. As you begin to make friends with folks who have printers' ink flowing through their veins, or people whose minds delight in words, some of their enthusiasm and skill is bound to rub off on you. Writing is a contagious disease. From such friends you will also learn about writing-related organizations and activities, such as meetings, seminars, and classes that might interest you. Local advertising clubs, for example, call in nationally known writers and editors, as do press clubs, communications clubs, and others. The public relations office at any college will keep you informed of authors and editors scheduled to speak at the school. (But of course you will make friends with the journalism professor, who will give you all the inside tips.)

Many writers' organizations are listed in *Writer's Market*, and these organizations will in turn help you locate local writer's clubs. Writing conferences, clubs, seminars, and retreats are listed in *Writer's Digest* each year, and there are other sources of helpful information. Like looking for a new love, the search for friends interested in writing brings surprises. You stumble upon them when you least expect them to appear.

I am reluctant to recommend local writing clubs. First of all, I can't bear to listen to somebody read aloud what he or she has written. I want to see it, to judge it. Secondly, many are operated by amateurs who have never experienced a grain of success. This leads to anthill introspection—death to good writing. If you choose someone to encourage you or give moral support, be sure that person has either top quality journalism credentials or a good portfolio of published works—preferably the latter. Amateur critics are either too hard on the victim, or too soft, gushing over unpublishable prattle.

I guess I'm English. I say that because Somerset Maugham, in *A Writer's Notebook*, said he found the practice of French writers reading their works to one another astonishing, insisting that no English author would subject himself to "the excruciating boredom of sitting for hours while a fellow novelist read him his latest work."

Maugham acknowledged that the English sometimes do ask a fellow writer to read a manuscript—to criticize it, if you please, "by which they mean praise, for rash is the author who makes any serious objection to another's manuscript!"

For a club to be worthwhile, someone in the group must know enough to lift the writing level beyond the beginner stage. Even if a person has headed such group for forty years to discuss reasons for rejection, that person's ability is stunted. He is still an amateur. To prove his credibility a group leader must either show exciting publishing progress himself, or produce students whose winning ratio progressively increases. I would not want to be part of a group unless a real-live professional was brought in to speak on occasion. Never attempt to learn from a loser.

Like Tennyson, I require, when writing, "myself to myself." Judith Krantz, who according to *Writer's Digest* has made more than $3 million on her Bantam novels, advised, "Don't talk about your work with your friends. This avoids the awful question, 'How's it going?' and prevents you from using up the vitality of your creative energy in conversation."

I need friends who think it's okay for me to go into a trance, becoming at least temporarily selfishly uncommunicative, with a sign on my door, "Keep out—Writer at Work," if not a band around my forehead which says, "No admittance. Talent developing." I don't need people who trip my creative panic button by talking prematurely about my thoughts. I would rather discuss my age, weight, checkbook balance, or sex life than my writing. Until it's developed enough to show, it's much to intimate to talk about it. When I do, I confide only in very close, trusted friends. Icy fingers clutch my heart when some outsider asks, "How's your book going?" I have no idea what to say. For the most part I keep my mouth shut about secret projects. Like having a baby, if a book comes to full term and turns out okay, the world will know it. If it miscarries, I'd rather cry alone.

In spite of that isolationist attitude, I believe everyone needs a writing buddy. You may be able to paddle your own canoe now, but when you hit rough waters, you'll wish you had an enthusiastic partner to lend a hand. Not to criticize your work, however. As a tough, professional editor, cruel at critiquing on the job, I despise reading a friend's material just to give my opinion. What can a friend say but "Terrific!"? That's like a surgeon saying your tumor is beautiful, when he would really like to get in there and hack away at it. Judson Jerome revealed immense insight with his words about the critic, which I think will be immortal: "I pretend I am asking for help, but the only opinion I am listening for is one or another form of Wow!"

I don't read my buddies' writing, and I rarely show them mine. We simply "communicate." I rely on professional editors to objectively critique my work. Either I pay them and heed their advice or I expect them to respond with a piece of paper I can deposit either in the trash can or in the bank. I rely on my writing friends to celebrate with me. Celebrating is one thing I don't do well alone.

In a family of writers, finding an understanding friend isn't hard. Ethel and I can run up a fairly good-sized phone bill with our common interest in writing, bouncing ideas off each other and sharing disappointments, success, or dreams. Jan locked herself up over Christmas one year to beat the deadline on a book; I hung out my "No Admittance" sign on my birthday. Not many families put up with that.

If you don't have a family as cuckoo as you are, you'll have to go out to look for a writing buddy. You'd be surprised if you knew who, right in your own neighborhood, is writing behind closed doors. Many writers don't know where to turn to find a shoulder to cry on or a true friend who will jump up and down and shout Wow! when they make even a two-buck sale. An error in a newspaper ad brought me a flood of such friends. In the *Professional Services* column, I advertised "Editing, resumes, ghostwriting"; the newspaper put it in the *Positions Available* column as "Editors, resumes, ghostwriting." Four editors, all apparently well qualified, applied for the nonexistent job, and I had calls from fourteen local writers! You can find writing buddies by advertising on bulletin boards or by news items to suburban shoppers about your neighborhood writers club—you being the sole charter member!

LEARN TO ACCEPT CRITICISM

Someday when a writer hands me a prematurely typed, unpolished creation and asks for my opinion, I believe I will honor the request.

"*Hmmm,*" I will say in a scholarly tone as I glance at it, "some weaknesses are immediately apparent. Your spelling is very bad, the word choice is lousy, the sentences are practically incoherent, and you appear to have an extremely limited knowledge of your subject."

Anyone daring enough to do that even by mail would be wise to have an unlisted home phone, use his real name only in private life, and never appear in public without a bulletproof vest. All of us are far too touchy. I turned down a book contract because I could not bear to associate with a slush editor who called my divinely inspired words garbage. Never ask to see what the slush editors have said about your work. Some low-rung secretary might be stupid enough to send their comments to you, resulting in either hari-kiri or murder. Top publishing firms hire public relations experts to correspond with writers because they are important to overall success. Letters are often approved by more than one executive before being mailed out.

The slush comments that angered me were subjective. No writer needs to put up with that. The critic's personal viewpoint on a subject may differ with a writer's, and often does. Marketing advisers find such differences of opinion vauable. They line up all comments, good and bad, to evaluate a cross-section of thought from which they can determine sales potential of a manuscript. Generally speaking, a writer reading the same cross-section of thought would not be helped at all, and probably would end up blinded by tears! Not *everyone* appreciates even the best of bestsellers.

Remind me never to write anything significant enough to be noticed by critics. If my writing ever is caught in reviews, I hope someone close to me censors the remarks. Thick-skinned I am not!

Constructive criticism, on the other hand, is a tool every writer must learn to use. It is important to find someone who is able to help you see weak areas in your writing, someone who can show you errors you have made and give you hints to strengthen, brighten, or expand your writing. Don't let just anybody do it. Search for a qualified critic among your "friends in the business," someone you can trust, someone you like, and someone who really helps you.

Merciless as I may be in tearing apart the work of others, I am not nearly hard enough on myself. Because expressing thoughts occupies my mind, I tend to overlook scrappy details that are terribly important. A friend in the business (Editorial Consultant John R. Harrison, Ph.D.) can look at my manuscript after I and everyone else who has seen it have pronounced it perfect, and see flaws galore. I tremble to see him pull out his red pen, but Ph.D. stands for "the highest degree awarded in the graduate school of a university." John pulls rank on me.

To give you an idea of what to expect from a critic of your work, let me tell you the kind of help I get from a person like John:

1. He tells me to be more specific. "Unclear" and "Imprecise" are two red scribbles I am sure to find. "Germane?" makes me look at the words more carefully, and I generally see that they are not germane to the thought. "This needs elaboration" means "add something," but "Is this necessary?" generally means "cut!"
2. He corrects minor errors and calls my attention to whoppers. A "What does this mean?" usually means I'm floundering, needing to do more thinking or more research to clarify what I have said, or correct it, if it is wrong.

No one succeeds better than John in ruining a beautifully typed page, but when I say a writer must learn to accept criticism, I am referring to specific, constructive criticism like his. Serious writers can find such good friends by gravitating to the right places, and it is important to locate them and line them up for future help.

I advocate taking writing classes and seeking every opportunity to attend seminars and conferences, for both the camaraderie and the learning experience. But you can't beat individual attention. Seeing a good private tutor even once a month is one of the best investments a beginning writer can make. Once a year would help! Anyone taking tennis seriously pays a tutor. An adult wanting to play the organ professionally scouts around for the best teacher available, and money is not an issue.

Finding a writing tutor is easy. Advertise and watch the ads, circulate in writers' circles and call local publishers and colleges. The problem is that would-be writers seek *free* advice. Paying for writing lessons is no gamble at all. It is a good investment. Two hours with a qualified writing tutor pouring over what you have produced will send you singing on your way.

Once you begin to see your work in print, you can compare the finished copy with the original you submitted and learn from the changes. My delight level is low, of course, but I smile broadly all day when my published work comes back with minimal editing. You should see me grin when a whole page comes back from my consultant clean!

Quality matters. You cannot scribble out a few random thoughts, type them poorly, and hope to sell them. It is not only unfair to expect distant editors to clean up your sloppy work, it is unsatisfying to you, the writer. Your whole attention must be given to improving the quality of your creative productions. Accepting criticism is one way to do this, so you will have to learn to swallow hard and say thank you to whoever is willing to stick his neck out to tell you the truth. You don't have to follow anyone's advice, but you do need to accept it with grace.

THE END, OR THE BEGINNING?

It's time now to lay aside your dreams of *becoming* a writer, in order to *be* one. A few people need to be reminded that they have not yet arrived, but the majority of beginners need constant encouragement. Since you can't always count on your family and friends to form a fan club to celebrate your every success, you must find ways to remind yourself that you are, indeed, a writer.

Something as simple as the awed look on the postman's face when he delivers your writing magazines will do it. You can drop comments to the neighbors like, "I've been so wrapped up in research for my latest article that I haven't talked to you in a month." When friends finally reach you by phone and ask where you have been you might say, "I had an appointment with my writing consultant," or, "I had a luncheon engagement with the newspaper editor today." Any of these comments will soundly establish you as a writer, especially in your own mind, which is very important at this point. You have every right to flaunt the greatest profession on earth. Furthermore, any confidence built up in your mind will inspire you to prove it is really so. I can take a deep breath and write like crazy wih the smallest pat on the back!

In addition to talking about your profession, you must start sharing what you write. Choice poems or quotations from your mini-articles can be decoupaged and given as gifts, or placed under the glass on the coffee table for visitors to read. Children's stories can be photocopied and bound in a simple manner to be given children you love. Short stories for adults, photocopied, make treasured additions to letters you write. Original greeting cards carrying your byline will be kept by the recipient forever, and if they are good enough you might get requests for reprints.

There are any number of creative ways to begin spreading your byline around without facing rejection. Whoever heard of a mother turning down an article about the antics of her child? Or a pet owner rejecting a poem about his pet? You might become the office poet, writing for every occasion.

Don't overlook any opportunity to be recognized as a writer, no matter how insignificant it may seem. You need to begin a brag book which should contain a copy of everything your publish (including personal photocopied efforts with which you begin). Special attention should be given to successes with the outside world: your byline in an office or club newsletter, a signed letter to an editor appearing in a paper or magazine, a news report you have written. Any printed material that identifies you as a writer should be added to the brag book. For example, if you were to speak at a club meeting, the program might identify you as a writer. Back the program with shiny gold paper and give it a special place of honor! If you list writing as a hobby on a resume, put a copy in the book.

The brag book is for your own personal enjoyment. Nothing

encourages one so much as reviewing past successes. As the years go by, you will be charting your growth. The day may come that you will draw from the brag book enough significant published material to make up a portfolio and apply for a writing job.

The steps to success start right at ground level:

1. See your byline in print and hear appreciative remarks from recipients of what you have written.
2. Get your writing published by newsletters, newspapers, and small magazines.
3. Sell an item, even if you only receive peanuts for pay.
4. Get a "yes" on a query.
5. Make a sale good enough to shout about.
6. Become recognized and well-qualified enough to have someone *ask you* to write for them.

Early in the game, you will begin to *feel* like a writer. The uphill grind continues no matter how much applause you may enjoy, but climbing is easier once your personal fan club starts to cheer you on.

THIS BOOK AS YOUR GUIDE

You will soon be on your own. Like any elephantine task, self-education in journalism will overwhelm you unless you organize well, breaking it down into portions you can handle. Self-education is tricky. Just when you think you've arrived at your destination, someone proves to you that you still have a long way to go.

The problem, you see, is that if you skipped the schools of higher learning (and goofed off in high school), you have huge gaps in your learning and no one to tell you what they are. Individuals who have come up through the higher education system have benefited from the organized study of people who preceded them. They have all the tools on the workbench; they are ready to go. If they have kept their knowledge alive those tools are sharp. If they don't *know* an answer, they know where to look for it.

You and I not only don't know; we don't know where to find out—or we didn't know until now. Now we know where to begin: at the library; and we know how to proceed: in a carefully organized plan of action.

Gaps in one's increasing store of knowledge may leave a person feeling hopelessly dumb, but self-education does not leave stupidity gaps. When you stand mouth agape wondering what is meant by what is said, or when a page you have read suddenly seems to be Chinese, you have not exposed a lack of intelligence. You have only entered a new area of learning. Recognize it for what it is, admit it, and tackle it. Run for the dictionary. Or call a knowledgeable friend.

It is important for the budding professional writer to understand that learning is a long process. Workable knowledge is best attained through a step-by-step coverage of what you need to know. Since no professor is outlining your courses of study, you will need to carefully plan them "all by yourself." To begin, you can use this book as your guide. Set up a plan to borrow and buy other material as textbooks and enroll in courses and seminars as you need them. Set up a supplementary reading plan to match the study courses you have planned for yourself.

In this book, Chapters 1, 2, 3, and 6, 7, 8, are introductory material. Their purpose is to acquaint you with the publishing system and to give you basic background for writing. You should familiarize yourself with this material as orientation to your self-planned course. Without a firm understanding of the system, you will probably flounder in spite of all your hard work.

Since this chapter is a wrap-up, it falls into the category of necessary background knowledge. Reread it and make marginal notes as you go along, to remind yourself of the things you ought to know or to do.

Seven chapters remain, on which you can base your course of study. How much time you take to learn will depend upon your schedule, your zeal, and your ability to absorb what you need to know before proceeding with the next lessons. I suggest dividing the seven chapters into a three-year course, a two-year course, or, if you are free of all other obligations, a one-year course.

THREE-YEAR COURSE

First Year:

Fall—Library/poetry (Chapters 4 and 11)
Spring—Articles (Chapter 9)

Second Year:

Fall—Style (Chapter 5)
Spring—Fiction (Chapter 10)

Third Year:

Fall—Editing (Chapter 12)
Spring—books (Chapter 13)

TWO-YEAR COURSE

First Year:

Fall—Library/Poetry
Winter—Articles
Spring—Style

Second Year:

Fall—Fiction
Winter—Editing
Spring—Books

EIGHT-MONTH COURSE

In these plans, you will work the foundational material in as a sideline (i.e., chapters 1-3, 6-8, and 14). Learning to relax and meditate, getting in touch with your feelings, collecting anecdotes, making friends in the business, and obtaining an understanding of journalism as a whole will come to the persistent writer naturally.

In a short-term crash course, the first month should be given to getting this background knowledge down pat. Do not pass it by. You will be the loser, if you do.

Month 1—Foundation of writing
Month 2—Library
Month 3—Articles
Month 4—Style
Month 5—Fiction
Month 6—Poetry
Month 7—Editing
Month 8—Books

If you plan now to write a book, I suggest you hold off long enough to do the crash course and study either articles or fiction, depending on which you plan to write, fiction or nonfiction. Writing a book without this basic background knowledge is absurd. Slush editors know all too well that most would-be authors are passing it by: driving a bus when they have failed to learn how to drive a car! I wish I could impress on you how much more satisified you will be with your finished book if you study diligently before writing it. Your chances of success will increase 100 percent if you give priority to learning, before trying to teach.

To speed up attaining mini-market success to support your writing habit, you could run through the eight-month course, followed by a repeat at some later date of the full study or portions of it.

However, it's *your* life. The dreams you dream are your own. You must decide, proceeding in the method and at the pace you believe you need. I hope I have made one thing clear: no matter what kind of writing you choose to do later, as a *professional* writer, you need full background. Bits-and-pieces studies will probably leave you in the amateur class, and I want you to reach up beyond that point, to bigger success and moon-distance goals. You can do it!

Well, I've come to the end of the line. I'd love to stick with you, and see this thing through to the end, but I can't. I hope you'll find a variety of helpful companions as you continue ever upward in your journey to The Top. But basically, from here on out, you're on your own.

God bless you with satisfaction,
contentment,
quality—
and success!

ASSIGNMENT 14 —Final Exam

You have completed the initial reading of a compact, but very intricate course of study. This test is designed to help you evaluate what you already knew and what you have learned, and to apply your knowledge in practical ways both now and in future study.

If you want to write the answers down, do so. Probably some of them will do just as much good if you mull them over in your mind until you have satisfied yourself and are ready to move on. Your personal journal would be a good place to capsulize the answers and record your goals.

I. EXAMINING YOURSELF

1. What have I got to show for my past interest in writing?
2. Have I ever allowed anyone else to read something I wrote?
3. If so, how did they react? If not, why not?
4. Why did I (read/buy/borrow/steal) this book?

II. EVALUATING THIS BOOK

The first time you take this test, go back and highlight important ideas in the book in yellow. After a few months or years of study and experience, highlight the answers to these questions in green. Each time you study it, use a different color. This will enable you to chart your progress. As you learn more, you will highlight less!

1. What thoughts in the book especially interest me?
2. What have I learned about publishing that I didn't know before? How can I expand that knowledge?
3. What new concepts have I learned about writing? How shall I apply them?
4. Which pages motivated me so much I said in my heart, "I can do that"?

III. ESTABLISHING GOALS

As you answer these questions, record the date. Your goals may change as time goes by.

1. What level of professional writing shall I shoot for?
2. Where must I begin?

Once you have answered these questions to your own satisfaction, proceed to "Go."

NOTES

Chapter 1

1. By Jolee Edmonson: *Writer's Digest*, October 1980.

Chapter 2

1. From *Peace Amidst the Pieces*, Copyright 1977, Adventure Publications, Staples, MN. Used by permission.
2. *Herald of Holiness*, July 15, 1981.

Chapter 4

1. *Getting People to Read*, Carl B. Smith and Leo C. Fay. New York: Delacorte Press, 1973.
2. *The Harvard Classics*, Edited by Charles W. Eliot, LLD. New York: P.F. Collier and Son, 1914.
3. *The Life and Adventures of Alexander Dumas*, Percy Fitzgerald; from Volume 2; London: Tinsley Bros., 1873.
4. *How to Write Best-Selling Fiction*, Dean R. Koontz. Cincinnati: Writer's Digest Books, 1981.
5. *The Paris Review Interviews/Writers at Work*; Fifth Series; Edited by George Plimpton; © 1981, Penguin Books; p. 169.

Chapter 5

1. *American Composition and Rhetoric*, by Donald Davidson; © 1953 by Charles Scribner's Sons, New York.
2. *Luther's Works*, Volume 26; Copyright 1963 by Concordia Publishing House, St. Louis; p. 263.
3. *Encyclopaedia Britannica*, 1964 Edition; Volume 21; s.v. "Style."
4. *Stay of Execution: A Sort of Memoir*, by Stewart Alsop. New York: J.B. Lippincott Company, 1973.
5. *Benjamin and Jon*, by Mary Ellen Heath. Minneapolis: Bethany Fellowship, Inc., 1979.

Chapter 6

1. The Holy Bible *New International Version*, Copyright 1978 by New York International Bible Society.
2. *Writer's Digest*, October, 1981.

Chapter 7

1. *Writing and Selling Science Fiction*, The Science Fiction Writers of America. Cincinnati: Writer's Digest Books, 1976.

Chapter 11

1. Adapted from *Walk Thru the Poets*, Copyright 1977, Walk Thru the Bible Press. Used by Permission.
2. Adapted from *Poems of Inspiration and Hope* by Annie Johnson Flint, "The Triumphant Story of Annie Johnson Flint" by Rowland V. Brigham. Used by permission.
3. From *Segelbind i Morgonbakt*, by Harald Stenbock, 1911, Dayton, Ia.
4. From *The Poet and the Poem*, by Judson Jerome, p. 26. Cincinnati: Writer's Digest Books, 1979.

Chapter 12

1. "The Unforgettable S.J. Perelman," *Reader's Digest*, March 1980.

Index

H

I

J

K

L

P

Q

R

T

U

V

W

Y

Z